'The most stimulating book I've read on the most important question facing Australian foreign and strategic policy. Brophy is not just answering questions others have asked, he's asking new questions.'
ALLAN GYNGELL, author of *Fear of Abandonment*

'Anyone who wants to know how and why Australia's China narrative has descended to such a dismal point needs to read *China Panic*. Brophy is that rare China scholar whose moral convictions, unflinching courage and probing intellect combine to deliver a devastatingly sharp critique. *China Panic* embodies a virtuous circle of formidable knowledge, dispassionate reasoning and surgically precise analysis, all of which are in desperately short supply in the current China debate. *China Panic* brings to light a wide array of uncomfortable truths about our collective neurosis when it comes to China, and highlights the urgent need for Australians to take a long, hard look at our own national consciousness and political process.

A powerful antidote to Australia's growing China-phobia, this book is long overdue.'
WANNING SUN, professor of media and communications, UTS

'In *China Panic*, David Brophy introduces much-needed nuance to the increasingly polarised discourse around Australia's relationship with China. He dissects the clichés and prejudices that are stifling Australia's ability to think clearly and act in a principled manner when it comes to dealing with China – revealing the flaws in the thinking of both the "China hawks" as well as elements of the left. With his detailed, knowledgeable and incisive analysis of everything from Xinjiang and Hong Kong to domestic politics, the independence of universities and the American alliance, he offers a unique and valuable perspective. *China Panic* is essential reading.'
LINDA JAIVIN, author of *The Shortest History of China*

CHINA

PANIC

CHINA

AUSTRALIA'S ALTERNATIVE TO PARANOIA AND PANDERING

DAVID BROPHY

PANIC

LA TROBE
UNIVERSITY PRESS

IN CONJUNCTION WITH BLACK INC.

Published by La Trobe University Press in conjunction with Black Inc.
Level 1, 221 Drummond Street
Carlton VIC 3053, Australia
enquiries@blackincbooks.com
www.blackincbooks.com
www.latrobeuniversitypress.com.au

La Trobe University plays an integral role in Australia's public intellectual life, and is
recognised globally for its research excellence and commitment to ideas and debate.
La Trobe University Press publishes books of high intellectual quality, aimed at general
readers. Titles range across the humanities and sciences, and are written by distinguished
and innovative scholars. La Trobe University Press books are produced in conjunction
with Black Inc., an independent Australian publishing house. The members of the LTUP
Editorial Board are Vice-Chancellor's Fellows Emeritus Professor Robert Manne and
Dr Elizabeth Finkel, and Morry Schwartz and Chris Feik of Black Inc.

9781760642501 (paperback)
9781743821497 (ebook)

A catalogue record for this
book is available from the
National Library of Australia

Cover design by Akiko Chan
Text design and typesetting by Tristan Main

Printed in Australia by McPherson's Printing Group

MIX
Paper from
responsible sources
FSC® C001695

CONTENTS

INTRODUCTION: AUSTRALIA'S CHINA PANIC   1

1. CHINA AND THE WORLD   23

2. THE US-CHINA RIVALRY TODAY   47

3. INFLUENCING THE REGION   71

4. INTERFERING WITH DEMOCRACY   95

5. COLD-WAR CAMPUS   121

6. HUMAN RIGHTS AND XINJIANG   145

7. THE BATTLE FOR HONG KONG   169

8. SOVEREIGNTY, VALUES AND RACISM   195

CONCLUSION   219

Acknowledgements   231
Notes   233
Index   249

INTRODUCTION:
AUSTRALIA'S CHINA PANIC

Browse through the section on Australia's foreign relations in any library, and you'll soon notice a consistent theme. *In Fear of China, Fearful Country, Anxious Nation* ... the list goes on. I'm well aware that by titling this book *China Panic*, I'm adding to that collection.

The warnings from government officials have certainly been frightening. Last September, the secretary of the Department of Foreign Affairs and Trade (DFAT) told us that 'the institutions we take for granted – our parliament, our democracy, our legal system, our freedom of speech and association – they really are at stake now'.[1] From 2018 to 2020, the percentage of the population who viewed China as 'more of a security threat than an economic partner' rose dramatically, from 12 per cent to 41 per cent.[2] In many ways, Australians have become afraid of China again.

Australia came into being as a settler colony far from Europe, and it's undeniable that geographic and demographic anxieties have lent its political culture a wariness towards Asia. Today's climate plays on sentiments of xenophobia that have never been far below the surface. In talk of 'invasion', and in caricatures of dragons menacing the continent with their grasping claws, it's possible to see the old genres of yellow peril being recycled. Historians debate the origins of these well-worn China tropes, but all recognise their tenacity.

After two decades of demonising Muslims, Pauline Hanson has returned to familiar themes of demographic swamping from Asia. 'The people have to move to somewhere,' she told *Sky News* in 2019, 'because they're ever increasing ... That's how I see the future.'[3] From the left, Clive Hamilton has made strikingly similar noises. When a business association in Fujian province held an information session on study and migration opportunities arising from Australia's 'Developing Northern Australia' plan, he took to Twitter to warn that 'Beijing is encouraging migration to northern Australia to populate it with people who'll promote [the Chinese Communist Party's] strategic power program of One Belt, One Road'.[4]

The centrality of 'foreign interference' in today's discourse, a drama of agents and operatives, easily calls to mind the Cold War red scare – most associated with the hunt for Soviet spies, but also a time of excessive, racialised policing of Australia's Chinatowns, which made it almost impossible for Chinese Australians to publicly support the newly established People's Republic of China (PRC). Back then, China was both yellow and red, though of course it wasn't the economic powerhouse it is today. For that, we might look to the example of the 1980s, when Japanese investment and buy-ups of Australian companies and real estate induced a paranoia that with hindsight looks well out of proportion to the facts.

Fears certainly do exist. They circulate through society and linger in ways often difficult to discern. I remember as a young boy the mixture of utopianism and unease with which my home state of South Australia debated the merits of Japan's Multi-Function Polis proposal, a futuristic satellite town to be built on Adelaide's dusty northern outskirts. For a while, the image in my mind of the Gold Coast was of something akin to a Japanese colony. I also briefly developed an acute sense that Indonesia might one day invade Australia. I'm not sure where I picked it up from, whether it was from looking at a map or from a snippet of conversation. It was obviously just something in the air.

But this book is not a cultural study of Australia's Asia insecurities. It's not a book about how China's rise is triggering an innate phobia of that country, or why Australia's policies are motivated by racism. As an explanation for the way Australia conducts itself internationally, I don't think racism and paranoia are the best starting points. The China panic I describe in this book is much more a *product* of Australia's policies than a motivation for them. To be precise, it's the result of a deliberate decision to wrench Australia away from deep, longstanding engagement with China, and to assume an active role in a campaign to preserve American dominance in the region.

Of all the spheres of policymaking, foreign affairs is probably the most immune to democratic participation. The most important decisions – including the ultimate one of whether to go to war – tend to be the last to be put up for public debate. Questions take shape and get decided by a narrow range of actors. When Tony Abbott famously described Australia's view of China as a mixture of 'fear and greed', he wasn't so much describing the attitude of ordinary Australians as the attitudes of two constituencies whose views carry the most weight in the formation of foreign policy: the nation's security and business elites. Their privileged policy role gives them a privileged role in shaping public perceptions of the outside world. Enemies need to be identified in stark, simple terms, and brought close to home. Alliances must be presented in idealised narratives of friendship, trade relations in rosy visions of liberal globalism: a win-win world of commerce whose benefits trickle down to us all.

Until recently, depictions of China in both guises – as friend and enemy – circulated in Australia in roughly equal measure. The PRC's rapid, seemingly inexorable, growth has almost single-handedly driven the Australian economy for the last two decades, winning it friends and admirers in the top end of town. The 'rise of China', and its growing rivalry with the United States, has been furrowing brows in security circles for just as long.

In the late 1990s, John Howard rejected the proposition that Australia would one day have to 'choose between her history and her geography'. Since then, the idea of a choice between the United States and China has dominated discussions, with many imagining Australia's path forward as a balancing act. Since Howard's time, politicians have tended to avoid his chauvinistic identification of Australia's 'history' with its Anglosphere allies but have held to the same basic view: 'Australia doesn't have to choose and we won't choose', as Prime Minister Scott Morrison confidently opined at a meeting in Singapore in late 2018.[5]

Talk of a simple binary choice between the United States and China, though, tends to obscure what the actual choice here is. The deeper issue has always been a recognition that China's growing economic, diplomatic and military heft in Asia might one day translate into relative American decline in the region. The corollary to this would be diminished US interest in Australia, rendering the ANZUS (Australia, New Zealand and United States) alliance an irrelevance. In such a situation, Australia's choice would not so much be a question of picking sides, as deciding whether or not to do more to sustain what Australia's elites have long viewed as the linchpin of a favourable status quo: American hegemony in Asia.

This scenario was already visible in 2009, the last 'all-time low' in Australia–China relations before the present one. It's instructive to look back to that period to see that many of the specific issues that dominate coverage of Australia–China relations today are not exactly new. That year saw the Rio Tinto bribery case and the application of China's opaque justice system to Australian citizens such as businessman Stern Hu. In July, riots broke out in Xinjiang's capital, Ürümchi, which Prime Minister Kevin Rudd described as indicative of a worsening human rights situation. Chinese officials responded with a clumsy intervention to prevent the Melbourne International Film Festival from screening a biopic on Uyghur exile Rebiya Kadeer, and PRC filmmakers withdrew their contributions. At the Copenhagen Climate Summit that December, Rudd clashed with Chinese representatives, his frustration famously boiling over in private: 'Those Chinese fuckers are trying to rat-fuck us.'[6]

Back home, suspicions swirled around Rudd's defence minister, Joel Fitzgibbon, and his relationship with a Chinese businesswoman whom Defence officials believed had ties to PRC military intelligence.[7] Heightened sensitivities towards Chinese investment were also coming to the fore, as the state-owned enterprise Chinalco bid to increase its stake in Australian iron-ore mining. Warning of the risks of putting Australian resources in Chinese hands, Opposition Leader Malcolm Turnbull told an audience at the Lowy Institute: 'If we wish to express our approach in Chinese, then we could paraphrase Mao Zedong and say: *Aodaliya renmin zhanqilai le* – the Australian people have stood up.'[8]

Published in the autumn of that *annus horribilis*, Rudd's Defence White Paper included in its draft version a section on Australia's ability to fight a war against China alongside the United States.[9] On a trip to Washington, he cautioned Secretary of State Hilary Clinton to keep the military option on the table should China fail to integrate into the 'international community'.[10] Back then, though, the military option was very much still on the table. If it wasn't obvious, President Barack Obama made it so when he took to the podium in Australia's Parliament House in 2011 to announce the 'Pivot to Asia' and the relocation of 60 per cent of the US Navy to the region.

Thus, the tense equilibrium between China panic and China pandering held. While many of the same elements souring relations with China today were present in 2009, they remained confined to separate spheres and did not catalyse a major shift in Australian policy. At a business forum on Hainan Island in April 2014, Tony Abbott declared Australia's desire to be China's 'true friend', standing ready to 'help build the Asian Century'. When negotiations for the China–Australia Free Trade Agreement were concluded that November, Chinese president Xi Jinping told the Australian parliament that a 'vast ocean of goodwill' existed between his country and ours.[11]

It's this equilibrium that has now broken down.

The End of Engagement

The mixture of fear and greed I'm describing here is as much a part of my own story as it is Australia's. After his bruising experiences in office, Kevin Rudd endowed a dedicated centre for Chinese studies at the Australian National University (ANU), intended to strengthen the country's ability to navigate China's rise. In 2011, the Australian Centre on China in the World gave me my first job after I returned from the United States to Australia. Around the same time, the University of Sydney, led by its Sinophile vice-chancellor Michael Spence, was enthusiastically embracing China, generating new strategies, new centres and new jobs. This eventually allowed me to land what is these days an extremely rare commodity: a secure academic position.

As a historian, I have not always focused on Australia–China relations. After moving to Sydney, though, the media began asking me for my opinion on various things China-related – from New Year festivities to Xi Jinping's rewriting of the PRC constitution. The queries sometimes felt like a distraction from my work. But as the questions became more complicated, the public debate more animated, I knew I had to make the effort to work out where I stood on issues such as Confucius Institutes, or the 'United Front'.

At the same time, in Xinjiang, the area of China I study and know best, the situation was deteriorating. That too required a response. To see with my own eyes what was going on, in 2017 I made my last trip to

China, as the 'expert' guide for a group of American tourists. Upon our arrival in Xinjiang, the signs of a security crackdown were immediately obvious – new police stations at every intersection, checkpoints slowing traffic, razor wire and blast shields in front of government buildings. The people I was travelling with were disturbed by what they saw. I shut the door of our train compartment and tried to explain what was going on, but I didn't have the full picture myself. One day, as we were driving through the heavily surveilled south, a Uyghur pointed out to me a new 'boarding school', where locals went to study during the week. I asked her: 'Why did they need to go to boarding school if they lived nearby?' I didn't get any response. A few weeks after I got back to Australia, news broke internationally of China's 're-education centres'. I realised I'd probably been looking at one of them.

Xinjiang today is probably the world's most disturbing example of security paranoia run wild, infecting all levels of an unaccountable bureaucracy. Without doubt, some of the negative turn towards China in Australian public opinion has to do with knowledge of this crisis, and of course with the crackdown on the Hong Kong pro-democracy uprising, which dominated coverage of China in 2019. It's impossible to think about China's role in Australia without being mindful of these things, because they often intersect: repression in China has serious consequences for Chinese citizens living here, be they Uyghurs cut off from contact with detained family members, or Hong Kong residents wondering if it's safe to return to the city.

We should be thankful for the checks against PRC-style security panics that exist in Australia. But the system here isn't entirely immune to such panics. Certainly, we don't consign Muslims to punitive 're-education' camps, but a similar policy logic, which interprets a turn to religion or rejection of liberal orthodoxies as a step along a pathway to 'radicalisation', has been at work here since 9/11 to frame Australian Muslims as a 'suspect community'.[12]

Returning to Australia in late 2017, I got the distinct sense that Chinese Australians were starting to face something similar. There was a shift in reporting on China-related issues, a tendency to stretch evidence beyond what to me seemed reasonable, a new innuendo surrounding ties with the country. Former Labor senator Sam Dastyari's scandalous dealing with real estate developer Huang Xiangmo was of course the headline-grabbing splash of 2017, but it was a speech by Malcolm Turnbull in December that crystallised the sense of a turn in Australia's official attitude towards the PRC. Here he again cribbed Mao's apocryphal phrase to declare that 'the Australian people have stood up', likening his stance to the Chinese Communist Party's struggle against foreign imperialism. Unlike in 2009, the disparate issues surrounding China were now to be welded into a single, all-encompassing narrative of its hostile intentions towards Australia, which would eventually cast a shadow over almost all spheres of contact with China.

Of course, this wasn't obvious at the time, and, like many people, I still had mixed feelings about the situation. No one could regret the exposure of corruption in the NSW Labor Party, and the heightened interest in China was giving the Uyghurs much-needed coverage of their plight. But the furious denunciations of 'Shanghai Sam' had more than a whiff of Cold War hyperbole about them. Synthesising many of the accumulating bad news stories on China, Clive Hamilton's *Silent Invasion* took the alarmism to a new level in 2018, arguing that Australia only had a short window of time to avoid becoming a vassal state of the PRC and lambasting those with dissenting views as apologists or 'capitulationists'.

At this point, Malcolm Turnbull's approach still wasn't entirely set in stone. In mid-2018, he went to the University of New South Wales, the Australian university most invested in exchange with the PRC, to give a speech that was reminiscent of earlier, more ambiguous rhetoric on China. Some interpreted it as an intelligent restatement of the new normal. Some saw in it a backdown from his previous bombast. Kevin Rudd, always on the lookout for point-scoring opportunities, went so far as to accuse Turnbull of 'grovelling' to Beijing.[13] Watching on from the United States, Donald Trump's campaign adviser Steve Bannon was worried by the conciliatory tone of the speech, and in an interview with the ABC complained that Turnbull was 'way too much of an appeaser [on China]'.[14]

It was late in 2019 when I finally decided I needed to write this book. That September, the outgoing chief of ASIO, Duncan Lewis, told the Lowy Institute that espionage and foreign interference constituted an 'existential threat to the state'.[15] In a post-retirement interview in November, he said that China was employing 'insidious' tactics to 'take over' Australia's political system.[16] 'China Wants to Rule Us' was the headline that dominated the front pages of *The Sydney Morning Herald* and *The Age* the following day.

This rhetorical escalation took place against the backdrop of the unfolding rebellion in Hong Kong, which I was doing my bit to support at the University of Sydney. With daily coverage of Hong Kong police cracking down on the city's teenage radicals, who were risking everything to preserve the ex-colony's autonomy, official warnings of PRC subversion of Australian sovereignty didn't require much evidence to have an impact. It wasn't hard to imagine that China was capable of such things.

Still, I was sceptical. What exactly were these 'insidious' tactics by which China was gaining control of the Australian political system? As far as I could tell, the various scandals and imbroglios involving China – as interesting, even alarming, as they might have been – didn't add up to a challenge to the foundations of Australian democracy. Even people inclined to believe ASIO's claims had been calling on the agency to release more details of what it knew, so as to convince the Australian public.

Then, within days of Lewis's pronouncement, two stories broke that seemed to lift the lid on the murky world of Chinese interference in Australia. To much fanfare, Fairfax Media announced that it was bringing in from the cold a world first – a defector from the Chinese intelligence services, with experience of kidnapping and cyber-espionage in Hong Kong and Taiwan, and valuable dirt on Beijing's spy network in Australia. 'A story that will be heard around the world' was how Chris Uhlmann heralded the emergence of Wang Liqiang on Twitter. The current affairs program *60 Minutes* promised that Wang would now help 'expose the secret army targeting our democracy'. The journalists who broke the story assured us that he'd been vetted by trustworthy eyes: 'Western security sources say Wang is telling the truth.'[17]

The story of Wang Liqiang was accompanied by a second scoop, this time purporting to shine a light on subversive activities at the local political level. A young Liberal Party member in Melbourne, Nick Zhao, was said to have been promised cash and political backing by people with links to the Chinese Communist Party (CCP) to run in upcoming elections. Zhao, we were told, had reported the plot to ASIO and was found dead in a hotel room within a few months.

These were sensational plotlines, promising to reshape the terrain of Australia's China debate. 'Suddenly, the Chinese Threat to Australia Seems Very Real', was how *The New York Times* summarised the situation by the end of the week.[18] A question was left hanging, though: the threat may have *seemed* real, but was it? China specialists soon queried elements of Wang's story – there was no new information in his testimony, and he seemed too young to be entrusted with the assignments he had described. ASPI's Alex Joske, who was involved in vetting Wang, admitted in *The Sydney Morning Herald* that 'we don't know the full story and we probably never will'.[19] In Zhao's case, a picture quickly emerged of a young man in serious financial and legal trouble before his death.

Just as pieces of the China puzzle seemed to be falling into place, the stories were beginning to come apart. That wasn't going to hold back the politicians, though. In parliament, independent senator Jacqui Lambie seized on the reports on Wang and Zhao to call for an official inquiry into PRC influence in Australia. Whether the stories were true or not, she railed, 'what is clear is that China is actively trying to reshape our democracy, and no one seems to be talking about that seriously enough'. 'This is not some wacky conspiracy theory,' she insisted. 'They're coming in by stealth. You need to wake up.'[20]

From the left, the Australian Greens joined the fray. Lining up to vote for the parliamentary inquiry with the independent crossbench, as well as One Nation and the Centre Alliance, Greens senator Nick McKim laid into the two major parties, which he said were 'riddled with CCP influence ... riddled with dirty CCP money'. The nation stood at a crossroads, McKim went on: 'History will record those who stood up and tried to address this situation, and history will record those who rolled over and let the CCP tickle their collective bellies. And unfortunately, it remains the case that both major parties in this place will be on the wrong side of history.'[21]

Rebuffing the calls for an inquiry, in December Morrison diverted the pressure in a direction more to his liking, announcing a $90-million dollar boost for the security agencies, with a new structure of collaboration between intelligence and police, all designed to bring foreign plots to heel.

It was an eventful few weeks, eventful enough to confirm for me that the new politics surrounding China was here to stay, and that it needed a response. There were already a lot of moving parts to the story, and I knew they would continue to move as I wrote. Writing with one eye on the daily news is an unusual and uncomfortable position for a historian to find himself in. What I couldn't predict, of course, is the way that in 2020, COVID-19 would intensify and exacerbate all of the tendencies already at work in Australia's dealings with China. Geopolitics seemed to speed up: talk in the early days of China taking a tumble quickly gave way to worries that the countdown for China to overtake the United States had accelerated. The international blame game, and Wuhan-lab conspiracy theories that refuse to die, have further poisoned an already toxic diplomatic climate. Anti-Chinese racism has spiked: one recent study finds that 47 per cent of Australians now have a negative opinion of immigrants from the PRC.[22]

Things could always be worse in Australia–China relations, but on both sides, analysts see a rift too deep to be mended anytime soon. Leaders of the two countries have not held prearranged talks since 2016, ministers since 2018. PRC officials now impose informal sanctions and bans on Australian exports on a regular basis, plunging some industries into crisis and spooking many of the rest.

Ostensibly, it was Australia's call for China to admit an international investigation into the origins of COVID-19 that triggered China's ongoing trade retaliation. It's not hard to see how this might have given offence – particularly Morrison's reference to UN weapons inspectors as a model. Beijing no doubt remembers how the Iraq inspection regime was infiltrated by US intelligence and then simply bypassed, as Washington fabricated a *casus belli*. But the truth is China is responding to a range of measures that represent a wholesale shift in the way Australia views it. Security laws, foreign-investment decisions, raids on Chinese journalists – the list is long. The combined effect of all these measures has been to cultivate an image of China as a uniquely dangerous country, with which business as usual cannot go on.

China has got that message and is now taking its business elsewhere. As I write, economists are debating the impact of China's trade actions with varying degrees of bravado and pessimism. The looming economic hit, along with the chaotic scenes of late-Trumpism in the United States, have returned Australia to certain basic questions about its China policy, questions that tended to be lost amid sensational talk of China wanting to 'take us over'.

That sensationalism, though, has left its mark. When Chinese journalists provided a list of fourteen grievances that China had with Australia, it met with a hostile response. All of Australia's policies were essential defences of national sovereignty, the retort went, and any modification would therefore be an unacceptable infringement on that sovereignty. The Australian Industry Group's Innes Willox, a voice from the business world, is only the most recent public figure to adopt this tone, accusing China of asking Australia to abandon its democracy.[23] We've got ourselves into a position where serious debate as to the rationale for, and wisdom of, Australia's foreign and domestic policies involving China is becoming hard to have. We need to get ourselves out of it.

The China Debate Today

In the last decade, China's rapid growth and political events in Asia and the United States have combined to erode confidence in America's ability to uphold its position in Asia. From the vantage point of 2021, it can feel as if Australia has gone along for the ride with an aggressive, anti-China Trump administration. It's the classic Australian nationalist critique – that when America tells us to jump, we simply ask how high. But this is not the perspective of this book. It's important for us to remember the way that in 2016, Donald Trump's 'America first' nationalism sent shockwaves through the US alliance network, seeming to presage a turn away from US commitments to Asia. It was that event, I believe, that triggered a sense in Australian security circles that it was time for the country to step up and do more. It wasn't US pressure, that is to say, but the worry that American resolve was flagging, its commitment to Australia's region waning.

Australia has independent initiative in this situation, but of course, there's very little that Australia itself can independently do to change the political dynamics in Asia. Australia's objective in this situation has been to rally a US-led response, and this gives its stance some unique features. Tough policies towards China have to be thought of, in part, as a form of international lobbying. They send signals to the United States and its regional allies of Australia's willingness to confront China. They

provide models of rhetoric, and strategies, that these 'like-minded' countries might themselves adopt. It's not enough, from this point of view, to
simply get tough on China: Australia has to ensure that it's *seen* to be getting tough on China. This explains something that is often pointed to as
a failing of Australia's China policy: its noisy, attention-seeking quality.
But this is not a mistake, it's a deliberate calculation. Advertising itself as
the 'canary in the coal mine' of China's rise, Australia has exported a narrative to the world that engaging with China is profoundly dangerous.

At the same time, because Australia's own policies cannot in any
way be determinative, there has to be a degree of hedging. There remain
doubts and misgivings that an American rally is possible. While leading
on certain issues, Australia has remained reticent, for example, to commit to provocative Freedom of Navigation Operations in the South China
Sea. Unlike the United States, Australia had avoided any formal redefinition of its relationship with China: officially, it remains a 'comprehensive
strategic partnership'.

The messaging can be confusing, verging on contradictory at
times. Last November, China and Australia both joined the Regional
Comprehensive Economic Partnership, the world's biggest free trade
bloc. Then, within a few days, the prime minister was in Tokyo, securing
a new defence pact with Japan – a step towards building regional military architecture capable of containing China. From there, he travelled
to London, where he spoke of Australia's 'mutually beneficial' relationship with China.

It's crucial for Australia's credibility as an ally, though, that any hedging does not create perceptions that Australia is backing away from the
fight. It is not only size, but economic profile that distinguishes Australia
from the United States: its economic complementarity with China remains
huge, with a whopping 49 per cent of Australian exports still destined for
China. While Chinese Australians have borne the brunt of the campaign
against 'foreign interference', the security scare also serves to intimidate
and sideline elite constituencies who prefer a more traditional 'engagement' policy. It's noticeable that if you travel today to countries such as
Japan or Korea, you'll find a public debate that has many features in common with Australia's, but with a far less panicked tone and few of the same
warnings that China is corrupting the nation's core institutions. To curtail

Australia's engagement with China has required a bruising campaign, one that is still in full swing.

Historians will eventually have a more precise picture of how Australia entered onto this path, but we can say with some confidence that security agencies have led the way. An inter-agency inquiry chaired by prime ministerial adviser John Garnaut has been widely cited as the catalyst for Malcolm Turnbull's policy shift.[24] ASIO has itself taken on an increasingly public role, issuing warnings from 2017 onwards that foreign interference was occurring at 'an unprecedented scale' in Australia. The defence department's public-facing think-tank, the Australian Strategic Policy Institute (ASPI), has likewise been assiduous in talking up risks from China. Headed by Peter Jennings, who advised John Howard on intelligence leading up to the Iraq War, ASPI has often been the brains behind Australia's interventionist policies in the Pacific and the Middle East, and now serves as a clearing house for 'get tough' strategies towards China. ASPI receives sponsorship from arms companies that have a material interest in stoking tensions with China, and these tensions have also won it large grants from Canberra and the US State Department.

Backbenchers from the right wings of both major parties have openly embraced the new mood, adopting the 'Wolverines' moniker from the 1980s film *Red Dawn*. While that image calls to mind plucky young Cold Warriors putting up a last-ditch defence, the definition of 'security' that Australia's hawks work with often extends well beyond the Australian continent and its maritime frontiers, making the line between defensive and offensive measures a blurry one. Wolverine Andrew Hastie calls on the West to wage its own 'hybrid and political warfare' against its adversaries.[25] Paul Monk, one-time director of China analysis for the Defence Intelligence Organisation, recently outlined a five-step plan to push back against Beijing. He advises Australia to configure its 'information warfare capabilities' for offence, which will include 'talking up the attractive prospects for a more open and tractable China'.[26] The definition of 'tractable', of course, is 'easy to control or influence'. It's notable that those most exercised by foreign influence are often the most interested in exercising it.

Yet Australia's abrasive new stance towards China clearly hasn't all been the initiative of typical hawks. The stand-off has given groups like the Uyghurs, or exiled Chinese dissidents, much more of a platform than they've ever had in Australia, and they naturally worry that talk of human rights and democracy will be discarded should tensions cool and a business-as-usual relationship with China be restored. With ASPI now devoting considerable resources to exposing China's human-rights violations, anti-CCP activists in these diaspora communities have tended to be drawn into alliance with such think-tanks.

Beijing's obvious abuse of dissidents and minorities; the charge, quite legitimate, that Australian foreign policy has put profits before people; and anxiety at the social impact of transnational capital flows have drawn a wide range of progressive voices towards some of the same security-centred critiques of China. In Richard Denniss's view, for example, Australia's politicians have prioritised free market dogma above 'very real threats to Australia's national security', which include the lease of the Port of Darwin to a Chinese company.[27] The most prominent voice decrying China from the traditional left has of course been Clive Hamilton, whose first foray into China punditry was on the question of rising real estate prices, but who now espouses a full-blown Cold War liberalism, arguing that progressives have no choice but to line up alongside the United States in a 'global war between democracy and the new totalitarianism'.[28]

Alignments like this often strike people as a case of strange bedfellows, but we have to ask: just how strange? Progressive political economy in Australia has a tradition of formulating ominous visions of Asian capital dominating Australia and strangling its democratic culture. In the 1980s, for example, Abe David and Ted Wheelwright depicted Australian big business as collaborating with Japanese investors to import that country's anti-democratic culture to the Australian workplace. Engulfed by 'Japan's tidal wave of capital', they anticipated that 'this will be the first time that world capitalism has *not* been dominated by an English-speaking country with a "Western" culture'.[29] Despite Japan's firm status as a US ally, its rise elicited a lot of the same anxieties, across the political spectrum, that China's is today.

There are, of course, many elite voices deeply critical of this turn. If a 'China lobby' describes those who advocate jumping ship and joining the PRC camp, then no such thing really exists in Australia. But for some security analysts, it is simply a foregone conclusion that Australia will have to get by in the future without the United States. Chief among them is Hugh White, who has long argued that American pre-eminence in Asia is coming to an end, and that Australia should therefore accommodate China's rise. Other dissenters from this policy tribe include former secretary of the Department of Defence, Dennis Richardson, who warns that 'national-security cowboys' are endangering the country's interests.[30] Angus Houston, chief of the Australia Defence Force from 2005 to 2011, maintains that 'China is Australia's partner, not an enemy'.[31] Prominent ex-politicians like Paul Keating likewise warn that it is foolhardy to align so closely with Washington.

In the economic sphere, meanwhile, those who first guided Australia's liberalisation and turn to Asia remain bullish on China and champion trade multilateralism as the alternative to what they see as America's turn to protectionist nationalism. Housed at the University of Technology Sydney, the Australia–China Relations Institute has remained positive amid the turbulence, constructing a counter-narrative of continued trade growth and pushing back against the fearmongering of rival think-tanks, such as ASPI.

What of capital itself? Are Australia's captains of industry tilting towards China, as many imagine? Some have certainly been sending signals. At the height of the COVID-19 pandemic, it was hard not to be struck by the scene of Andrew 'Twiggy' Forrest bypassing the government to engage his 'Chinese friends' in the medical equipment industry, and then ambushing health minister Greg Hunt by inviting a PRC consul to the press conference announcing his purchase. But the mining industry as a whole has remained fairly mute so far; the only vaguely political note in a recent Minerals Council of Australia report is a cautious recommendation that it 'would welcome more high-level policy action by Australia to seize opportunities linked to China's Belt and Road Initiative, as well as to clarify potential risks'.[32]

Some in the immediate firing line of China's trade shutdown have been more forthright in their views. When wine shipments were held up last November, one angry vigneron complained: 'It's no one else's fault, it's the Australian government's fault'.[33] Many who do business with China probably feel the same way, but there can be a cost for speaking up. So effective has been the suspicion cast on corporate ties to China, that even the mildest critics from that milieu can find themselves pilloried for selling out the national interest. The studiously middle-of-the-road China Matters think-tank, whose donors include Rio Tinto and PricewaterhouseCoopers, found this out last July, when the government withdrew its funding, and the tabloid press went to town on accusations that it was doing Beijing's bidding. Clearly anxious at the sidelining of the corporate, pro-engagement perspective, members of the Australia–China Business Council have recently established the G.E. Morrison Institute as a new voice of business in the public debate, named after an influential Australian journalist for *The Times* during China's transition from empire to republic.

Many of these calls to face up to the reality of US decline, or tilt towards engagement, hark back to a Labor-centred narrative of Australia turning towards Asia in the 1970s, but so far they've made little impact on today's Labor Opposition. A 'bipartisan compact on national security' is a point of pride for the Australian Labor Party (ALP), and almost anything to do with China these days is seen as a question of national security. Criticisms centre on tone, not the substance of policy. The only prominent exception to this has been the party's pro-coal agriculture spokesman Joel Fitzgibbon, who holds that Turnbull 'drew first blood' in the dispute, through measures including foreign investment restrictions, and that Australia has put its exports at risk by 'demonising the Chinese and their system of governance'.[34]

For all the speculation that Labor is soft on China, it's worth remembering that the party in fact has a history of trying to out-hawk the Liberals: prodding them, for example, to reconsider their opposition to Freedom of Navigation Operations. As leader of the Opposition Anthony Albanese recently reiterated in a speech at the USAsia Centre in Perth, Labor views American power as an indispensable pillar of Australian foreign policy and believes it is in Australia's interests to 'encourage the restoration of that power'.[35]

To the left, the Greens have been divided on China. Foreign policy, it must be said, has never been a priority for the party or its following. A recent Essential poll found that when asked whether Australia should strengthen its relationship with the United States or China, Greens supporters were the most likely to say neither (37 per cent), but they were also twice as likely as ALP and Coalition voters to say that they didn't know (21 per cent).[36]

Where the party has its roots in environmentalism, for example in Tasmania, some Greens politicians have embraced the new talk of the PRC eroding Australian sovereignty. MP Rosalie Woodruff, for example, describes the Cambria Green development, a joint-venture healthcare and tourist facility, as an 'essential building block for the Chinese Communist Party to take residence in Tasmania and to use it as a launch pad for its various strategic objectives'.[37] In New South Wales, by contrast, where the party has firmer affiliations with the left, opposition to ANZUS militarism and anti-Chinese racism has dominated the response. Caught in the middle, party leader Adam Bandt has stuck to a limited set of talking points: that Australia is too reliant on the United States politically and too reliant on China economically, and it therefore needs a more 'independent' foreign policy.

Not much remains in Australia of the Old Left and its misplaced insistence that China – for all its flaws – still represents a superior social system to the capitalist West. Most of the organised far left in Australia is critical of both China and the United States. Elsewhere, though, US–China antagonisms have led to the revival of 'campist' politics, tying opposition to American imperialism to support for the CCP and a wilful blindness to, if not outright apologism for, issues such as repression in Xinjiang. Online, 'tankies' fill their profiles with neo-Stalinist insignia and the flags of countries they imagine to be 'anti-imperialist', and adopt positions in accord with the principle that Mao once articulated: 'We should support whatever the enemy opposes and oppose whatever the enemy supports.'[38] For all its ostensible radicalism, this style of leftism boils down to a liberal vision of a more multipolar world system, in which the PRC will have freedom to manoeuvre without resistance from the United States. It's a sad reflection of the absence of more transformative visions for global affairs on the left today, at a time when precisely such a vision is needed.

The far right, meanwhile, is lurking, though it has to be said that their efforts to make hay out of the new climate have been complicated by the embrace of anti-Chinese paranoia across the political spectrum. Hamilton is no racial chauvinist, but when *Silent Invasion* was published, one far-right organisation proclaimed that 'Professor Hamilton is not revealing much more than what the Australia First Party has been saying for years!' Such organisations have also made alliances with anti-CCP dissidents, such as the Falun Gong spiritual movement, a situation that requires them to tone down racial animosity to ethnic Chinese and focus on COVID-19 conspiracy theories and similar anti-CCP talking points. Strange to say, but there are also pro-China groups on the Australian far right. The Australian Citizens Party, formerly the Citizens Electoral Council, hails China's Belt and Road Initiative as the realisation of their guru Lyndon LaRouche's vision of a 'Eurasian land bridge' and attacks American influence in local politics from an Australian nationalist standpoint.

A Different Kind of 'China Choice'

This book is both a critique of Australia's China policy and a critique of what the politics surrounding China is doing to Australia. It's not a book about how we need to return to a traditional 'engagement' stance or how anti-China politics is ruining Australia's trade surplus. Getting back into China's good books is not my interest. While I'm not blasé about the impact that the end of the China trade might have on Australian livelihoods, there are more important things to consider than simple economic imperatives. Yet by the same token, I don't share the conviction that incurring the wrath of Beijing is in and of itself the hallmark of good policy.

My basic motivations for writing this book are quite straightforward: I see as dangerous any efforts to uphold a flagging American hegemony in Asia, which is now of an almost exclusively military nature. I worry at the visible rise in anti-Chinese racism we see here. And I worry at the worsening levels of state repression in China. The fate of the Uyghurs, the future of civil liberties and democracy in Hong Kong – these are things we should all be worried about. Indeed, I'd go so far as to say they should be the top priorities for any Australians dealing with China. But the seriousness of these situations requires equally serious reflection on how best to engage with them. I don't believe we advance the cause of human freedom in China by lining up with its enemies here in Australia, or by driving away ordinary Chinese Australians with Sinophobia.

I'm sure a lot of people would agree with this as a starting point. This book is written, though, with an understanding that foreign policy is not so much a field of competing ideas as a field of competing interests. As much as Australia's major parties are resolute in their loyalties to the US alliance, they also remain deeply beholden to corporate interests. In a field of foreign policy dominated by these two outsized influences, it can often feel as if our options are constrained. China hawks don't so much challenge the corporate influence on Australian policy as use it as a foil: if we don't side with the United States, they ask, then what's to stop Australia dropping its criticism of China for the sake of a buck?

I take this question seriously. Certainly, nobody wants corporate lobbyists writing Australia's China policy. Even if that's not on the cards, certain truths have been exposed about the nature of Australia's transactional relationship with China, and about China itself, that naturally make people hesitant to endorse any return to 'business as usual'. The standard critique of 'engagement' – that the West learnt to live with a repressive party-state so as to advance its own political and economic interests – has much truth to it. Compromises that were made to preserve and cultivate 'the relationship'; a revolving door between politics and the corporate world; the blurry line between political lobbying and more dubious forms of influence-peddling: all of these issues and more have come into view. Certain things that were unsayable (or if said, were ignored) have now become sayable. But they've become sayable in a particular way – a way that draws the focus away from any systemic critique and keeps it fixed on China. This is the point where I dissent.

A catalogue of the various accusations levelled at China and its activities in Australia has already filled one book. Reviewing and evaluating the accuracy of these various claims could easily fill a second. This is part of what I do here. But the more important task is to engage with the framing of Australia's China panic. Beyond the news cycle and the day-to-day policy debate, Australia's 'China choice', as I see it, is about the lens through which we view China's place and role in the world.

Is there something uniquely corrosive about Chinese influence, for example, or do episodes of political corruption involving China reflect flaws in Australia's political system? Is the PRC a uniquely dangerous actor in world affairs, or should we interpret its actions in light of a global system of which it is a part? Even at the level of China's domestic policies, we can ask similar questions: is China's persecution of its Muslim minorities of its own making, or is it tied to wider international trends?

In an intellectual sense, of course, everyone will admit to the need for a degree of self-criticism. But in practice, Australian policies have consistently singled out China at the expense of any wider critique. On a range of issues, it's hard to make sense of Australia's stance without coming to terms with the fact that China is already being thought of as an enemy state. This sense of mission gives the hawkish stance a certain coherence, moral force even, that elite criticism of it sometimes lacks. But it ends up undermining the very values that it invokes for its justification.

Criticism, for it to count as criticism, has to be made on the basis of certain standards against which we measure everyone – including ourselves. If we're not doing that, then we're doing something else. If we're more forgiving of bullying diplomacy when America's interests are at stake, rather than China's, then we're simply not a credible critic of bullying diplomacy.

What's more, when the emphasis is put on the Chineseness of an actor, and not the nature of the action itself, associations with China in and of themselves quickly become stigmatised. A national-security lens extends across all sorts of diasporic ties to China that until very recently were thought to be harmless, even positive. Any and all such associations, indeed the very presence of Chinese in Australia, are seen to have security implications. Far from defending the rights that Chinese Australians value here, the response to China puts these rights at risk.

If business-led engagement with China is an unlikely vehicle for the promotion of democracy and human rights, then so too is the new paradigm of strategic competition. Australia has hit upon a response to China that is not only unconvincing for its inconsistencies. With its heavy reliance on security measures, the increasing use of inscrutable 'national interest' determinations, and an implicit, and sometimes explicit, view of PRC citizens as a fifth column, this new paradigm is undermining democratic rights and rule of law in a way that only legitimises China's desire to do the same thing.

The solution seems obvious. What we need is a position not beholden to the paranoid vision of the security agencies or to the priorities of trade, but one that lives up to its profession of universal values. This, of course, is where the structural constraints of foreign policy get in the way. To reorient Australia's China politics in a more progressive direction, one capable of both defusing the brewing cold-war conflict *and* extending solidarity to people in China, there's no getting around the fact that those constraints will need to be broken down and a wider range of voices and interests represented in the making of Australian foreign policy.

This is not a perspective that I imagine many members of the major parties, or the foreign policy establishment, will embrace. I'd be delighted if they did, but this book isn't written for them. I sometimes talk about what 'Australia' should do, but most of the time I'm really talking about what *Australians* should do. I'm sceptical that the Australian state, as it exists today, can be a principled humanitarian actor on the world stage – it's simply not built for that purpose. Similarly, with occasional exceptions, I avoid referring to a national 'we'. The lesson to draw from today's conflict over China policy is not that Australia is having trouble identifying its national interest, but that there's really no such thing as a single national interest. Global rivalries for economic and political dominance serve elite interests, but for the rest of us, they deplete public resources and endanger political freedoms. To get out of the rut into which Australia's China debate has settled, we need to recentre it on the interests that ordinary people in Australia and across Asia share in both combating oppression and resisting warmongering.

The array of questions that China raises for Australia today is daunting, far too diverse for anyone to claim expertise in them all. I've written this book not because these questions require a specialist, but because they're too important to leave to the specialists. Although the study of China is my full-time job, what I've written here is as much a reflection of my recent experience as a participant in debate, and as an activist, as it is a reflection of my academic pursuits. It's as much an exercise in Australia-watching as it is in China-watching, and Australia-watching is something that everyone who lives in this country should be doing.

I begin here with the other two corners of the geopolitical triangle that Australia finds itself in – first China, and then the United States – before turning to Australia itself, and the interests and objectives that shape its standpoint on the growing trans-Pacific rivalry. My focus then switches to domestic politics and one of the key features of Australia's recent shift on China: the new, heightened focus on 'foreign interference', both at the political level and in the more specific field of Australia's universities, where much of today's China anxiety is centred.

In the two chapters that follow, I take up the twin political crises that have dominated discussion of China of late, and the global response to them: the crackdown in Hong Kong and the mass repression of Turkic-speaking Muslims in Xinjiang. Here, I ask a difficult question: what will it take for Australia to make a meaningful difference to the victims of repression?

The last chapter brings us back to Australia and the controversial question of anti-Chinese racism: what is it, where is it, and what should we do about it? To conclude, I outline possible scenarios for the future and some principles to guide us forward, through what may well turn out to be difficult times.

1. CHINA AND THE WORLD

At the beginning of the COVID-19 pandemic, when Scott Morrison consigned returnees from China to Christmas Island for quarantine, then put up those from elsewhere in hotels on the Australian mainland, a question naturally arose: had Chinese people been singled out? A century ago, the same question might have been asked. As Alison Bashford observes, the 'infectious disease' provision of the 1901 *Immigration Restriction Act* was often applied in ways that blurred the distinction between epidemiological and racial exclusion, with Chinese arrivals being routinely associated with disease and contamination. Like the dictation test, Bashford argues, quarantine 'functioned quite centrally in the production of Australian racial purity: it was a technology of White Australia.'[1]

Chinese inscriptions left on the walls of Sydney's Quarantine Station record the anxieties of epidemics past: 'I am very frightened of having the disease, and the doctor is helpless to control it.' But they also register political resentments: 'Down with imperialism!' reads one. Alongside a picture of an Englishman, another reads: 'Down with this kind of people!' Some Chinese internees linked their individual plight to that of their beleaguered home country: 'This is all because the country is weak. Whatever the obstacles, everyone must struggle to avenge the nation.'[2]

Similar sentiments can be found on the walls of Angel Island in San Francisco Bay, which also served as a holding pen for Chinese exclusion. 'If my country were strong, it would not be like this,' one says. 'Confined here, I know it's because the country is weak,' says a second. Brooding before their likely deportation, their thoughts turned to retribution for the insult. 'The nation weak, we Chinese sigh bitterly at the lack of freedom. The day my country becomes strong, I swear to cut off the barbarians' heads.'[3]

The 'century of humiliation' is not a figment of PRC propaganda. It was a lived reality for such people. In 1949, when Mao Zedong stood atop the main gate of the Forbidden City in Tiananmen Square and declared the founding of the People's Republic, he was marking the end of a century in which China had experienced multiple foreign invasions. Its finances had been drained by crushing indemnities, and its tariff policies and customs ceded to outsiders – predatory practices that today we might call neo-colonialism. It had lost large chunks of its territory and seen its citizens stigmatised as an unwelcome presence in countries worldwide. Of course, today the CCP puts all these facts to the service of its own interests, but they are no less facts for that.

My point here is not to induce pangs of guilt. Nor do I think that history alone justifies any particular vision of the future. I don't intend to argue that Australia must now expiate the sins of empire. But history can help explain how we got to where we are today.

No modern country has travelled quite the same path as China – from a state of semi-colonial subservience to its current position of a heavyweight in the global system. It has done so in a world not of its making, and its rise can't be considered in isolation from that wider world. From the nineteenth century onwards, China's options were constrained by the various sticks and carrots wielded by an international system of trade and diplomacy. Australia only had a bit part in the design of that international system, but it nevertheless belonged to an alliance of nations that tried to influence China's path – at times by isolating it, at times by conditionally accepting it into the fold. Our histories have long been intertwined.

Some sense of these interconnections is worth holding onto at a time like this, when China looms before us as a very different place. Any notion that the People's Republic of China was ever on a path to convergence with Western-style political systems must be dismissed as wishful thinking. China is adamantly not a liberal democracy; in fact, its ruling Communist Party considers liberalism its enemy.

These facts engender genuine disappointment among people who until recently vested hope in a path of 'reform' in China. As in the 1950s, when the West 'lost' China to communism, ideology is again becoming a popular explanation for failed expectations and the evident differences between China and the West.

John Garnaut, one of the chief architects of Australia's shift on China, took up this theme in a speech in 2017. In China, he told his audience of Australian officials, a newer 'totalitarian' communist ideology has been 'grafted onto an existing ideological system – the classical Chinese dynastic system'. In his view, the political choices of China's elite can be explained by their interpretations of the historical classics that chronicle the dynastic cycle, as well as Stalin's turgid theorisations of party rule.[4]

A 'totalitarian ideology' deriving from ancient texts and Marxist dogma provides a handy theory of everything to do with China, one likely to find favour among those who anticipate an inevitable showdown with it. According to one account, Garnaut's speech struck the 'Wolverine' Liberal MP Andrew Hastie with the force of revelation.[5] Part of the theory's attraction lies in the way it obviates any need to look for more proximate, contingent factors to explain China's direction today. China's been that way since ancient times – what do you expect?

The view that the CCP embodies Chinese tradition while remaining faithful to its Marxist lineage is a curious point of convergence between China hawks and the party itself. Yet if you examine the twists and turns of official Marxism as expounded in China's institutes and universities, you'll see a school of thought that's been relied upon to justify ex post facto all sorts of contradictory positions – from autarky to free trade, from expropriating the bourgeoisie to welcoming them into the ranks of the CCP. It's hard not to conclude from this that ideology is subordinate to policymaking in China. Garnaut, in fact, knows this and undermines his thesis by acknowledging that the indispensability of CCP rule is the only principle that China's party elite consistently adheres to: 'All that remains is an ideology of power, dressed up as patriotism.' The CCP wants to preserve its dominance, and it increasingly relies on plain old nationalism to achieve that. On this point, I think everyone can probably agree. The ongoing centrality of party rule is indeed a pillar of today's CCP.

It's also true that as long as the party is seen to be making good on its promises to improve the lives of PRC citizens, many in China seem comfortable with the status quo. Allowing for the pitfalls of opinion polling in China, where citizens have no obvious political alternatives and no free press, polls usually register strong levels of satisfaction with China's single-party system. An emphasis on ideology in the way we explain the popularity of the Chinese party-state can easily invite conclusions that the population as a whole has simply been brainwashed or has different 'values' to us. We need a better explanation for the illiberal, even anti-liberal, features of China's system.

This is where some ideology of our own begins to show. For some, it's simply inconceivable that, given a choice between Western-style democracy and party rule, anyone could prefer the second option. The absence, or unpopularity, of liberalism in China can therefore only be from lack of acquaintance with it. At an event at Stanford's Hoover Institution in June 2019, the sociologist Larry Diamond outlined a plan to penetrate what he imagined to be an ideological blockade surrounding the PRC and to expose its population to liberal thinking: 'We could take … quite a large swathe of the classic canon of liberal ideas, … put it on thumb drives and infiltrate quite a large number of them, at very low cost, into the People's Republic of China.'[6]

It's a funny anecdote, I know, but the Hoover Institution is a serious actor in US–China affairs. Diamond himself is the co-author of the 2018 report 'Chinese Influence and American Interests', the publication of which was an important step towards establishing a new hawkish consensus among America's China specialists. Alongside him at the 2019 event was H.R. McMaster, who had recently departed the Trump administration, where he was responsible for the now declassified 2018 US Strategic Framework for the Indo-Pacific. The event was chaired by historian Niall Ferguson, an outspoken advocate of a new cold war with China.

I'd be curious to know which texts from the liberal canon Diamond had in mind for the influence operation he outlined. John Stuart Mill's *On Liberty*? Maybe Alexis de Tocqueville's treatises on parliamentary democracy? Whichever they were, smuggling them into China on a thumb drive would be a waste of time. Works like Mill's have been available in Chinese translation since the nineteenth century and are still available online and in bookshops. They've been debated in China for just as long. Even hard men of the Politburo, such as Li Keqiang, are said to be fans of Tocqueville and his warnings that if you give the people reform, the people will give you revolution. (Liberalism, let's remember, isn't a philosophy of unbridled democracy.)

Following the fall of the Qing dynasty, liberalism was about as popular in China as Marxism – which is to say not particularly popular at all, but with advocates in the professoriate and support from foreign devotees living in China. Liberalism's failure to gain traction requires us to reflect on the merits of competing philosophies – not in the abstract, but in specific historical conditions.

Liberal thinking arose in Europe through the efforts of new social groups to restrict feudal privilege and pave the way for capitalist enterprise. An indigenous product long in the making, laissez-faire individualism had radical, even revolutionary, force – although realising its democratic potential required centuries of struggle from below. Outside Europe, liberalism took on a different role, justifying the violent imposition of free trade and Western 'civilisation' on societies that held out against these things – among them China. A decade after the First Opium War, Tocqueville wrote to a friend: 'It would be difficult for me to console myself if, before dying, I did not see China opened and the eye of Europe penetrate there with its arms.' When the Second Opium War broke out, Mill was convinced of its justice. In his view, 'the prohibition of the importation of opium into China' violated 'the liberty ... of the buyer'. The Chinese were 'barbarians', and there could be no 'ridiculous appeals to humanity and Christianity in favour of ruffians, & to international law in favour of people who recognize *no* laws of war at all'.[7]

Of course, being on the receiving end of this kind of liberalism didn't stop Chinese revolutionaries from championing individual freedom in their attack on the old, oppressive social structures of the Qing dynasty. But in societies penetrated by foreign capital, liberal orthodoxies offered little guidance on how to build up new structures in place of the old. What's more, from the vantage point of China in the early twentieth century, what many saw in Europe or America was not so much the intercourse of free individuals, but strong states whose various elements – their diplomats, their captains of industry, their churches – all seemed to be working in remarkable coordination to achieve the West's political and economic ends. To survive in such a world, Chinese thinkers almost unanimously concluded, China would need a strong state of its own. It would need the same unity of purpose, the same degree of organisation they saw in the West, and a social theory celebrating the self-interested individual would not help them achieve that.

We conventionally talk about modern China's two revolutions: the 1911 revolution, which brought the Qing dynasty to an end, and the communist revolution of 1949. But it can help to think of the two as one long revolution, with many of the questions raised by the first only receiving a semblance of resolution in the second. Unable to rouse sufficient support to topple the Qing in their own right, the 1911 revolutionaries ceded that task to a decidedly non-revolutionary elite of ex-officials and regional warlords. Early efforts to unite China behind a system of parliamentary democracy ran up against this elite's anti-democratic instincts and the centrifugal force of their rivalries – all of which was exacerbated by the ongoing competition for commercial and political influence among foreign interests.

Watching on from enclaves in the south, and the relative safety of the foreign concessions in treaty ports such as Shanghai, China's two major political parties – the nationalist Guomindang and the Chinese Communist Party – drew similar conclusions. Only a disciplined party with its own army would have any hope of staving off internecine war and rescuing China from its subordinate position in the global system. The chief difference between the two parties was in their attitude towards a second issue raised by the collapse of the Qing dynasty: a social revolution that was taking place in China's countryside. Drawing much of their support from landlords and treaty port elites, the Guomindang sought to subdue this agrarian uprising and win Western backing by accommodating foreign interests. The communists, by contrast, seized on this revolution as a vehicle for the construction of a more self-sufficient China, one able to stand on its own two feet in a hostile world. Guided by Stalin's theory of 'socialism in one country', the rapidly industrialising Soviet Union seemed to provide the best, indeed the only, available template for achieving this. Republican China had its share of liberal intellectuals, along with dissident leftists who had a more democratic and internationalist vision of the future, but neither faction had solutions to the immediate crisis facing China that were as persuasive as the CCP's.

None of this is to say that the CCP embodied some abstract 'will' of the Chinese people, as the party itself claims. Its rule was the product of a divisive civil war. But it was a civil war in which neither side was offering a pluralistic, democratic China. Australia's first envoy to China,

Frederic Eggleston, described the Guomindang as a fascist organisation, which presided over 'a one-party government, bolstered by military force and a powerful, well-organised system of political espionage'.[8] In that, he was right. By contrast, his estimation of the CCP as agrarian radicals who 'desire the reforms in land tenure, in resistance to land abuses, landlordism and usury, which are needed' was far from the complete picture. Having steeled itself though guerrilla war and vicious intraparty conflicts, by the 1940s the CCP already had at its disposal the techniques of purge and repression that would mar the politics of coming decades. Like the Bolsheviks in Russia, the CCP would identify the survival of its country with the survival of the revolution, and the survival of the revolution with the survival of party rule. Eggleston eventually came to recognise this, but still saw the communists as perfecting a system that the nationalists had pioneered.

It's misleading therefore to imagine that Chinese nationalism, with its scepticism of the overtures of Western liberalism, is a product of Communist Party brainwashing. These attitudes predate the Communist Party and gave impetus to its rise. The legitimacy of the basic grievances that drove Mao and the Red Army to victory was something that some outsiders were willing to acknowledge at the time, but in the Cold War climate of the 1950s those voices fell silent, or were silenced. For the next two decades, the dominant narrative was one of communism as a deceptive foreign conspiracy. It took the disastrous war in Vietnam for the West to once again grapple with the fact that communism expressed native Asian aspirations for independence and self-determination. Of course, all forms of nationalism distort political realities to some degree. But when they look at their country's modern history, enough Chinese people find enough validation for basic claims of Western hostility to China to sustain the CCP's evolving nationalism to the present day. Any perception that contemporary conflicts reflect longstanding ambitions to keep China down will only be grist to that mill.

From Isolation to Engagement

In putting an end to decades of civil strife and freeing China to begin charting its own independent way in the world, the 1949 revolution was a major achievement. But the CCP's vision of socialism had little to do with the Marxist vision of an urban working class emancipating itself. China's cities were often the last places to be occupied by the CCP's People's Liberation Army (PLA). The nation's actual proletarians were discouraged from taking too much initiative in the construction of the 'proletarian dictatorship', lest they disrupt production. Nationalisation, along with top-down economic planning, meant that capitalist competition would play little role in shaping China's domestic economy. But the country's new bureaucracy was acutely aware of the need to build up its military and heavy industry, and to this end they siphoned off surplus from China's peasantry and state employees as assiduously as any corporate CEO.

How exactly to characterise the social structure of Mao's China is still a vexed debate. The party certainly made good on some of its egalitarian promises. Significant advances were made in health and education, without which the rapid growth of China in the post-Mao period would have been impossible. The socialist ethos of the time still inspires a certain nostalgia, both inside and outside China. But none of these facts is incompatible with the idea that the People's Republic of China has been, in essence, a heavily nationalised state capitalist system from its founding, with a party-led bureaucracy standing in for a non-existent capitalist class. As early as the 1930s, core Leninist principles, such as the self-determination of nations, were jettisoned in favour of a more centralised vision. The CCP denied that there was any division between 'oppressor' and 'oppressed' nationalities within China: all of its citizens were victims of colonialism alike. They therefore claimed the remaining territory of the Qing dynasty as inseparable parts of the new China, turning Tibet and Xinjiang into 'autonomous regions', with little genuine autonomy given to their inhabitants.

China's communists believed that disengaging from the global economy was necessary to stabilise the new nation's economy and accumulate capital, but the bootstrap development plans that we associate with the Maoist period were not simply a policy choice. Beijing held out hope that friendly relations could be established with the West, bringing with it reconstruction aid, but in this they were disappointed. Rejecting the advice of many of its 'China hands', Washington remained faithful to Chiang Kai-shek and shielded the Guomindang as it took refuge in Taiwan. As Washington redefined its post-war mission as the containment of communism, tensions across the Taiwan Strait soon deteriorated into direct US–China conflict on the Korean Peninsula. With China on its knees economically, the United States isolated it diplomatically. Despite wartime promises that parts of Japan's colonial empire would revert to 'China', Beijing was excluded from all post-war negotiations on the status of these colonies – a decision that left a legacy of ambiguity surrounding the disposition of territories such as Taiwan. Japan itself quickly went from being an enemy of the United States to a friend, as Washington identified it as a pillar of the new anti-communist alliance it was constructing.

In Australia, the small cohort of China hands in the Department of External Affairs were mostly in favour of immediately recognising the new People's Republic, but here too the politics of anti-communism intervened. The Menzies-led Liberal Party took up the anti-communist cause with gusto on the eve of the 1949 elections, scaring Labor away from any move to recognise Mao's government. Then, with the beginning of the Korean War, the newly elected Menzies government firmly took the US line on China and withheld diplomatic relations from the CCP for the next two decades, making anti-communism a pillar of Australian foreign and domestic policy.

Bereft of friends, the Chinese communists had no choice but to fall back on their testy relationship with the Soviet Union. Stalin had never shown much confidence in Mao's brand of 'Sinified' Marxism. During the Chinese Civil War, the Soviets had been far less forthcoming in support for the CCP than America had been for the Guomindang, and the Soviets had even carried off some of Manchuria's factories as war booty. While Soviet finance and expertise now contributed to China's economic stabilisation, the two sides remained at odds on many issues. Lingering territorial disputes were never fully resolved; Beijing vied with Moscow for influence throughout the Communist Bloc and the developing world; Mao took umbrage at the Soviet Union's criticisms of Stalin and its friendly gestures to the West. The friendship was not destined to last long.

Domestically, Mao's impatience to industrialise the country required massive – and tragic – sacrifices from China's people, as well as a political conformity drilled into them by dulling political campaigns. While the period saw a huge increase in life expectancy and a reduction in mortality, the disastrous 1958–61 famine, triggered by the policy failures of the Great Leap Forward, cost as many as thirty million lives. Mao was still enough of a materialist to recognise the practical obstacles in China's way; his heterodox solution was to try to crash through these barriers with revolutionary enthusiasm – and he was willing to risk fracturing his party to generate it. The decade of Cultural Revolution from 1966 to 1976 was many things: factional manoeuvring at the top and an element of revolutionary play among the Red Guards (even if it often got deadly). But it also bore witness to a genuine grassroots hostility towards party elites, as well as experiments in popular democracy that resembled more classical models of proletarian socialism – something anathema to the 'Communist' Party.

Coming at the height of the Cultural Revolution in the early 1970s, America's opening up of relations with the People's Republic of China caught many observers of East Asia – both on the left and the right – by surprise. Initially the détente was little more than a political gambit on the part of the United States, designed to lay the foundations for a respectable withdrawal from the quagmire of Vietnam and to capitalise on the Sino–Soviet rift in the international Communist Bloc. For Nixon's adviser Henry Kissinger, preventing the economic and political integration of the Eurasian continent, and thereby allowing the United States to rule by dominating either end of it, was a sine qua non of American strategy.

When Mao's death in 1976 seemed to presage a turn to pragmatism by the CCP, a new rationale was built into US policy on China, which became known as 'engagement'. Since 1949, social science orthodoxy in the United States had held that China had been thrown off a natural pathway to modernisation by irrational revolutionary exuberance. In this view, communist regimes were irredeemable: short of intervention and regime change, the only sensible response was to contain their aggressive tendencies and hope they would one day collapse. Political reconciliation with China led the United States to rethink this approach. If America could show China the benefits of entering the global capitalist system, the theory went, incentives would arise for China to collaborate with, and not oppose, the exercise of American primacy. At their most optimistic, proponents of this view anticipated China entering a more 'normal' transition to modernity, with a rising middle class exerting pressure on the party-state to democratise. A liberalised, open China would peacefully reconcile itself to the world that the United States had built around it. Engagement may have been a stark reversal of America's previous stance in practice, therefore, but it was still consistent in its avowed aims – the pursuit of freedom and democracy.

The theory reflected longstanding liberal beliefs in the civilising role of capital. On its own, it was never likely to be all that persuasive, but there were strong incentives for Western elites to believe it. China became cautiously receptive to foreign capital from 1978 onwards, and by the 1990s it was actively courting investment with special economic zones and other inducements. Economic integration with China became a bonanza for corporations and economic and policy advisers alike. The charge that advocates of engagement with China were motivated by self-interest isn't entirely wide of the mark: those who supported the policy shift often did become active investors in the country themselves. But amid a declining rate of profit worldwide, the need for new sources of profit was a structural one. With rural–urban migration controls that kept labour costs down, and its absence of trade union militancy and environmental regulation, China was an ideal place to relocate Western factories. Deng Xiaoping, the man most often credited with China's economic transformation, was feted as a hero in the West.

Just as America justified its volte-face in terms of world peace and US national security, China came to see its growing ties to world capitalism as a hedge against more dangerous times. First in the countryside, then in the cities, China's economic experiments let market principles work their way through the system, prompting the restructuring (or dismantling) of parts of the public sector, while private enterprise grew up around it. Benefiting from the influx of capital and technology, China sought to follow a similar path to some of its neighbours, such as Japan and South Korea, by gradually building up the technological base for its own enterprises to go out into the world. The bargain with the West was a fairly simple one: a healthy, low-cost workforce in exchange for know-how and intellectual property.

Of course, like all countries, China also spies for commercial, as well as diplomatic and military, advantage. But today, when Westerners accuse

China of intellectual property theft, they often elide the nature of the commercial transaction they've entered into. On a recent flight to California, I sat alongside a Silicon Valley entrepreneur who was agitated by China's acquisition of American IP. 'They don't exactly force you to give it up, though, do they?' I queried him. 'Isn't it more the price of doing business in China?' 'That's true,' he replied, 'but if we don't manufacture in China, we'll go bankrupt!'

As Australia's Opposition leader, Gough Whitlam had already made overtures to Beijing by the time of Nixon's secret diplomacy, and as prime minister he was happy to have his policy direction vindicated by America's own move towards engagement. No less than the United States, Australia switched rapidly from virulent hostility to the enthusiastic embrace of China and the opportunities it presented. The words of two young Asia specialists in the Department of External Affairs illustrate this dramatic change. In 1967, having tendered his resignation in opposition to the Menzies government's containment policy, Gregory Clark wrote that 'few countries, Western or non-Western, are more hostile to China than Australia'.[9] By 1989, his one-time colleague Stephen FitzGerald (who had also quit External Affairs under Menzies, before returning to serve as Australia's first ambassador to the People's Republic of China) was of the view that, 'in the whole of Asia, Australia has probably been the most Sino-friendly, and the closest to being single-mindedly so'.[10] Writing in the wake of the Tiananmen crackdown that June, FitzGerald realised that Australia's paranoia had given way to pandering. Some self-criticism was required.

Going Out

Engagement gave rise to a state of mutual dependency between China and the West that exists to this day. America's appetite for low-cost consumer goods was insatiable, while China reinvested its huge dollar surplus in US treasury bonds, thereby sustaining America's supply of credit. In the fallout from the 1989 massacre in Beijing, China increased its investment in US debt, while hundreds of American corporations spent millions of dollars lobbying for the maintenance of normal trade relations. (Australia lent its voice to this cause too.) With corporate America on its side, China has tended to hold back from lobbying Washington directly. To this day,

Chinese government and corporate spending on Washington lobbyists is still only a fraction of that of South Korea and Japan.

Still, engagement wasn't quite the policy U-turn that it's sometimes depicted as. Friendly relations were always conditional on a set of expectations for China's conduct. What exactly were those expectations? As with the 'rules' of today's 'rules-based order', the terms of engagement were never really spelled out officially. But in 1996, amid a tense stand-off in the Taiwan Strait, a Council on Foreign Relations (CFR) study entitled *Weaving the Net: Conditional Engagement with China* put forward a set of 'ten principles for acceptable behavior'.[11] Many of these were laudable principles, among them 'peaceful resolution of territorial disputes' and 'respect for basic human rights'. But they were one-way injunctions on China, not firm principles of an international system that the United States intended to abide by itself.

The primary rule that China was being told to accept was one that wasn't on the list – the same rule that the rest of the world was told to accept at the highpoint of American triumphalism in the 1990s: that the United States gets to set the rules. The first and most important of the CFR's 'principles' was that there was to be 'no unilateral use of offensive military force'. Also high on its list were 'respect for national sovereignty' and 'moderation in military force build-up'. No one can credibly argue that America's foreign and defence policies have consistently embodied these principles. China, therefore, has been told to play by 'rules' that are not the *actual* rules of the system. Put in this unenviable position, it has continued to do what it's done since the nineteenth century: extrapolate those actual rules from observing the way the system's members, particularly its leading members, behave. When we look at things this way, what we see is that China is not so much breaking the rules as beginning to play by them. It's this, I think, that should worry us.

The CFR's eighth principle, 'market access for trade and investment', might suit established capitalist economies, but no country has ever risen from the bottom rungs of the global system on that basis. For that, you need foreign technology and a protective shelter for local industry. America itself knows this well. In the nineteenth century, it stood outside liberal orthodoxies and put up protectionist barriers. Reflecting on the country's post-war hegemony, a 1971 study found that three-quarters of major industrial innovations of the 1950s occurred at America's universities and concluded that 'it is the official US research and development program that has generated US overseas dominance'.[12] This public–private partnership continues to the present day. In the case of Apple, for example, the political scientist Clinton Fernandes writes that the twelve 'major technologies that make the iPhone so distinctive were all developed by public investments backed by the American taxpayer'. 'It was decades of public subsidy,' he concludes, 'that made the smartphone smart.'[13]

Another rule is that any country liable to incur the wrath of the United States had better acquire a military deterrent to ensure its survival. When the end of the Cold War removed the strategic rationale for US–China collaboration, America's blitzkrieg invasion of Iraq sent alarm bells ringing in the Chinese military. In 1992, the Bush administration broke with precedent and resumed the sale of fighter aircraft to Taiwan. At the same time, the US Navy and Marine Corps unveiled a revision to its strategic thinking: the US Navy would shift its focus away from ocean operations against the Soviet Navy to a battle space of coastlines and their hinterlands. Naval forces would 'maneuver from the sea using their dominance of littoral areas to mass forces rapidly and generate high intensity, precise offensive power'.[14] 'It is not difficult to imagine,' historian John Dower writes, 'how potential adversaries like China might have viewed such an aggressive redefinition of the American strategic mission.'[15]

The basic dynamic in regions such as the South China Sea has been in place ever since. With its long, exposed coastline, America once justified its domination of the entire Pacific as a defensive necessity, including its seizure of Hawaii and the Philippines. Today, it insists that its 'defence' interests require it to thwart China's ability to deter American military action inside the 'first island chain' – the seas off China's coast. It's a highly aggressive posture: just imagine if a country thousands of kilometres away made it an express part of its 'defence' strategy to deny Australia the ability to secure its immediate coastline. China, unsurprisingly, is responding by building up its capability to do just this. Beijing expresses its defence needs in far less expansive terms than the United States, but by pressing its dubious historical claims in the South China Sea it is acting aggressively towards neighbouring countries, including Vietnam and the Philippines. In any such situation, what counts as defensive and what counts as offensive is very much in the eye of the beholder.

By introducing reform and opening itself up to foreign investment, China reduced the risk of any immediate rupture with the United States, but Beijing officials were conscious of a second risk: that too much integration with the global economy might erode the party-state's capacity to guide Chinese development. With the CCP's legitimacy resting in large part on its promises of ever-increasing prosperity for the Chinese population, it could not afford to ignore the deleterious impact that free trade and international financial institutions were having on other developing countries. This was highlighted by the Asian financial crisis of 1998 and the conditions that the IMF imposed on countries such as Indonesia and Thailand, which exacerbated the contraction of their economies and severely compromised their sovereignty. By contrast, China – having ignored advice to liberalise its financial sector – was shielded from the crisis.

These events – and the worldwide critique of globalisation they gave rise to – were part of the background to the Chinese debate on whether or not to seek admission to the World Trade Organization (WTO). Entry promised a massive increase in trade and investment, but some worried that an influx of foreign corporations and the constraints of WTO membership would bind China to the dictates of global capitalism. Beijing nevertheless pressed on, signing an onerous protocol of accession that exceeded the normal requirements for membership. Since signing, China has maintained its resolve to rise up the global value chain through a deliberate industrial policy, involving state-owned enterprises, subsidies and the ongoing acquisition of foreign intellectual property. 'Made in China 2025' – a strategic plan to shift the Chinese economy to higher-value products and services – exemplifies this national ambition and brings China into direct competition with sectors currently dominated by the United States.

China began promoting its own outward investment in the early 2000s, after some tentative forays in the 1990s. Energy and transport infrastructure were early priorities, but the CCP has of late encouraged a more diverse portfolio, including agriculture and healthcare. China's state banks have become the world's most active international lenders, willing to provide commercial loans at a below-market rate to countries unable to secure finance anywhere else. Meanwhile, excess capacity in domestic industries requires China to raise external consumption of its goods and services. Since taking office in 2012, Xi Jinping has rebranded these ventures as part of the 'Belt and Road Initiative'. The initiative aligns with China's strategic priorities in various ways: by opening up trade corridors across the Eurasian continent to China's west, for example, China will reduce its vulnerability to maritime blockade. Beijing's Belt and Road Summit, as well as similar platforms such as the Forum on China–Africa Cooperation, has become a major international networking event. But far from the coordinated plan for global dominance it is sometimes depicted as, the Belt and Road Initiative remains a messy, and in many ways unfulfilled, scheme, with China's rate of lending now much reduced from the high point of 2015–16.

China's global presence has been accompanied by the same corruption, labour disputes and environmental damage we associate with Western lending in the developing world. Arguably, any kind of indebtedness puts the sovereignty of poor nations at risk. But China has been able to ingratiate itself in regions such as Africa in part by refraining from the practices of the International Monetary Fund (IMF) and other institutions, which dictate domestic policies of austerity and privatisation to borrowing countries. China's lending, of course, may still exacerbate a country's vulnerability to such pressure. Belt and Road debts, for example, contributed to Pakistan's dire fiscal condition in 2019, which led Imran Khan to contract a new US$6 billion extended fund facility from the IMF, requiring huge cuts to government spending. But China itself is primarily interested in the commercial viability of the ventures it supports, not intrusive reforms to smooth the way for private enterprise. With its strong emphasis on the specificity of China's national conditions, Beijing lacks the impulse of the West to propagate its system worldwide; political, not structural, alignment is its main priority.

This naturally allows for a certain meeting of the minds with fellow authoritarians. On a trip to Tajikistan in 2019, I was working in the National Library one day, when I came across a conference dedicated to the launch of the Tajik translation of Xi Jinping's collected speeches and articles, *The Governance of China*. I can't imagine too many Tajik bureaucrats engaging deeply with the work as a manual of governance, but the event was a sign of the times. Next to the hostel I was staying in, a PRC trade office was being fitted out with a Chinese-style facade. Locals told

me it was the first of its kind; until then, China had avoided advertising its presence in that way. Deep in the Pamir Mountains in the east of
Tajikistan, an outpost of the PRC's People's Armed Police overlooks the
sensitive Wakhan Corridor, a thin strip of Afghan territory that offers a
route into China. With half of its foreign debt owing to Chinese lenders,
Tajikistan is in a poor position to say no to Beijing.

Progressive political economists have often imagined that China, possibly as part of the BRICS (Brazil, Russia, India, China and South Africa)
alliance, might democratise international relations by challenging the
dominance of the Bretton Woods institutions and Euro–American hegemony within them. The United States has tended to resist efforts by China
to bring its IMF quota, and hence its voting share, into line with its position in the global economy. This was one of the motivations for China to
set up the Asian Infrastructure Investment Bank, which America declined
to join (Australia signed up at the last minute). But contrary to those who
imagine China catalysing a shift to a world in which developing countries
have more of a say, China's growing influence in international financial
institutions has tended to come at the expense of the rest of the developing world. In 2012, for example, when the IMF was recapitalised, China's
vote share went up from 3.8 to 6 per cent, but many countries in Africa
saw their share reduced. China's evolving role in global finance has so
far been far less disruptive than either pro-China or anti-China pundits
might have predicted. In many ways, China has taken up the mantle of
the United States as the leading advocate of corporate globalisation.

Meanwhile, China has become active at all levels of the UN, championing its role with far more rhetorical support than America or Australia.
This development came after the decade of the 1990s, in which the United
States effectively rendered the UN a multilateral proxy for its war and
sanctions regime on Iraq. The mood of that time was encapsulated in
new doctrines of humanitarian intervention, such as the 'responsibility
to protect'. Instinctively wary of Western claims to advance human rights
by force of arms, China has gradually tried to shift the UN back towards
a stance that respects the principle of state sovereignty. A key turning
point was the 2011 military intervention in Libya. China, to the surprise
of many, initially endorsed UN resolutions to condemn Libya's dictator Muammar Gaddafi's bloody repression of the local opposition and

refrained from vetoing a resolution to establish a no-fly zone above the country. NATO then took advantage of this unlikely consensus to launch massive air strikes on Libya, staging an intervention that China believed to greatly exceed the UN mandate. Since this time, China has been much firmer in its opposition to any resolutions that might serve as a pretext for Western military action. It has repeatedly opposed, for example, resolutions against Bashar al-Assad's government in Syria.

While China sees itself as curbing America's trigger-happy interventionism, Western diplomats criticise it for coddling a set of dictatorial allies. A deputy assistant secretary of state in George W. Bush's administration, Thomas Christensen, complains in a recent book that 'a more assertive China sometimes directly defies the wishes of the United States and like-minded nations by wielding a veto or threatening to do so to block unwelcome resolutions aimed at some of Beijing's more unsavory diplomatic partners'. But in the same discussion, Christensen describes how, in 2006, when two Chinese peacekeepers (along with around a thousand Lebanese citizens) were killed in what Human Rights Watch calls 'indiscriminate Israeli airstrikes' on Lebanon, the American mission to the UN did much the same thing. As he explains, 'We needed to maintain China's cooperation with the UN while *preventing the organization from adopting language and actions unacceptable to Israel*, the key US partner in the region' (my emphasis).[16] If we're honest with ourselves about what the rules of the system actually are, we see that China is playing by them.

Whither China?

As China rises towards the top of the world system, it is beginning to carry itself in a more imperious fashion. This is not something to welcome, but it's not something that should surprise us either. From a historical point of view, Xi Jinping's desire to translate economic weight into political influence is similar to the desire articulated by Commodore Perry, who drove America's nineteenth-century imperial expansion into Asia: 'In the development of the future, the destinies of our nation must assume conspicuous attitudes; we cannot expect to be free from the ambitious longings of increased power, which are the natural concomitants of national success.'[17] Of course, Xi has different language to describe

China's success and its attendant ambitions. Domestically, he celebrates 'the great renewal of the Chinese nation'. Internationally, he would like to see a 'new type of great-power relations'. Xi's nationalistic boilerplate, a mix of hardly recognisable Marxism and classical allusions, has now been enshrined in the Chinese constitution as 'Xi Jinping Thought on Socialism with Chinese Characteristics for a New Era'.

In a 2017 speech, Xi outlined three domestic objectives for China to meet by 2020. The first, poverty reduction, aimed to raise Chinese society to a level of a 'moderate prosperity'. Has this been achieved? It's a cliché, but anyone who visits China today can't help but be impressed by the transformation – the high-speed rail and ever-expanding subways, the cash-free economy with its ubiquitous QR codes, the recognisably middle-class lifestyle of many in China's cities. China has massively contributed to global poverty reduction: some seven out of every ten people who have escaped poverty since the 1980s are Chinese. With economic resources come freedoms unthinkable only a couple of decades ago: the freedom to buy a car, to start a company, to live and study abroad.

Yet while China now ranks second in the world in terms of GDP, the per capita average has only just risen above US$10,000, a fifth of what it is in Australia. Keep in mind, too, that per capita GDP elides the huge levels of inequality in China. The raw figure also fails to take into account what Chinese citizens have lost in the course of liberalisation: universities now charge tuition fees comparable to those in the West; healthcare is a privilege for those who can afford it; only the small percentage of the population who remain in state employment receive pensions. There's a case to be made that, along with reducing poverty, China has actually exacerbated global levels of inequality. There are more billionaires in China today than anywhere else in the world, and policies continue to favour cities and urban residents at the expense of the rural population.

In November 2020, China claimed to have fully eradicated extreme poverty, but this measure is set at an annual income of a mere ¥4000, around A$800. While Chinese media spoke of a 'final push' into moderate prosperity, the lifestyle that we in Australia might associate with that term is still beyond reach for most in China.

Will they get there? Many inside and outside China worry about the stability of China's development. Looming before it is what is known as the 'middle-income trap', which occurs when a country's export-led growth runs its course without spawning enough higher-productivity industries for the country to keep rising up the value chain. Equally worrying is the thought that, while China escaped the impact of the last global financial crisis, conditions may be ripe for it to detonate the next one. With returns on savings kept deliberately low so as to redirect resources to state-led investment, Chinese with cash to invest have migrated between real estate and stocks, inflating speculative bubbles in both sectors. In 2015, a crash wiped out 40 per cent of the value of the Shanghai stock exchange, which development economist Walden Bello describes as being 'as much a casino as Macau'. Limits on bank lending have given rise to a large 'shadow banking' sector, outside the state banking system but nevertheless tied to it. After the Asian financial crisis and the 2007–08 global financial crisis, Bello argues, 'the Chinese bubble could be the third phase of the global financial crisis'.[18]

Mitigating this financial risk was the second of Xi's policy objectives to be ticked off by 2020. The recent crackdown on billionaire Jack Ma's Ant Group, known for its Alipay financial platform, is only the most eye-catching episode in an ongoing campaign. In articulating his vision of a 'dual circulation' economy', Xi has restated the need to increase domestic consumption and move away from an investment-led economic model, which many see as a field of bad debt and diminishing returns. China has a long way to go, though: private consumption as a share of GDP is still extremely low. At 39 per cent, it is well below the world average of 63 per cent.

The third objective on Xi's list was to rein in pollution. China's emissions remain high and are still growing, though some parts of the country have seen small-particle air pollution drop significantly. China builds, and drives, the most electric cars in the world, and it imposes high quotas on local governments for the production of renewable energy – often outstripping consumption. Air quality is of course only one of China's many environmental problems; others include desertification, deforestation, the loss of biodiversity – the list could go on.

China's technocratic, state-driven environmentalism divides opinion. The huge social cost of some of its campaigns and crackdowns, including land grabs and the forcible relocation of populations, has led some to conclude that China's 'green authoritarianism' is better thought of as a new

style of totalising social control. 'The green cloak of Chinese authoritarianism is ... more ornamental than functional,' as one recent study puts
it.[19] By contrast, others see in China's non-democratic system, free from
the influence of climate-change scepticism, the kind of state-imposed
emergency response that will be necessary to save the planet.

The truth is probably somewhere in the middle. Without popular
input, many of China's environmental campaigns have in fact backfired.
As the world discovered with the onset of the COVID-19 pandemic,
China has also neglected important tasks, such as ending the trade and
consumption of wild animals. But it would be too cynical in this day and
age to dismiss China's ambitious commitments – including a pledge to
be carbon-neutral by 2060 – as in some way invalidated by its repressive
political system. There's far too much at stake for that.

As China celebrates the centenary of the founding of the CCP, you
don't need to be an economist or environmental scientist to see that, in
domestic terms alone, the country could be in for a bumpy ride ahead.
Since becoming general secretary in 2012, Xi has clearly signalled that
he intends to negotiate any risk of instability through the strengthening
of party authority.

Some of this tightening involves traditional tactics of purge and co-
option. The CCP is an organisation of some 90 million members, drawn
from all walks of life. With its origins in an intellectual cadre commanding an army drawn from the peasantry, its top echelons still see the
party as a one-way transmission belt for imparting to the populace correct thoughts and actions. In practice, though, party membership has
often been exploited as a ticket to insider perks. Xi's widely publicised
crackdown on corruption recognises this obvious fact and has won him
considerable popularity. He has also increased the presence of the party in
the private sector, set up new party bodies (many of which he directs himself) and brought sections of the state bureaucracy under party control.
One of these strengthened institutions is the party's United Front Work
Department, the role of which is to win friends and combat political enemies in wider Chinese society. Part of its brief, and one that now causes
much angst internationally, is to 'guide' the overseas Chinese community.

Of course, if its persuasive powers fail, the Chinese state is as willing as ever to engage in outright repression. The year 2015 saw a major

crackdown on 'rights-defence' lawyers, brave individuals who stick their necks out to defend dissidents or those who have been stripped of their property by unscrupulous local officials. In 2016, after a string of terrorist attacks in Xinjiang and elsewhere in China, Xi appointed the party secretary of Tibet to Xinjiang, where he would introduce a scheme of mass-scale internment and indoctrination.

Xi's centralised authority and strict insistence on the party's leading role often inspire comparisons with Mao. In his anti-corruption campaign, too, there is an echo of Mao's attacks on party privilege (and probably a similar degree of hypocrisy). A kitschy, nostalgic reverence for the 'Great Helmsman' Mao is observable across the country today. But Mao is not simply a symbol of party authority. Some critical Maoists agitate within the party to rein in the logic of capital and its social costs. There are also self-identifying Maoists who view the party as irredeemable and imagine the chairman's slogans once again inspiring revolutionary struggle at the grassroots level. There is a tension between the party's need to canonise Chinese Marxism while blunting its message of anti-capitalist radicalism. In 2018, members of Marxist study societies at some of China's most elite universities put their principles into practice and went south to Shenzhen to support an organising drive in factories there, eventually provoking a major police crackdown. Yet an ostensibly Marxist party couldn't possibly abolish the Marxist clubs from which these radicals had emerged, they could only 'reorganise' them.

Far from a return to communist traditionalism, Xi's authoritarianism carries many of the marks of China's engagement in global affairs. In the ethnic policy debate, for example, a shift towards assimilationism has been justified in decidedly liberal language: advisers wish to do away with rigid structures inherited from the Soviet Union and adopt a US-style 'melting-pot' approach. This, of course, raises anxieties among non-Han populations that ending the bureaucratic recognition of their national distinctiveness will be a step towards erasing it in practice. From their point of view, it would be preferable for China to come good on Mao's original promise of national autonomy – a perspective that is more faithful to China's communist past than that of today's policy elites.

The CCP's denial of basic democratic rights to a fifth of the world's population is a dismaying reality, one that should vex us all. But the West does the cause of democracy a disservice when it constructs it not as a measurable quality of a political system but as one side of a simplistic democracy–authoritarianism binary, with the contemporary West held up as the democratic archetype. Worse still is the tendency to reduce this debate to one between two different 'models': the Chinese and the American.

If the perils of doing so were not already obvious, they should be now, in the wake of COVID-19. When the pandemic hit, systemic comparisons in binary terms proliferated. Almost immediately, commentators held forth that China's authoritarianism would be its downfall, while democracy would shine in its response. The truth, of course, has been precisely the opposite. As expected, China has been secretive and insensitive to human rights in combatting COVID-19, but it has also kept the disease in check. Many Chinese have been aghast at the seeming inability of wealthy nations, such as the United States and Britain, to do the same. Clearly, glib, self-congratulatory characterisations of the systemic difference here – for instance, that in authoritarian China officials are accountable to those above them, while in the democratic West they are accountable to the people below – will not do. The increasingly shambolic functioning of Western polities, with their own obvious corruption and spheres of impunity, points to the need for a revival of democratic principles at a global level.

China has survived COVID-19 with its system well and truly intact, and domestic confidence in that system likely only enhanced by comparison with a disease-ridden wider world. Its economy has slowed but not stalled. China was the only major world economy to grow in 2020, and predictions for 2021 have it returning to around 8 per cent growth. It is now the most attractive destination in the world for foreign direct investment. In light of COVID's impact, some analysts have revised their predictions for China's GDP to surpass that of the United States, bringing the date forward to 2028, or even as early as 2026. It seems very likely that at some point in the next decade America will be displaced from its leading position in the international economy, a position it has held since 1890, when its industries eclipsed those of Great Britain.

2. THE US-CHINA RIVALRY TODAY

'There is a growing consensus,' Jake Sullivan and Kurt Campbell write, 'that the era of engagement with China has come to an unceremonious close.'[1] Sullivan is now President Biden's national security adviser, while Campbell is his 'Asia tsar'. Both bring experience of service in in the Obama administration, an administration which had remained rhetorically hopeful for a collaborative relationship with China. 'The United States welcomes the rise of a stable, peaceful and prosperous China,' wrote the authors of the 2015 National Security Strategy. 'While there will be competition, we reject the inevitability of confrontation.'[2] By contrast, the Trump administration all but embraced that notion of inevitability.

In 2018, for the first time, it became the official US view that China intended to supplant US hegemony, not only in Asia but worldwide. The Trump administration's National Defense Strategy predicted that China would continue 'its economic and military ascendance, asserting power through an all-of-nation long-term strategy', and would 'pursue a military modernisation program that seeks Indo-Pacific regional hegemony in the near-term and displacement of the United States to achieve global pre-eminence in the future'.[3] On this basis, the 2018 Strategic Framework for the Indo-Pacific spelled out the goal of maintaining US 'diplomatic, economic, and military pre-eminence' in the region.[4] The term that America's strategists have hit upon to describe this mission is 'great-power competition'.

American foreign policy elites still exhibit a range of views on China. Many would dissent from talk of a long-term Chinese strategy to achieve global dominance – a perspective associated with a cohort of 'hawks' who rose to prominence in the Trump era. These included people such as Mike Pillsbury, author of a book on how ancient military texts inform China's every move, and Pete Navarro, who believes China is slowly killing Americans with its low-quality exports. But the shift in how China is discussed should not be dismissed as mere rhetoric, and it is unlikely to be undone by the new Biden administration. Since the end of the Cold War, the United States has shown no interest in modifying or revising a view that crystallised at that time: that the emergence of a regional competitor *anywhere* endangers US dominance *everywhere*, and Washington should act to prevent such an eventuality. Although this view is identified as the brainchild of neo-conservative thinkers, many more 'dovish' US analysts share their conclusion: that American primacy in Asia must be defended. US debate, therefore, centres not so much on whether to set limits on China's emergence as an independent actor on the world stage, but on how to set such limits.

In essence, America's 'containment' versus 'engagement' choice has always been a choice between actually containing China and simply threatening to do so. Writing on the cusp of Trump's 2016 election, Thomas Christensen was among those who still expressed optimism about a cooperative modus vivendi with China, but he also spelled out the implicit message of 'or else'. 'Chinese anxiety about a US containment effort could carry some benefits for the United States,' he pointed out. 'The potential for future encirclement may encourage Chinese strategists to be more accommodating.'[5] In DC think-tanks, only a handful of outliers still advocate something like a classical engagement policy. The free-market fundamentalist Cato Institute, for instance, still aims to reconcile China's behaviour with US interests through deepening economic ties and WTO mechanisms. The anti-interventionist Quincy Institute calls for dialogue and diplomacy, not cold-war rivalry. Across the rest of the spectrum, however, most of America's China hands are putting their minds to more confrontational strategies.

For those who adhere to a realist philosophy of international relations, there's nothing remarkable about any of this: states pursue their interests at the expense of other states. A rising power presents a challenge to a reigning power, which can be expected to meet that challenge with all the policy instruments at its disposal. The laws of realpolitik render any debate as to moral superiority beside the point. This stripped-back,

pretence-free perspective is, I think, more accurate than many alternatives – and it's certainly Beijing's view of the situation. But it jars with the
sensibilities of many, if not most, in the US foreign policy world, who
prefer to see US–China relations through the lens of a morality tale. This
tale has its roots in America's self-image as a force for anti-colonialism in
the world. Its belated arrival in East Asia and advocacy of an 'open door'
trade policy towards China – in place of territorial concessions or an
exclusive sphere of influence – was spun into a narrative that the United
States was uniquely mindful of China's wellbeing. In the wake of World
War II, the CCP's view of America as a predatory foreign intruder was
met with bemusement, if not incomprehension. According to one participant in State Department discussions in 1951, 'In seeking liberation
from Western imperialism, the Oriental peoples are contending against
something that isn't there anymore.'[6]

A sermon-like speech by Vice-President Mike Pence at the Hudson
Institute in 2019 reprised many of these historical tropes: China had welcomed America's message of free trade and Christianity, Washington had
held back while Europe and Russia preyed on a vulnerable China's sovereignty, and the United States and China had made common cause against
imperialism in World War II. Spurning this beneficence, China had sadly
chosen 'to pursue authoritarian expansionism', and therefore only had
itself to blame for Washington's Cold War policy of blockade and military
intimidation. Pence even held up China's admission to the United Nations
as evidence of Washington's goodwill, neglecting to mention that US support for Taiwan prevented the PRC from joining the body until 1971.[7]

The same tragic cycle, of America extending a friendly hand, only
to have it bitten by a recalcitrant, aggressive China, plays itself out in
common narratives of the 'engagement' period. To be sure, there is consensus among China's elite that America did help the PRC by offering
it a path of export-led growth, self-interested as that stance may have
been. But regrets that China has not reciprocated by acquiescing to US
pre-eminence in Asia often strike a paternalistic tone – positioning the
United States as a forbearing patron now obliged to discipline its way-
ward apprentice. Consider how journalist John Pomfret concludes his
2016 history of the tribulations of the US–China relationship, sighing that
'the United States has no choice but to redouble its efforts to complete

its historic mission to pull China into the world'.[8] America still imagines itself engaged in this 'historic mission'.

Washington's charge sheet against China is a long one – from trade practices to bullying diplomacy, to the repression of the Uyghurs, and more. But above and beyond the specifics of these disputes, there is what John Dower calls the 'the mystique of exceptional virtue' – the faith that American primacy has delivered to humanity the best of all possible worlds.[9] It is this faith, more than anything else, that allows the China challenge to be depicted in moral terms, and no one will rise to high office in American diplomacy without declaring themselves a true believer. 'America's leadership is needed around the world,' declared Biden's secretary of state, Anthony Blinken, at his Senate confirmation hearing.

Domestic politics plays a decisive role in promoting this claim: because the United States practices a form of electoral democracy at home, its foreign policy must be favourable to democracy worldwide. The corollary is that China's lack of democracy will incline it to promote authoritarianism. 'If the international order is a reflection of its most powerful states,' Campbell and Sullivan argue, 'then China's rise to superpower status will exert a pull towards autocracy.'[10] As I've already noted, there are few grounds to be optimistic that China's rise will encourage democracy internationally. But is it true that the global order simply mirrors the constitutions of its most powerful states? A characteristic of modern Western empires, political scientist Mahmood Mamdani argues, is that 'they combine a democratic political system at home with despotism abroad'.[11] The entire history of colonialism, after all, was one of denying colonised peoples the rights enjoyed by citizens in the metropolis.

In the wake of post-war decolonisation, America's respect for democratic elections elsewhere was often dependent on their outcome, and Washington has employed every tactic at its disposal – from psychological warfare and support for terrorist proxies to outright coups – to destabilise countries that made the 'wrong' choices. To this day, Washington shows little discrimination in the regimes it aligns with and financially supports. Besides its support for the self-defined Jewish ethno-state of Israel and its ongoing military occupation of Palestine, Washington's position in the Middle East rests on deep military and political ties with countries such as Egypt and Saudi Arabia that Freedom House classifies as 'not free'. The liberal order that China is said to be disrupting is not now, and has never been, particularly liberal.

So what can we anticipate today from a US policy to check China in a competition for global influence? Some imagine that an overt rivalry with China could revive America's flagging democracy mission, and that Washington should seize the 'opportunity to restore faith in democratic capitalism', as a Brookings Institution study puts it.[12] But if the last Cold War is anything to go by, the more likely outcome is just the opposite: strategic imperatives will trump any qualms about violating democratic practices and human rights. We see the beginnings of this tendency, for example, in the reconciliation of the United States and the ruling Communist Party of Vietnam, hardly a friend of freedom. Similarly, while the US State Department has campaigned loudly against China's human rights violations in Xinjiang, it has expressed little to no public criticism of India's military clampdown in Kashmir, busy as it is courting Delhi as an anti-China ally.

What of a second claim made for the international system, that on the United States' watch it has been orderly and 'rules-based'? Although it was the chief architect of many post-war global institutions, the United States was immediately wary of the constraints of international law. In its 1946 Connally Reservation, Washington reserved the right to determine for itself what disputes fell within its domestic jurisdiction and, therefore, outside the jurisdiction of the International Court of Justice, the UN's judicial organ. It has stood apart from many international treaties, neutralised others with extensive provisos, and undermined UN bodies and officials who have incurred its displeasure. In 2002, George W. Bush enacted a law authorising military force to free any American service member brought before the International Criminal Court in The Hague, which investigates and tries war crimes. Donald Trump then continued the assault on that institution, sanctioning its officials for investigating American actions in Afghanistan. In the course of his presidency, Trump withdrew from the Joint Comprehensive Plan of Action with Iran, the Paris Accord on climate change, the Intermediate-Range Nuclear Forces Treaty, the Arms Trade Treaty and the Open Skies Treaty. All of this leaves America with precious little credibility left as a good-faith negotiator.

While Biden may undo some of this damage, competition with China will continue to exacerbate the superpower's natural proclivity to slip the constraints of treaties and international law.

The Pivot Towards Competition

'Chimerica' was the term coined in the early 2000s to describe the deeply intertwined nature of the American and Chinese economies, and this connection remains a reality in many ways. If we analyse economic activity not in terms of national GDP, but according to the home base of corporations, it turns out that a large proportion of China's economic output remains in foreign, particularly American, hands. This kind of data serves as evidence for those who criticise the notion of America's relative economic decline.[13] The same data shows that American business has acquired a large, at times dominant, share of China's domestic market in a range of spheres. Coca-Cola, for example, controls 48 per cent of China's soft drink market, and Boeing holding roughly the same position in the aviation market. Among coffee chains, Starbucks commands more than half of all sales in China. On the eve of Joe Biden's inauguration, Xi Jinping himself penned a letter to the chair of the company, calling on Starbucks to 'play an active role in promoting US–China trade cooperation and bilateral ties'.[14]

This state of affairs certainly stands in stark contrast to the original Cold War, which was a competition between two insulated economic blocs. It raises questions about what it would look like to 'decouple' the two economies that make up Chimerica, or whether such a move would even be possible. As one of the chief beneficiaries of a decades-long feeding frenzy in China's low-wage, low-rights economy, America has much to contemplate if it's to extricate itself from its ties to China. There is a degree of confusion, therefore, possibly even incoherence, in the US response, caught as it is between disengaging from the Chinese economy and continuing its drive to prise it open for American profit-making. If you listened closely, the Trump administration's China-bashing was at times tempered by hints of business as usual between the two countries. When the secretary of state Mike Pompeo told a Sydney audience that 'you can sell your soul for a pile of soya beans or you can protect your people', it was generally interpreted as a warning not to do business with China. What he said next wasn't as widely reported: 'Our mission set is to actually do both.'[15]

Yet corporate America is nowhere near as bullish on China as it once was. As the global economy's centre of gravity shifts towards Asia, America's stake in, and therefore control of, world capitalism is slipping. The sociologist Ho-fung Hung describes the global financial crisis of 2007–08 as a key turning point.[16] In its wake, Beijing's massive stimulus helped domestic companies push American competitors out of the Chinese market and establish a firmer platform from which to compete internationally. This change undermined the longstanding Beijing–Wall Street nexus, quietening the normally vocal US corporate lobbyists and opening the way for security hawks to gain the ascendancy in the policy debate in Washington. The age of mutual enrichment had ended, and the time for more direct competition had arrived.

In the Obama era, America responded to its relative decline in Asia with the two instruments it has long relied on to enforce its international mission: the hidden hand of free trade and the iron fist of the US military. The first objective was to claw back America's position and reorientate Asian economies away from China through the enticements of a new free-trade pact, the Trans-Pacific Partnership. The second was to renew the US military's emphasis on Asia, a policy that became known as the 'Pivot to Asia'. In Secretary of State Hilary Clinton's view, the American military presence had been, and would remain, indispensable to the region's prosperity: 'Asia's remarkable economic growth over the past decade, and its potential for continued growth in the future, depend on the security and stability that has long been guaranteed by the U.S. military.'[17]

The economic dimension of this approach ran up against the contradictions of America's own domestic predicament. By the time of the 2016 presidential election, with mounting opposition to free-trade doctrine on both the right and left of US politics, Obama had failed to 'fast track' the ratification of the Trans-Pacific Partnership, and Clinton herself had ditched her commitment to it as the Democratic Party's presidential candidate. In the wake of his surprise victory, Trump set his course away from alliance-building and free-trade compacts, and towards 'America first' economic nationalism. The new US president took his philosophy to

the region at an Asia-Pacific Economic Cooperation (APEC) summit in
Vietnam in November 2017: 'We are not going to let the United States be
taken advantage of anymore. I am always going to put America first the
same way that I expect all of you in this room to put your countries first.'[18]

As for the military dimension, many critics deem Obama's 'Pivot to
Asia' a failure. American defence analysts, now fixated on Russia and
China, rue time lost to costly engagements in the Middle East throughout his tenure. At the same time, and in a slightly contradictory vein,
some hawkish voices fault Obama's unwillingness to intervene more
aggressively in the Middle East – to enforce a 'red line' on Syrian dictator
Bashar al-Assad, for example – arguing that this contributed to the ongoing erosion of US credibility in possible flashpoints in Asia. The Pivot's
advertised commitment to relocating 60 per cent of the US Navy to the
Pacific by 2020 has in fact been met, but this has so far done little to dissuade China from pursuing its military modernisation and enclosure of
the South China Sea, which Washington worries will inhibit its own war-
fighting capacity in maritime East Asia.

Arm Wrestle in Asia

China's military spending as a percentage of GDP is approximately the
same as Australia's (1.9 per cent), and its total outlay is less than a third of
America's. For 2020, US Congress signed off on a whopping $720 billion
spending bill, a total that rises close to $1 trillion when all military-related
expenses are tallied up. This buys the United States a massive military
presence worldwide, some 800 overseas facilities at rough count, while
China has only one official base in Djibouti (alongside its paramilitary
presence in Tajikistan). From its headquarters in Honolulu, the United
States Indo-Pacific Command has the most wide-ranging brief of any
part of the US military, covering a region in which half the world's population resides. Alongside Hawaii, the US territory of Guam – effectively a
colony – also serves as a strategically significant military hub on US soil.

Elsewhere in Asia, America's position rests on a network of alliances
and overseas bases that reflect complex historical relationships. Many
Asian countries now find themselves in a similar position to Australia:
habitually reliant on a US military presence, but economically intertwined

with China. While most elite opinion remains in favour of an ongoing American presence in Asia, far from all welcome an intensifying US–China rivalry. Countries close to the conflict zone have to weigh up the likely benefits of increasing defence ties with Washington against the possible costs, and question America's intent and resolve in pushing back against China. Trump, for his part, similarly questioned the value of America's Asian allies when he took office, calling on Japan and South Korea to stop 'free-riding' and foot more of the bill for the US presence in their countries. There is second-guessing on all sides, and the stability and longevity of this alliance network is in doubt.

Hardly had the ink dried on Japan's post–World War II constitution before the United States realised it would have to roll back the strict pacifism outlined in Article 9 so as to enlist Japan as a military ally. The same objective is written into the constitution of Japan's ruling Liberal Democratic Party, which is now expanding the role of the national 'Self-Defence Forces' in close coordination with the United States. Twenty-three facilities in Japan host some 50,000 American troops, most of them on the heavily militarised island of Okinawa. In the face of considerable opposition, Japanese prime minister Yoshihide Suga is continuing construction on a new base there. Fifty-seven warships of the US Navy's Seventh Fleet occupy a base in Yokosuka, south of Tokyo.

The product of Cold War partition, South Korea hosts 25,000 US troops across fifteen installations. While it is often at odds with China diplomatically, South Korea also has ongoing territorial and trade disputes with Japan, and historical grievances centring on wartime abuse of Korean 'comfort women'. Its interest in gradual unification with North Korea also brings it into conflict with Japan, as well as the United States, which has sought to apply 'maximum pressure' on North Korea to denuclearise. South Korea, much more than Japan, is seen as hedging its bets between the United States and China.

To the south, America retains a small troop presence in the Philippines, which was once a US colony, and a Visiting Forces Agreement allows its ships and aircraft full freedom of movement there. In Taiwan, America has remained the island's unofficial patron since switching diplomatic recognition to the PRC. Like Australia, America maintains a deliberately ambiguous 'One China' policy on Taiwan's status: acknowledging but not endorsing the 'One China' principle that is Beijing's official position. At the same time, America refuses to construe the PRC–Taiwan stand-off as a civil conflict, a stance that allows it to fulfil the terms of its 1979 *Taiwan Relations Act* and continue selling arms to Taiwan.

America holds periodic military exercises with Malaysia and Indonesia, both of which entered an American-led Cold War 'arc of containment' after crushing local communist movements in the 1960s. A longstanding agreement, recently renewed, gives the United States air and naval facilities in Singapore. In the last decade, exercises and port calls have signalled growing ties between America and Vietnam. The most pressing alliance-building priority of late, though, has been to woo India into the fold, hence the recent redefinition of the 'Asia-Pacific' as the 'Indo-Pacific'. While India's Himalayan rivalries with China often serve to justify the pursuit of a revived Quadrilateral Security Dialogue – involving India, the United States, Australia and Japan, and commonly known as the 'Quad' – the Indian Ocean is the more valuable strategic space. As Australian Quad enthusiast Rory Medcalf points out, it is here that, in the case of conflict, 'China's far-flung outposts and resource supply lines would instantly become liabilities and vulnerabilities'.[19]

In a region with no shortage of flashpoints, the South China Sea has emerged as a focus of contestation. China is far from the only country pressing controversial claims there, with island-building and brinkmanship, but its claims are the most expansive, encompassing all islands within its 'nine-dotted line', which often cuts into the internationally recognised exclusive economic zones of its neighbours. Local conflicts centre on fishing and drilling rights, but Beijing's principal objective is to deter the presence of Washington, which still insists that its ability to take action along China's coastline is a non-negotiable national security imperative. 'Beijing will have to accept,' write Campbell and Sullivan, 'that the United States will remain a resident power in the region, with a major military presence, naval operations in its major waterways, and a network of alliances and partnerships.' The question is, what if Beijing refuses to accept this state of affairs?

Although it has had no shortage of disputes with China – forty-five since President Duterte took office in 2016 – the Philippines is one example of a country now adopting a cautious stance towards the US–China rivalry. In 2015, with American backing, it took a case against PRC and Taiwanese claims within its exclusive economic zone to a tribunal of the United Nations Convention on the Law of the Sea (UNCLOS), and won. It was a moral victory of sorts, but neither the PRC nor Taiwan recognised the tribunal, and both immediately rejected the ruling. Australia had itself withdrawn from UNCLOS arbitration mechanisms (in its case, to avoid an unfavourable outcome in its dispute with Timor-Leste), but that did not prevent it from weighing in and criticising Beijing's failure to respect the decision. Likewise, America seized on China's response as evidence of its violation of international law, though the United States has yet to even sign UNCLOS. One American specialist on the convention believes that the tribunal's ruling on the Philippines case renders it even *less* likely that the United States will eventually sign on, as the precedent calls into question many American territorial claims in the Pacific.[20]

The tribunal's ruling was good political sport, therefore, but did little to help the Philippines in practical terms, leaving Manila with little choice but to negotiate directly with Beijing. Critics in the Philippines argue that America is unlikely to intervene militarily to support it in its small-scale stand-offs with Chinese fishing vessels and naval patrols. Military collaboration with the United States therefore can only figure as part of Washington's planning for a wider war with China, and will endanger the Philippines by situating it at the centre of such a war. Rhetorically anti-US, Duterte initiated a six-month countdown in February 2020 to terminate America's Visiting Forces Agreement, a move that would all but void the US–Philippines Mutual Defence Treaty. Duterte eventually hit pause on the clock, but in December he threatened to restart it should the United States fail to provide the Philippines with enough doses of COVID-19 vaccines. The tensions between the two countries worry Washington's hawks, some of whom argue that America should abandon its formal position of neutrality on territorial claims in the South China Sea.

Tensions have also risen across the Taiwan Strait since Donald Trump entered the White House. After he unwittingly took a congratulatory phone call from Taiwanese president Tsai Ing-wen in 2016, Trump's administration exchanged high-level diplomatic visits with Taiwan, and in its final days lifted all self-imposed restrictions on interactions with Taiwanese officials. The Trump administration also sold some US$13 billion worth of arms to Taiwan, more than was sold during the two terms of Obama's presidency. Beijing, which is committed to one day 'reunifying' Taiwan with the Chinese mainland, vows that any move towards Taiwanese independence will be met with force, and views such strengthening of US–Taiwan ties as a step in that direction. Having suffered badly for its perceived proximity to Beijing, the Guomindang has now joined Tsai's Democratic Progressive Party in its call for normalising diplomatic ties with the United States, a move China has predictably denounced. In the months preceding the 2020 US elections, China responded to American warships patrolling the Taiwan Strait by conducting its own exercises off the Taiwanese coast. The week of Biden's presidential inauguration witnessed similar wargaming.

The right of people in Taiwan to decide their future for themselves is one that should be defended. Their aspirations to do so predate the Chinese Civil War – in fact, it was once CCP policy to support self-determination for Taiwan. But as the mainland's military strength grows, so too does the view that Taiwan's only path to preserve its de facto independence is to draw deeper into the US embrace, and this will ensure that the 'unfinished civil war' framing of the issue predominates. This is a gamble that some Taiwanese may be willing to take, but at best this scenario offers the island a future as a militarised protectorate amid a permanently heightened state of US–China tensions – a return to the chilliest days of the Cold War. At worst, China will decide to test Washington's resolve, and in that case Taiwan will either find itself in the firing line of a hot war or be left to its fate, and in a worse position to negotiate with Beijing. What these troubling calculations point to is the need for alternative strategies to uphold the principle of self-determination for Taiwan.

The risk of an incident in the Taiwan Strait – or the South China Sea – igniting a major conflagration is one that everyone recognises. The American military doctrine known as 'AirSea Battle' – which aimed to 'offset' the PLA's 'unprovoked and unwarranted military build-up' with a massive cyber-strike and a barrage of missiles aimed at the Chinese mainland – was popular for a time.[21] But American wargaming has shown that China can now hold its own in a conventional conflict in its neighbourhood, meaning that any such conflict will invite escalation and ultimately risk going nuclear. America's withdrawal from arms-control treaties and 'modernisation' of its nuclear arsenal signals its willingness to fight such a nuclear war; it now has a fleet of submarines equipped with 'tactical' nuclear missiles. Unlike China, which has held to a no-first-use policy since it first developed the atomic bomb in 1964, the United States reserves its right to a 'pre-emptive' nuclear strike on adversaries. It's likely that China would nevertheless be able to fire off a 'second strike' if hit, putting at risk population centres in the United States itself, or in allied countries such as Australia.

Logic says that there is no way for anyone to 'win' a war between America and China. But instead of pulling back from the brink, the United States is determined to find ways to do precisely that, including by extending the arms race into space. In December 2019, Trump inaugurated the United States Space Force as the newest branch of the military. Biden's secretary of defence, Lloyd Austin, told the Senate in his confirmation hearings that 'space-based platforms' would be among the innovations required to 'to present a credible threat' to China and 'hold large pieces of Chinese military inventory at risk'.[22] A study of space warfare envisages that a kinetic-energy weapon 'would enable the US to strike ground systems anywhere in the world from space, as well as work to mitigate any anti-access environment that would restrict the operation of conventional forces'.[23] Given present US priorities, it is hard to see this as anything but thinly veiled code for a plan to circumvent China's defences.

From Trade War to Tech War

In the economic sphere, the United States has registered its grievances against China more forcibly, but it has exhibited less and less faith in institutions such as the WTO to act as forums to resolve them. China, in fact, has a strong track record in complying with WTO dispute rulings against it, one that compares well with those of the European Union and the United States. Liberalising reformers in China have often welcomed such rulings as providing them with the political leverage they otherwise lack. But as America continues to view China's trade practices as hostile, China's compliance is increasingly interpreted as evidence that the WTO has become unfit for purpose. Needless to say, China has relished the opportunity to pose on the world stage as a defender of the international trading system.

In place of a complicated set of international obligations reflecting the different historical trajectories of members of international organisations, Washington now prefers the principle of 'reciprocity' in its dealings with China. This new language was part of Trump's 2017 'America first' speech to APEC and one of the battle cries with which he launched his 2018–19 trade war. Trump's first round of tariffs – on US$34 billion of Chinese goods – went into effect in July 2018, in response to a report by US trade representative Robert Lighthizer into PRC trade practices, in particular the issue of intellectual property rights. That same month Trump said he was willing to impose tariffs on *all* Chinese imports and would subsidise American agriculturalists for lost export revenue. China raised its own tariffs in response, and tit-for-tat tariff hikes continued throughout 2019. Eventually, a large proportion of the US economy was brought within some kind of trade protection.

Despite critics accusing him of harming the US economy, Trump kept up a brave face. When one of his campaign advisers said in August 2019 that the trade war was bringing China to the brink of its first-ever recession, Trump advertised the claim with relish on Twitter. Then, with his trade war arriving at an inconclusive Phase-1 armistice, he proclaimed in his State of the Union address that 'we have the best relationship we've ever had with China'. The verdict, now, is that the trade war failed to achieve any of its key objectives: to reduce America's trade deficit, increase its competitiveness relative to China and revive American manufacturing. From Australia's point of view, the impact of the conflict was worrying, if not dire. Slowdown in China caused a fall in stock prices here, and a drop in commodities such as wool. More alarming for Australian business was the political message sent by Trump's actions, which legitimised the use of tariffs in a way that has made it easier for China to use the same tactics against Australia. Trump's economic nationalism has also put Australia in a worse position to resolve its disputes with China, as the WTO's dispute-resolution mechanism was crippled by America's decision not to appoint new members to it.

With hindsight, we can see that Trump's trade war was but a prelude to a much more serious 'tech war', in which the United States is attempting to check the growth of Chinese corporations expanding into fields that until recently have been dominated by the West. In the early 2000s, telecommunications giants such as Huawei served as flagships for China's 'going out' strategy, which encouraged companies to invest and do business abroad. Huawei and ZTE were soon provoking alarm by entering traditional US preserves such as Latin America, where economic instability was dissuading Western investors. Since then, these companies have made significant inroads into more developed economies and stolen the edge in certain fields, such as 5G internet technology.

From 2008 onwards, America has invoked national-security concerns to block the sale of software to Huawei, and to prevent the company's participation in certain domestic networks. Australia did the same thing in 2012 by banning it from the country's National Broadband Network rollout. In December of that year, a US intelligence investigation identified both Huawei and ZTE as security risks, citing their opaque ties to the Chinese state, which had 'the means, opportunity and motive to use telecommunications companies for malicious purposes'.[24] That may well be true, though the force of this warning was considerably reduced within a few months, when Edward Snowden exposed the scale of the US National Security Agency's own global data-collection program. One of the most shocking facts to come to light involved the agency's Special Source Operations division, the mission of which was to 'leverage unique key corporate partnerships to gain access to high-capacity international fiber-optic cables, switches and/or routes throughout the world'.[25] To this end, it had secured the collaboration of major US tech companies, such as Google and Microsoft. The Snowden files also revealed that as early as 2007 the National Security Agency had penetrated Huawei servers to study its technology and spy on its executives. While America's telecommunications sector may be more privatised than China's, this was obviously no impediment to state spying.

All governments spy, and many have laws requiring their tech companies to help them. China's National Intelligence Law, enacted in 2017, requires Chinese organisations to assist and cooperate in national intelligence work, and for all their protestations, companies like Huawei are not exempt from this. But the implications of China's law for tech companies are not all that different from those of Australia's 2018 *Assistance and Access Act*, according to which companies can be required to assist in intercepting information, or to add new interception capabilities to their products. While hypocritical, then, today's national-security warnings are not necessarily without basis. What they highlight is the extent to which extreme, worst-case conflict scenarios – Beijing flicking a 'kill switch' to shut down a network, for example – have come to impinge on Western policymaking towards China.

In America, government officials initially lobbied behind the scenes for US providers to curb their sale of Huawei and ZTE products, before Trump issued an executive order in 2019 that prohibited companies from using telecommunications equipment made by firms the government deemed national-security threats. At the same time, Trump made use of extensive export controls, which impose stringent licensing requirements on those doing business with foreign companies, and can deny companies the crucial pieces of American hardware and software on which they rely. Primarily, this involves the sale of silicon semiconductors, the key to modern computing. On the basis that the company was 'engaged in activities that are contrary to US national security or foreign policy interest', the Department of Commerce added Huawei – and many of its affiliates – to its 'entity list' in 2019. The long arm of US political sanctions has also been a tool in this struggle, allowing Washington an avenue to punish Chinese companies that conduct business with designated enemies. In 2018, the Commerce completely banned exporting products to ZTE, which had been selling its products to Iran, forcing the company to temporarily cease operations. If wielded to full effect, the suite of restrictions the United States has at its disposal could severely damage China's telecommunications industry.

Internationally, the United States has lobbied hard to limit Chinese companies' penetration of its domestic telecommunications, often threatening to cut off intelligence sharing with anyone who defies its will. Australia has made its own contributions to this effort – for example, by pressuring the Solomon Islands to ditch a submarine cable contract with Huawei in 2017, then providing foreign aid for an Australian company to build it. According to *The Wall Street Journal*, intelligence chiefs of the Five Eyes countries met in Canada in July 2018 to coordinate their activities in containing Huawei.[26] Of the five member countries of this intelligence-sharing partnership, Australia embraced the most wide-ranging ban, excluding Huawei and ZTE from all 5G infrastructure. New

Zealand soon prohibited Huawei from supplying its mobile phone company Spark. Canada's intelligence agencies were divided on the question at first, but Canadian wireless providers have now effectively shut Huawei out of the country. Outside the Five Eyes, France and Germany have shied away from outright bans, but will use licensing restrictions and regulatory oversight to effectively limit Huawei's presence in their markets.

Elsewhere, additional arm-twisting has been required. Despite extensive lobbying from both the United States and Australia, Conservative UK prime minister Boris Johnson initially admitted Huawei into Britain's 5G rollout, no doubt conscious of post-Brexit trade opportunities with China. The decision gave Huawei a brief flush of vindication, but Washington responded by tightening the screws, and in 2020 it widened the scope of its entity list to prohibit all foreign companies that use American software (Samsung, for example, in South Korea) from doing business with Huawei. China is now accelerating its drive to reduce its reliance on imported technology, but many are sceptical of its ability to do this in a short space of time. Describing it as a 'herculean task', Britain's National Cyber Security Centre revised its position on Huawei and now questions the company's ability to produce the necessary technology on a commercially viable scale.[27] These considerations, combined with pressure from the Atlanticist wing of his own party, led Johnson to reverse his position, banning new sales of Huawei technology and demanding that existing equipment be removed from the system by 2027. In the absence of any cooling of political tensions between the United States and China, the fracturing of the globe into two rival technological blocs seems a looming reality.

Belting the Belt and Road

Washington has held an unrelentingly negative attitude towards the Belt and Road Initiative. A 'constricting belt' and a 'one-way road' was how Mike Pence characterised it in his speech to APEC in Papua New Guinea in 2018.[28] Australia is among the countries that the United States had tried to dissuade from collaborating with China on infrastructure and investment schemes. American pressure has clearly had a role in keeping the lease of the Port of Darwin to private Chinese company Landbridge a live issue in Australian politics. Although the Foreign Investment Review Board, the defence department and ASIO all gave the green light to the lease in 2015, Obama was angry he was not consulted, and the State Department secretly conducted a poll to gauge Australian opinion on the lease. Leaked to *The Australian*, the poll found that 90 per cent of Australians thought the lease presented 'some risk' to national security. The State Department's spin was that the lease had 'made strategic elements of China's maritime economic initiatives apparent', and that the poll's results would 'likely force Australians to rethink their choices of when to put national security ahead of economic gain'.[29] This wasn't the only possible interpretation, though. A second poll by the Australia–China Relations Institute demonstrated that Australians viewed any foreign ownership of infrastructure with scepticism, regardless of the nationality of the investor.[30]

Belt and Road detractors decry what they call 'debt-trap diplomacy', arguing that China aims to deliberately ensnare small countries in financial traps so as to take control of their strategic infrastructure. The chief, and in fact only, evidence provided for this claim is the case of the Hambantota Port in Sri Lanka, where a Chinese operator now holds a ninety-nine-year lease, prompting claims that China has similar designs on ports in Africa and Europe. But Sri Lanka is not mired in Chinese debt: the bulk of its repayment obligations remain to international financiers. It was to service this sovereign debt that an incoming Sri Lankan government decided in 2017 to lease out the poorly performing port.[31] The 'debt trap' narrative has been effectively debunked, but such is the degree of suspicion of the Belt and Road Initiative that talk of similar transactions still hits the press on a regular basis. Recently, Marco Rubio accused China of luring El Salvador into a 'debt trap' by gifting the country a US$150 million non-refundable grant.[32]

Unsurprisingly, there is little appetite among Chinese lenders to seize unprofitable infrastructure, with refinancing or debt forgiveness a far more common outcome of Belt and Road debt negotiations.[33] Some, in fact, describe the Belt and Road Initiative as not so much a debt trap for recipients as a lending trap for China. The piling up of bad debts has led to a cooling off in Chinese lending since the heady days of 2015–16; one estimate of 2019 lending shows a 94 per cent drop. Of course, these fluctuations give Washington its alternative line of attack: that the Belt and Road Initiative is all hype and no substance, a 'vanity project', as one White House national-security spokesperson put it.[34]

America has put forward a range of regional initiatives that are explicitly or implicitly designed to combat the Belt and Road scheme, with the vaguely defined 'Blue Dot Network', which also involves Australian and Japan, signalling approval or disapproval of specific ventures. Supporting these initiatives, the *Better Utilization of Investment Leading to Development Act* has established a new US government agency, the Development Finance Corporation, to finance private development collaborations (with preference given to American corporations). In Africa, for example, the 'Prosper Africa' initiative aims to double trade and investment between the United States and the continent. In Latin America, the 'America Crece' initiative saw Ecuadorian debt refinanced in return for the country signing up to Washington's 'Clean Network' program, which commits Ecuador to excluding Chinese firms from its telecommunications. In addition to US agencies, Washington still holds a commanding stake in the IMF, which seems to be loosening the finance tap for Africa. The growth of Chinese investment in Ethiopia, Angola and Equatorial Guinea has been cited as a factor in recent decisions to lend to these countries. Human rights organisations voiced loud opposition to a recent IMF bailout package for Equatorial Guinea, a highly repressive regime led by the world's longest-serving president.[35]

Although America's 'Pacific Pledge' investment plan is relatively meagre in financial terms, US–China competition surrounding aid and lending in the Pacific is as evident there as anywhere else in the world. In September 2018, with Chinese investment on offer, the Solomon Islands became the most recent nation in the region to cut ties with Taiwan and extend diplomatic recognition to the PRC. The move exacerbated a longstanding rivalry between the two most populous islands in the Solomons – Guadalcanal and Malaita – a rivalry that was at the centre of a civil war in the early 2000s. Malaita's premier, Daniel Suidani, rejected the government's tilt to Beijing and declared he was calling in foreign support: 'We've asked the US and Australia to be part of Malaita security.'[36] Brandishing the flags of Taiwan, the United States and Israel, a cavalcade of 'Christians for Taiwan' drove through the provincial capital, while a 'Malaita People's Resolution', heralding an imminent declaration of independence, circulated online and by hand. Since then, America has sought to work the emerging fault line by provocatively offering a US$25 million aid package directly to Malaita province – a large increase in US support for the Solomons, but designated for a single province alone. The dangerous implications of this approach should be obvious.

A Biden Reset?

America's turn to great-power competition has had predictable consequences domestically. When FBI director Christopher Wray said he viewed the 'China threat as not just a whole-of-government threat but a whole-of-society threat on their end', he was encouraging a generalised suspicion of all things, and all people, Chinese.[37] America has enough on its plate that China is not the front-page issue in the same way it is in Australia, but its intelligence agencies have been willing to do things Australia's has not: cancelling the visas of PRC citizens studying in the United States, for example, or prosecuting Chinese American academics for failing to disclose collaborations with PRC institutions. The administration has applied pressure on universities to close Confucius Institutes, and it has taken steps towards banning the Chinese apps WeChat and TikTok. When COVID-19 hit, Trump poured fuel on the fire with his xenophobic rhetoric about the 'China virus', and indulged conspiracy theories of the disease as a manufactured bioweapon.

In the last months of Trump's tenure in office, calls for the president to take more drastic action only increased. A committee of Republicans calling themselves the China Task Force delivered a report urging Trump to take inspiration from Ronald Reagan and adopt an explicit policy of regime change: 'America's goal must not be indefinite coexistence with a hostile communist state, but rather, the end of the [Chinese Communist] Party's monopoly on power'.[38] Inspired by a similar vision, some liberal Chinese dissidents, including Tiananmen exiles, came out strongly in support of Trump. Meanwhile, fugitive businessman Guo Wengui (Miles Kwok), partnering with Steve Bannon, pitched for American backing for a 'New Federal State of China', as much an investment scheme as a serious political venture. Guo's catchy rap song, 'Take Down the CCP', briefly rose to the top of the US iTunes chart.

The charge that Biden – Trump's Democratic Party rival and now the president – was soft on China was a feature of the 2020 Republican campaign, which saw millions poured into advertisements pushing this point in swing states. If Biden wins, 'you're going to have to learn to speak Chinese', Trump told conservative talk radio.[39] Biden took the bait, unfortunately, and hit back with his own accusations against Trump: that he had 'rolled over for the Chinese' on trade and failed to 'hold China accountable' for its actions in the face of the COVID-19 pandemic. China-bashing took hold on both sides of the aisle, sending public opinion on the country into a downward spiral.

As president, Biden brings a change in style to American foreign policy. One of his initial executive orders instructed federal agencies to ensure their pronouncements 'do not exhibit or contribute to racism'. How much substantive change will there be, though? There is fresh talk of collaboration on climate change, but anyone hoping the United States will extend an olive branch to Beijing will be disappointed. Secretary of State Blinken believes that 'President Trump was right in taking a tougher approach to China' but went about it the wrong way. 'China is a strategic adversary', said new UN ambassador Linda Thomas-Greenfield during her 2021 confirmation hearing, in rhetoric hardly distinguishable from Trump's top emissaries. 'Their actions threaten our security, they threaten our values, and they threaten our way of life, and they are a threat to their neighbors and they are a threat across the globe.'[40] Many of Biden's China hands with experience of the Obama administration have chided their former boss for being too conflict-averse. They will now be hoping to provide a more palatable, internationalist face to America's confrontation with China, undoing the damage that has been done to its alliance system, but with the same determination to take on Beijing.

What might a revived Pivot to Asia look like? The US Navy is pushing to create an entire new fleet in the Indo-Pacific, and suggestions for its home base have included Singapore, close to the Strait of Malacca. The Navy secretary imagines 'a NATO that takes in all democratic nations of the world ... you're talking Indonesia, Australia, Japan, India ... in addition to the Western European nations ... China wouldn't be able to stand against us.'[41]

On the economic front, Campbell and Sullivan have envisaged 'a rules-setting initiative of democracies layered over the WTO system'.[42] It's hard, though, to see much international buy-in for a new trading bloc that excludes China, along the lines of the original Trans-Pacific Partnership. The tone of US politics is itself sceptical of any new free-trade push, with both Republicans and Democrats embracing the rhetoric of economic nationalism. Marco Rubio is calling for a '21st-century pro-American industrial policy'; during her primary election campaign, Elizabeth Warren outlined a 'Plan for Economic Patriotism'. Biden's own 'Made in America' plan is no less nationalistic, and so far he has shown no inclination to reduce Trump's tariffs on China.

Influential sections of American industry are pushing on this protectionist door, with major tech CEOs now reconciling themselves to a 'bifurcated' world, and lobbying for a strategy of state investment in American and allied countries' tech capacities.[43] In this world, talk of 'democracy' and 'values' will serve not as a moral justification for free trade but as a rationale for the construction of American-centred production chains designed to compete with China. The revival of the industrial policy debate presents a familiar conundrum: how to make the case for investment in well-paying, unionised jobs without ceding the political terrain to divisive 'America-first' nationalism. The attraction of industrial policy will be enhanced for some by the possible resonance it may have with calls for a Green New Deal. But linking much-needed environmental restructuring to a campaign to check China's rise is a dangerous game to play. Imperatives of economic competition and national security can only undermine the kind of international collaboration that will be necessary to actually save the environment.

For the time being, America's course seems set. Recent high-level US–China talks in Alaska resulted in no change to Trump-era policies, with a public slanging match between the two sides marring their opening. This was prepped in large part by secretary of state Blinken's repeated assertion, on the eve of the talks, that America intended to approach China 'from a position of strength'.[44] Such talk sends an unmistakable signal that Washington thinks it's time to put China back in its place – a place that Washington reserves the right to define. But it's uncertain whether America can come up with a workable, thought-out plan to constrain – let alone contain – China's ambitions. Of late, its actions seem more a series of 'ways to fuck with China' (as the National Security Council reportedly asked officials to provide) than part of an actual plan.[45] Biden may style himself as more of a diplomat than Trump, but hawks who rail against the idea of stabilising relations with China have a point: should America gets its way on issues such as intellectual property, it would do little to slow China's economic growth, which is the source of its challenge to American capitalism's global dominance. They argue that as long as America entertains the notion that it can simply 'compete' with China – without any more deliberate plan to curtail its rise – the rest of the world will hedge its bets, and America's position will continue to slide. If America wants to stay top dog, the clock is ticking, and more drastic action will be required.

This is the dangerous logic of great-power competition: there's not much point announcing an intention to compete with someone if you don't intend to win. It's a logic that the Biden administration will likely remain captive to – and if not, the Republicans will be on hand to hold them to it. China will be optimistic that America's domestic crises will distract Biden from focusing too keenly on Asia. But, the fact is, the centrist Biden is not the kind of progressive reformer who is capable of delivering the racial justice and economic redistribution his country needs. In such circumstances, the temptation to try to prop himself up with a unifying anti-China message will remain strong.

3. INFLUENCING THE REGION

On 1 January 1901, the day Australia's colonies federated into a single commonwealth, our troops strode proudly through the centre of occupied Beijing. The reigning Guangxu Emperor had already fled the capital for the country's west, any remaining authority vanishing with him. Because of the special occasion, the Australians were given pride of place in the parade, carrying the Union Jack at the head of the British Empire's expeditionary force. Australia's contribution to putting down the Boxer Rebellion wasn't a large one, just two small contingents of Victorian police and New South Wales marines. They'd arrived too late for any serious fighting against the Militia United in Righteousness (better known as the Boxers), an anti-foreign uprising that had laid siege to the diplomatic residences in Beijing. Mostly, the Australians spent their time on guard duty and were only occasionally required for the dirty business of shooting prisoners, or blowing up temples that had been identified as rebel rallying points. Still, it was enough of a contribution to claim a share of the loot from the smoking ruins of the Forbidden City.

Historian Henry Reynolds has described Australia's 'endless deference' to Washington as a habit of mind inherited from the nation's colonial past. Long conditioned to subservience to the metropole in London, Australia's turn to Washington after World War II, Reynolds believes, has prevented Australia from claiming its full sovereignty. Offering us no genuine protection in case of conflict, the ANZUS alliance requires Australia to blindly follow Washington into its wars, in the vain hope of 'topping up a flimsy insurance policy'. As Reynolds says, this has led us into a quagmire in the Middle East: 'We are not even clear about what we are there for or what possible advantage we are likely to gain from the lives lost and blighted, and the billions of dollars spent since the turn of the century.'[1] It's a common refrain that Australia's pro-US stance deprives the nation of its initiative, even its independence. Reliance on Washington is described as an ingrained habit, an irresistible urge, not something with a considered rationale. Reynolds' critique voices the horror that many Australians feel at the atrocities we've committed in American-led wars – recently on full display in the Brereton Report's exposé of war crimes in Afghanistan.

But Reynolds' profession of incomprehension reflects a blind spot in Australian thinking. Even in the age of 'empire nationalism', when most Anglo-Australians felt themselves to be British through and through, local support for London's military ventures – be they in Sudan, South Africa or China – reflected a growing sense of distinct Australian interests. It's true that, at first, Australians didn't make much of a distinction between colony and metropole: what was good for empire, it was believed, was good for Australia. But as an Australian perspective on world affairs emerged, Australians lobbied to make the opposite case to Britain: that what was good for Australia was good for the empire. Made anxious by the colonial ambitions of France and Germany in the Pacific, nineteenth-century Australian politicians urged Britain to incorporate more of the region into its empire. In the early twentieth century, they cautioned London against being too friendly to Imperial Japan. During World War II, they campaigned for the Allies to modify their policy of defeating Nazi Germany first and to invest more in the Pacific conflict.

These actions are very different to those of a 'lapdog'. By tying itself to a 'great and powerful friend', Australia tries to influence its friend and – through its friend – the wider world. Australia wants its patron to factor in Australian interests when formulating its own policies and to direct more of its attention to Australia's part of the globe. This tactic gives an indirect shape to the country's foreign policy. Australian sets aside, sometimes even sacrifices, things that seem to obviously benefit ordinary citizens to do favours that it hopes will one day be returned. With one eye on the immediate region, it acts far from home, with the objective of staying in the empire's good books. There is a price to be paid here, but Australian politicians have always believed the price to be worth it.

The world today looks very different to the way it did in 1901, during the occupation of Beijing, but the dynamics of Australian foreign policy remain recognisably similar. The question that sits at the centre of today's elite foreign-policy debate is whether or not American primacy can last. This prompts a second question: how far should Australia go in trying to shore up America's position, or even reverse its slide, with all the risks this poses for conflict with China and damage to the Australian economy?

At one end of the table sit those who argue that Australia's historical reliance on the United States has passed its use-by date, and that America's relative decline vis-a-vis China will translate into eventual US withdrawal from East Asia, bringing with it a waning commitment to its alliance with Australia. The chief representative of this camp has long been the defence analyst Hugh White. For more than a decade now, White has warned that efforts to sustain America's flagging position will fail and only exacerbate the risk of a catastrophic war. While he was once optimistic that America might negotiate some kind of condominium with China, his 2017 Quarterly Essay, *Without America*, has a blunter prognosis: 'America will lose, and China will win', and Australia will simply have to accommodate the new reality.[2] Where White was once criticised for predicting a showdown between China and the United States, today his critics assume that the fight is on, and only denounce him for his reluctance to commit to it.

Analysts sitting around the sides of the table think there is scope for a balancing act. China is a challenge, they concur, but America is stumbling and prone to unpredictable outbursts. Their hope is that clever diplomacy will allow Australia to muddle through with its relationships with both countries intact – that we won't have to choose a side. But to imagine America and China voluntarily shifting from their collision course requires a degree of wishful thinking. In a recent article, Allan Gyngell spells out three possible future scenarios for the China–US relationship. The first is a full-blown cold war; the second a wary decoupling and economic isolationism; the third is the only scenario that might allow Australia to maintain the US alliance while doing business with China, and it strikes me as improbable: 'the PRC will come to understand that China can prosper best if it accommodates the security and economic anxieties of its partners, and the United States will resolve the current dysfunction of its government and accommodate itself to a more multipolar world.'[3] How likely is it, though, that China will 'accommodate' America's security and economic anxieties, when these stem from a desire to maintain primacy all the way up to China's front door? Others on this side of the table are more frank about the fact that concessions may be required to mitigate the rivalry. Brendan Taylor, for example, advises Washington to back away from Taiwan and the South China Sea, and retrench to North Asia.[4]

At the other end of the table sit those who argue that Australia must actively encourage America to stay engaged and impose conditions on China's rise, even if this requires more of Australia as an ally. This course of action will require Australia to enlist Asian nations in the same mission, with much hope invested in the Quad. In his recent book, *Contest for the Indo-Pacific*, Quad advocate Rory Medcalf presents the forum as a continuation of the West's longstanding 'conditional engagement' policy towards China. In his view, the Quad serves as a platform for 'an American strategy that is competitive but not confrontational, confident but not complacent'.[5] But as we've seen, America's leading strategic thinkers, including top officials of the Biden administration, have declared the end of engagement. The alternative, of course, is the policy that dare not speak its name: containment.

Since colonisation, Australia has never had to face the world without the comforting presence of an ally capable of calling the shots in Asia. While retrenchment from Asia might come as a blow to America's global standing, for Australia it will erode the very foundations of the nation's foreign policy. The thought that US dominance in Asia might be more important to Australia than to the United States provokes deep anxiety. If that's the case, Australia can't afford simply to 'tag along' with America's efforts to uphold its dominance: Australia has to encourage Washington to step up to the fight. In 2018, Labor's shadow defence minister, Richard Marles, spelled out the task in a speech to a Washington think-tank: Australia must 'demonstrate to them that we can help share the burden of strategic thought in the Indo-Pacific' so as to 'retain the American presence we need in the East Asian Time Zone'.[6] That is to say, Australia has to present plans for pushing back against China, and prove its own willingness to adopt a more confrontational stance. It has to do what it's done before in these situations, and be more imperialist than the empire itself.

There's enough difference of opinion in this debate for it to be a bruising one. Nonetheless, it's a debate that has been fought, for the most part, on a terrain of common assumptions. Australia's foreign-policy establishment has a deep conviction in the benign, beneficial nature of American primacy. The acceptable positions are either regret that the status quo cannot last or a stoic faith that it will. White is no less guilty of this than anyone else, describing America's role in the Western hemisphere – the history of which is littered with coups and clandestine interventions – as 'exercising primacy with a light touch'.[7] John Mearsheimer's appraisal is more accurate. In a debate with White at the Centre for Independent Studies in 2019, he frankly acknowledged that the United States was no benign hegemon: 'we have a rich history of doing horrible things in South and Central America.'[8] As I'll discuss later, something similar can be said of Australia's history in its Pacific 'backyard'.

The Dynamics of Alliance Diplomacy

Australia's desire to prove its relevance and thereby retain the interest of an easily distracted patron is a strong one. After a phone call with incoming president Donald Trump ended badly for Prime Minister Malcolm Turnbull in 2016, Joe Hockey, Australia's ambassador to Washington, sprang into action. Hockey pitched what eventually became an hour-long History Channel documentary celebrating a 'century of mateship' between Australia and the United States. The start date of the trans-Pacific friendship was revised backwards to 1918, to a battle on the Western Front at the town of Le Hamel, where a small body of American troops served under Australian command. The theme of the documentary was a predictable one: it chronicled the many wars in which Australians had fought and died alongside Americans. To accompany it, a 'mateship' lapel pin was cast, featuring a kangaroo superimposed on an American bald eagle. Well may we cringe, but the campaign seems to have got its message across. Hockey would've no doubt felt he got bang for his buck when Donald Trump solemnised in a September 2019 speech that 'our bond was sealed in blood at the Battle of Hamel'.[9]

In this rewriting of history, the signing of the ANZUS alliance in 1951 was the consummation of a natural friendship. The facts, of course, tell a different story. With Britain's swift capitulation to the Japanese advance in World War II, Australia became anxious for a new protector in the Pacific, and the continent offered a valuable platform for America's fightback. But even at this high point of wartime camaraderie, Washington's generalissimo Douglas MacArthur had little time for sentiment. Arriving in Melbourne to take up his command, he told Prime Minister Curtin bluntly that his country 'had no sovereign interest in the integrity of Australia'.[10]

Consistent with this, America expressed little interest in a postwar alliance with Australia, and certainly not a robust mutual-defence pact of the kind it was building in Europe through NATO. In the end, America acquiesced to Australia's campaign for a treaty for two reasons: to placate Australian opposition to Japan's remilitarisation as a Cold War bulwark against the Soviet Union, and to secure an Australian commitment of troops to join what Britain and the United States imagined to be an impending world war against Moscow.

While formally an instrument of collective defence, the ANZUS treaty was therefore motivated in large part by an offensive objective: for Australia to send troops to the Middle East. History clearly has a sense of irony, because the only time ANZUS has ever been invoked was precisely to that end. In the wake of 9/11, Howard triggered the treaty to support George W. Bush's War on Terror, committing Australian troops to the invasion of Iraq and Afghanistan. Howard did this in spite of the fact that both invasions violated the first article of ANZUS, which requires signatories to resolve international disputes peacefully and in accordance with the purposes of the United Nations.

From day one, it has been obvious that the ANZUS treaty is far from an ironclad security guarantee; it only requires its signatories to 'consult' on occasions when they feel their 'territorial integrity, political independence or security' to be threatened in the Pacific. Yet Australia's official rhetoric on the benefits of ANZUS tends to obscure this point. In a 2019 speech on this topic, defence minister Christopher Pyne began by stating that 'potential adversaries understand that an attack on Australia is an attack on the alliance'.[11] True enough, but in a time of war, with doubts surrounding Washington's willingness to come to Australia's aid, this fact could equally motivate an attack on Australia. Pyne then claimed that

'Australia benefits from the extended nuclear deterrence provided by the US'. In reality, America has never confirmed that its nuclear shield extends as far as Australia. There may be some basis for Pyne's confidence, but it has never been made public. If there is uncertainty about America's commitment to Australia in the case of a conventional attack, though, how can we be confident of its response to a nuclear attack? In the end, Pyne's third point was the only one resting on solid foundations: that ANZUS gives Australia 'unparalleled access to the most advanced technology, equipment and intelligence, which is central to maintaining the potency of the Australian Defence Force'. America is willing to sell Australia more, and tell it more, than it would were it not a treaty ally.

What does America derive from its military relationship with Australia? Primarily, a convenient location for a string of intelligence and military facilities. A recent study identifies seven such 'joint facilities', including the Pine Gap satellite station, the North West Cape naval communications station, the Shoal Bay Receiving Station outside of Darwin and a satellite communication facility east of Geraldton.[12] Long justified in terms of arms control and surveillance of Soviet nuclear testing, these facilities now provide signals intelligence and satellite data for a range of offensive activities. Since the 1980s, Australia has claimed to have 'full knowledge and concurrence' of all activities on its soil, but this formula only gives the government knowledge as to the *purpose* of these activities, not the details of specific actions. In his 2019 speech, Pyne sought to reassure Australians 'that these activities are undertaken in accordance with Australian and international law', but we know for a fact that Pine Gap supports America's extrajudicial drone strikes.

This state of affairs represents a serious compromise of Australian sovereignty, one far more serious than anything China is said to have been responsible for in recent times. Given the intelligence and communications role that the 'joint facilities' will play in any future American confrontation with China, it is hard to say whether Australia will actually have any choice about whether to involve itself in such a confrontation or not. For example, in the event of a conflict with China, America's fleet of nuclear submarines will receive targeting and firing instructions from the North West Cape. Australia's reliance on America's willingness to use nuclear weapons also calls into question Australia's commitment to the

Nuclear Non-Proliferation Treaty and has prevented it signing the recent United Nations Treaty on the Prohibition of Nuclear Weapons.

But Australia doesn't risk becoming embroiled in a war not of its own choosing simply to obtain US intelligence and arms. Nor is that the justification for its internationally unpopular pro-nuclear posture. Pyne's speech to parliament failed to mention what is probably the chief value of ANZUS to Australian strategic thinkers today: its symbolic role in retaining 'the American presence we need in the East Asian Time Zone', to cite Marles again. Allowing US facilities on Australian soil serves the same end.

Australia emerged from World War II on the winning side, with ambitions to translate that victory into an expanded sphere of influence in its immediate region. But harmonising this objective with Washington's interests was never a given, and it has required delicate, at times difficult, diplomacy. In the 1950s, for example, Australia lent support to US efforts to destabilise newly independent Indonesia, but was hesitant about supporting Washington's aggressive stance towards the PRC. The following decade, Australia was disappointed by Washington's more accommodating line on Indonesia, when President Nixon remained unconvinced that Australia's *konfrontasi* with Indonesia in Borneo should trigger ANZUS.

With Britain departing the scene, Canberra nevertheless saw binding itself ever more tightly to Washington as its only option. In the 1960s, previously measured diplomats took up the domino theory of communist expansion with gusto, fulminating against 'Peking's brand of militant communism, and communist armed aggression and subversion in South-East Asia'.[13] The Vietnam War presented itself as an ideal opportunity to entrench an American presence to Australia's north. As Prime Minister Harold Holt is said to have told one of his cabinet members, 'We will win there and get protection in the South Pacific for a very small insurance premium.'[14] At a crucial time in Washington's decision-making, Australia lobbied hard for Nixon to take strong action against the Viet Cong.

In the end, of course, 'we' didn't win the war in Vietnam, and the collapse there occasioned a twofold shock to the alliance. First, in words not dissimilar to Donald Trump's in 2016, Richard Nixon remarked in an interview that nations looking to the United States for support would now have to take responsibility for their own defence. Second was the election of Labor's Gough Whitlam as prime minister of Australia. Hardly a radical, Whitlam nevertheless took Nixon at his word and demonstrated sufficient foreign-policy independence to be deemed unreliable in Washington.

When Malcolm Fraser came to office in 1975, he was determined to undo the damage to the alliance. By now, Beijing had come in from the cold and was aligned with Washington against the Soviet Union. In Indonesia, America's Cold War ally President Suharto was ruling with an iron fist. Australia could afford to scale back its own military ambitions and discard the previous doctrine of 'forward defence' for the more limited 'defence of Australia'. But this went hand in hand with an increase in military spending, as Fraser whipped up a climate of hostility to the Soviet Union.

Bob Hawke, Australia's next prime minister, was no less an enthusiast for American primacy, although he had to face down 'residual anti-Americanism and pacifist naivety' on the left of the ALP. He did this through a series of compromises, including a review of ANZUS, which was set up to deliver a vote for the status quo. (CIA analysts recognised Hawke's sops to the left as 'cosmetic gestures'.) So supportive of ANZUS was Hawke that he redefined it an ALP initiative, crediting wartime prime minister John Curtin – a man who had never enjoyed Washington's confidence – with laying the foundations for the alliance. But as the Cold War drew to a close, Australia once again had to confront the possibility of American withdrawal from Asia. Addressing the Senate in 1989, the foreign minister Gareth Evans cautioned that 'it would not be wise to assume that the United States will continue to maintain its present level of security activity in this part of the world'.[15] When America rallied support for its invasion of Iraq in 1991, Hawke's hand was one of the first to go up.

Australia's Balancing Act

Australia's post–Cold War involvement in American wars has helped to shore up the alliance and cure Australia of its 'Vietnam syndrome'. Yet something else occurred in the Hawke–Keating era that would come to complicate Australia's calculations. Until this time, Australia's ties to Britain had made foreign policy a field in which questions of security and

economics were mostly confined to separate spheres; the Department of
Foreign Affairs and the Department of Trade were two distinct entities.
When Hawke merged them in 1987, it symbolised the way that Asia, once
a space in which security thinking had dominated, was becoming increasingly important as a destination for Australian exports. Even today, Britain
and the United States still account for almost half of Australia's outward
foreign investment, and they invest in Australia's economy to roughly the
same degree. But in the quest to sell its products to the world, Australia
now set its eyes on Asia – 'North-East Asia' in particular. Exports to Japan
were the initial priority, but by the mid-1990s it was obvious that China
would be 'the most important focus of economic growth in Asia.'[16] That
prediction has since been amply confirmed, with China now the destination for almost 50 per cent of all Australian exports, accounting for some
8.5 per cent of Australia's GDP.

It was equally obvious at the time that China's economic growth could
undermine American influence in Asia. Indeed, in the wake of its Cold
War victory, a degree of US retrenchment from Asia seemed inevitable.
The 1994 Defence White Paper, 'Defending Australia', predicted that the
United States would 'neither seek nor accept primary responsibility for
maintaining peace and stability in the region', prompting Paul Keating to
formulate his view of Australia seeking 'security *in* Asia, not *from* Asia'
(my emphasis). This was heresy to conservatives like John Howard, not
simply from a strategic standpoint but from a cultural perspective too.
'It would not be in Australia's interests', argued the Howard government's
1997 Defence White Paper, 'for China's growing power to result in a diminution of US strategic influence.' Once again, a campaign to revitalise the
alliance was on the cards.

As usual, Howard's 'alliance maintenance' had a military dimension;
in the 2000s, he enthusiastically participated in the 'coalition of the willing'. Army analyst Albert Palazzo, discussing the 2003 invasion of Iraq,
encapsulates Australia's attitude to all such interventions: 'Australia joined
the war to advance its own policy objective: to improve its relationship
with its great power protector ... For Australia, what mattered most was
not what was happening in Baghdad but in Washington.'[17] Howard's strategy had an economic dimension too: the Australia–United States Free
Trade Agreement, which was signed in 2004. Everyone knew this was

a dud deal in economic terms, and DFAT advised the prime minister against it. But for Howard, economics and politics were intertwined, and integrating the Australian and American economies had value in and of itself. It wasn't the first time that Australia had defied economic logic to cultivate its relationship with the United States, and it probably won't be the last. Australia has always believed that the alliance trumps more tangible interests. Those hoping today that economic self-interest will dissuade Australia from going too far down a hostile path with China should keep this episode in mind.

In expanding the horizons of Australian military action, Howard envisaged a navy and air force that could fight a major war in Asia alongside the United States. Since this time, as Hugh White observes, 'building our capacity to support America in a war with China has quietly become the central aim of our defence policy'.[18] Publicly, though, what Howard described as Australia's 'economic strategic partnership' with the PRC gave him pause in depicting China as motivation for his 'alliance maintenance' with the United States. The rhetorical caution paid off for the Liberal Party, and saw them secure massive gas export deals and open negotiations on what eventually became the China–Australia Free Trade Agreement. In 2004, foreign minister Alexander Downer infuriated Washington by expressing his view that ANZUS wouldn't necessarily oblige Australia to join the United States in a military defence of Taiwan. In response to the State Department's insistence that it would, Downer made only a partial concession: while a Chinese attack on US warships might indeed trigger ANZUS, the treaty still wouldn't oblige Australia to go to war.[19]

The logic here is simple: while maximising the American presence in its region, Australia tries to minimise any direct insult to China. Public and private language can therefore vary considerably. In 2016, Kim Beazley privately told the US ambassador that 'Australia would have absolutely no alternative but to line up militarily beside the US' on Taiwan, but no Australian politician has ever said so publicly.[20]

A corollary to this is that when America seems to be stepping up to play the role Australia wants it to, Australia can afford to back off on China. In 2011, Australian MPs welcomed Barack Obama's reassuring declaration that 'the United States is a Pacific power, and we are here to stay', which came on the heels of his announcement of a US Marine Corps rotation in Darwin.[21] Amid optimism about the efficacy of the Pivot to Asia, there was little to dissuade Australia from clinching its free trade agreement with China, bringing with it all the fanfare of Sino–Australian friendship. It's when American resolve is in doubt that Australia becomes more hawkish. Australia's confrontational turn on China in 2017 – to return to a point I made in the introduction – was due less to American pressure than to the perception that Trump might downgrade America's commitment to the Pacific.

There is no doubt that America has political influence in Australia. There's a long history of American officials lecturing Australian politicians or making their opinions known in more indirect ways. It visibly irks them when Australia says that it doesn't have to choose between America and China. As one Obama administration official is said to have complained to Hugh White, 'Dammit, you *do* have to choose, and it is time you chose us!'[22] On his 2019 visit to Sydney, sitting alongside Australian foreign minister Marise Payne, US secretary of state Mike Pompeo told his audience that 'the ANZUS alliance is unambiguous' on Australia's future role in any US–China conflict in the Taiwan Strait. Payne awkwardly declined the invitation to confirm Pompeo's interpretation.[23]

There are also networks that comprise an identifiable 'US lobby' in Australia – groups such as the American Australian Association, established by Keith Murdoch, which now funds think-tanks at two Australian universities. In the early 1990s, at a time when Australia's relevance to America seemed on the wane, the Australian American Leadership Dialogue came into being to shore up the pro-alliance orthodoxy in elite opinion. The Leadership Dialogue's annual events bring Australian politicians and journalists into contact with their top-level American peers, aiding the formation of an elite consensus. With that consensus holding strong across both major parties, Australian politicians regularly participate in other trans-Pacific networking opportunities, such as the Harvard Trade Union Program.

Yet we need not make too much of direct American pressure or local lobbying. The influence that America has in Australia is the product of a view that was arrived at independently, according to which an embedded American presence in the region – and naturally, therefore, in

Australia – is seen as a worthwhile political end in itself. Too much talk of American influence can easily obscure the more important question: why do Australian elites maintain this view?

Rules and Orders

The Australian government explains its pro-US stance in terms of America's role in constructing a particular kind of world. As the 2017 Foreign Policy White Paper puts it, 'without sustained US support, the effectiveness and liberal character of the rules-based order will decline'. But there's an obvious contradiction between the idea of rules (which by definition apply to all) and the privileged role of a lone superpower in maintaining them. Australia's alliance with the United States prevents it from almost any public criticism of American rule-breaking and often makes it complicit.

We also have to ask how sincere Australia's own commitment to 'rules' is. On a visit to the United Nations in 2019, Scott Morrison held up the international body as 'the prime custodian of the rules-based order'. As its prime custodian, you would think it would be deserving of a certain respect. But on his return to Australia, Morrison made very different noises, attacking what he termed 'negative globalism', and insisting that Australia would not be constrained by an 'unaccountable internationalist bureaucracy'. In words that call into question Australia's commitment to any notion of international law, Morrison said bluntly that 'we can never answer to a higher authority than the people of Australia'.[24] Indeed, in certain spheres of international governance, Australia has become notorious for neglecting its obligations. At its most recent review before the UN Human Rights Committee in 2017, it was criticised for 'chronic non-compliance' with the committee's work. It was adopting an approach, the committee's chair said, that 'in essence challenged multilateral, expertise-based treaty monitoring by declaring the power to self-assess its own record of compliance and to pick and choose which obligations to implement'.[25]

To the extent that Australia's professed preference for 'rules' has any basis, it reflects the liberal free-trade orthodoxies that inform both major parties' view of the world. Rules that facilitate market entry, that create a safe international environment to trade, invest and repatriate profits from – these are rules that Australia supports. They're rules that sustain a global hierarchy of nations, which sees hundreds of billions of dollars annually transferred from the developing to the developed world. Given its own limited size and influence, there's a preference in Australia for multilateral trade bodies, such as the WTO, but it's important to appreciate the role that Australia often plays in such bodies. Although its economic profile, heavily weighted towards raw materials exports, more resembles that of a developing country, Australia's loyalties lie with the club of wealthy nations to which it belongs. As Clinton Fernandes has discussed, during the 1970s push for a 'New International Economic Order', Australia made use of its position among global resource exporters to thwart the efforts of developing countries to revise the terms of global trade in the interests of the poor. Multilateral negotiations can also be a site of 'alliance maintenance'. In international negotiations on trade-related aspects of intellectual property rights (known as TRIPS), Australia has sided with America's highly restrictive position, to the detriment of its own industries.[26] Ultimately, Australia looks to America, not multilateral institutions, to uphold this global system, and aligns closely with America so as to seek advantage within it.

In its immediate environment, however, Australia has more on its mind than free-trade principles. The logic of interstate competition was present at Australia's founding. Britain wasn't only interested in Australia as a dumping ground for convicts. It was equally motivated by the thought of deriving economic benefit from its new colonies and the need to prevent rivals gaining a foothold in the Pacific. Naturally, the colonists themselves inherited this worldview. From the first days of settlement, Australia identified a large sweep of Pacific as its own field of colonial activity, seeing in these islands a source of labour and resources, a destination for exporting capital and a field of missionary activity. This gave rise to an expansive definition of Australian security. In 1896, a meeting of the Intercolonial Military Committee deemed that 'the defence region of Australia be extended to include New Zealand, New Caledonia, the New Hebrides, New Guinea, and portions of Borneo and Java'.[27] Early twentieth-century politicians termed it a 'Monroe Doctrine for Australia'. After World War I, Australia secured the colonial mandate to Papua New Guinea and Nauru, eventually guiding these nations to a fragile independence on Australian terms. Elsewhere, Australia has exercised indirect influence through investment, finance and aid, all the while keeping its military options on the table. Here, Australia seeks to maintain what the 2016 Defence White Paper terms a 'secure nearer region, encompassing maritime South East Asia and the South Pacific'. Lodging an American presence in Asia, and indeed on Australian soil, is the preferred method to do this.

On his 2019 visit to Sydney, Mike Pompeo declared that 'the days of Australia as a middle power are coming to an end'. The line elicited a laugh from the audience. I imagine most assumed he was just buttering them up. But it's a piece of flattery worth reflecting on. Australia's willingness to 'pick and choose' from its international obligations, its determination to exercise a decisive influence on its wider region – these tendencies *do* reflect the instincts and practices of a great power. Instead of a 'middle power', a more accurate description of Australia's role in the world is that of a great power writ small, whose ability to act in such a way is enabled by, indeed dependent on, its relationship with an actual great power. 'Sub-imperial' is the term some use to describe this situation. A sub-imperial Australia effectively asks America to underwrite its ambitions for its own mini-empire, which extends well beyond the boundaries of the island continent and into the Pacific. It's in this sphere of influence that Australia and China are beginning to face off directly.

Fencing off the Backyard

On the assumption that China is compromising the sovereignty of small nations in the Pacific, Australia describes defending this sovereignty as its mission in the region. Remaining the preferred 'partner of choice' of these nations is also part of Australia's mission. In truth, Pacific countries have had few partners to choose from until recently, but China is beginning to provide them with an alternative. What happens, then, when Pacific nations make sovereign decisions to work with China? When the principle of sovereignty runs up against what Australia declares are its 'legitimate security interests', which wins out?

As I write, one test case for this question is a mooted deal between the government of Western Province in Papua New Guinea and a Chinese commercial fishing company. Locals who are supportive of the partnership see in it an opportunity to obtain more of the revenue they're entitled to from fishing rights in the Torres Strait, and to build bridges to China's huge seafood market. Australia's response, however, has focused on the deal's security implications. ASPI's Peter Jennings claimed it was 'guaranteed' that any such fishing plant at Western Province's capital would 'be designed with PLA military needs given priority'.[28] A DFAT delegation lobbied the provincial governor directly against the partnership, but Governor Taboi Awi Yoto was unimpressed with the meeting and took to Facebook to accuse these officials of plotting his downfall.

It's too early to say how this particular episode in Papua New Guinea will play out, but it calls to mind an earlier Cold War security scare in the Pacific – the 'Tuna Wars' of the 1980s. At the time, many newly decolonised nations found their economic development hindered by foreign resource exploitation – in this case, tuna fishing. With Ronald Reagan's backing, America's fishing fleet was defying international laws that would require them to pay Pacific nations a licence fee to fish in their exclusive economic zones. To secure much-needed revenue from these fees, first Kiribati, then Vanuatu, entered into fishing agreements with the Soviet Union, which was just beginning to turn its eyes to the Pacific. The move made obvious economic sense, but Western nations were no less horrified for that. Conjuring up images of a Soviet spy station in the Pacific, maybe even an island base, Australia, New Zealand and the United States all piled on the diplomatic pressure to dissuade the struggling nations from pursuing economic ties with Moscow. Canberra could not allow a 'Cuba in our backyard'.

Of course, this was not the first time that Vanuatu had sent Australian alarm bells ringing. In the nineteenth century, French occupation of the islands was greeted with howls of outrage in the colonies. Similar noises were made in April 2018, when a story ran that the Chinese Navy was in talks with Vanuatu to establish a base there, possibly by converting a Chinese-financed wharf development. 'Pacific Push: China Plans Military Base in Vanuatu' ran the banner headline in the Nine newspapers, citing anonymous Defence officials and think-tank analysts.[29] Vanuatu's officials vehemently denied there had been any such discussion, and the foreign minister affirmed that the country was 'not interested in any sort of military base'. The ANU's Graeme Smith, a keen observer of China's Pacific engagement, found talk of any prospective base to be 'baseless'.[30] Yet Peter Jennings insisted it was 'certain' that Beijing was eyeing a naval facility and urged Australia to respond by securing rights to permanently station its own naval vessel in Port Vila.[31] Clive Hamilton felt that not only Vanuatu, but the entire Pacific, had to be reminded of its place in the world: 'It really is of strategic importance for Australia to make it clear to the Pacific island nations that you remain in our backyard.'[32]

Australia's ability to uphold its dominance in the Pacific is seen as an important test of its credibility as a US ally. But even in this restricted sphere, it can be hard for Australia to act without American support, as the case of the 1999 intervention in Timor-Leste shows. We now know that John Howard only decided to dispatch Australia troops to the island once America had pressured Jakarta to accept a peacekeeping mission and scale back the militia violence. Until that time, the Howard cabinet had preferred to continue Australia's longstanding policy of support for the Indonesian occupation, even going so far as to withhold intelligence on the ongoing violence against Timorese civilians from the United States. When the decision was finally made for the Australian-led International Force East Timor force to go in, Howard was desperate to secure an American troop commitment to accompany it, but Washington was wary of getting too involved. Eventually a single warship with 900 marines was dispatched to keep a watching brief off the Timorese coast.

We now know a lot more too, about Howard's purpose in 'liberating' Timor-Leste, as the sordid details of Australia's efforts to spy on Timorese officials and swindle the impoverished nation of its resources have come to light. The close collaboration between Australian officials and Woodside Petroleum in seeking to maintain the lion's share of the Greater Sunrise oil and gas fields exemplifies the way that Australian policy prioritises the interests of elite corporate actors above the welfare of the people of the region.

Howard derived huge political benefit from the mission at the time and capitalised on it to give the Australian Defence Force a more interventionist form. Disseminated by think-tanks such as ASPI, the discourse of the 'failed state' justified Australia's efforts in the 2000s to police the Pacific and liberalise the region's economies. The 2003 Regional Assistance Mission to Solomon Islands served to reinforce the structural reforms demanded by the IMF, reforms that had been a major factor in the crisis to begin with. Using aid as leverage, the sovereignty of Papua New Guinea was compromised by the appointment of Australian officials to key public-service positions and the granting of extraterritorial immunity to Australian police. Across what security specialists termed the 'arc of instability', Australian interventions served to undermine the state's capacity to fend off the predations of foreign capital, creating a narrow elite of winners but offering the majority little chance of meaningful development.

For much of its history, the PRC's interest in the Pacific was almost exclusively political: to persuade countries to switch their diplomatic recognition from Taipei to Beijing. Kiribati and the Solomon Islands have recently done so, and now only the Marshall Islands, Palau, Nauru and Tuvalu remain as Taiwan's friends in the region. A new piece of American legislation instructs the State Department to use pressure to deter countries in the region from recognising the PRC, but as China ups its aid and lending programs, the cost of remaining loyal to Taiwan is increasing.

China's actual aid spending in the Pacific has not yet lived up to its large commitments: the Lowy Institute's data shows China stumping up roughly a quarter of what Australia provides, with figures in a similar ballpark to New Zealand. Nevertheless, the narrative of a Chinese invasion has been irresistible for the Australian media. As Nine News put it, 'China is on the move in the Pacific and the communist country has already begun a slow invasion of Australia's neighbouring islands.'[33] Critical of this alarmism, authors of a 2019 Jubilee Australia study point out that China is 'acting just like any other aid donor', and therefore 'current security concerns may be overstated'.[34] This is obviously true in a sense, but it also misses the point. Australia itself now defines foreign aid as part of its 'economic diplomacy': that is to say, as a tool of political influence, not an act of altruism. It naturally sees Chinese aid in the same way, and any Chinese influence as a security risk.

Australia's proprietary claim on this region is such that it simply doesn't see itself, or America, as outsiders here. 'Australia would be very concerned if anybody from outside of the Pacific decided they wanted to set up a military base in the Pacific,' assistant minister for the Pacific Anne Ruston said, shortly after Australia announced it was collaborating with the United States to revive the Manus Island military base in Papua New Guinea.[35] Scott Morrison has come up with a new formula for the relationship: 'We are connected as members of a Pacific family', he said at Lavarack Barracks, announcing his Pacific 'step-up' policy.[36] The step up, Australia's primary vehicle for countering China, aims to increase Australia's regional defence collaborations, envisaging more training for Pacific militaries and police in Australia. Australia's diplomatic presence is also being expanded, and more Australian TV will be broadcast to the region. But the chief selling point is the Australian Infrastructure Investment Fund for the Pacific, a $2-billion commitment, combining $500 million in aid grants with $1.5 million worth of loans.

In stumping up this cash to compete with China's Belt and Road Initiative, Australia has advertised the superior quality and transparency of its infrastructure support. China is building 'roads to nowhere', while Australia has the experience and local know-how to bring development to where it's needed. But history shows otherwise: the region is littered with ill-considered and even harmful investments that have done little to lift people out of poverty. One notorious example is Exxon Mobil's liquefied natural gas plant in Papua New Guinea, built with the backing of Australia's Export Finance and Insurance Corporation (EFIC). A 2018 report on the failing venture found that, far from paving the way to prosperity for Papua New Guinea, the investment had the net effect of reducing household incomes, employment and public spending on health and education. Yet Australia continues to prioritise such initiatives, and has increased EFIC's available funds and the discretionary scope of its 'National Interest Account'.

As a consequence, Australia is doing precisely what it keeps accusing China of – using finance as a political tool, and lending with little transparency and accountability. In 2019, after the Papua New Guinean prime minister hinted he might go to China for help to refinance the national debt, Australia countered with a $442 million loan package, the terms of which were kept secret. Naturally, corporate interests have been playing up the China angle too. In lobbying to widen EFIC's remit, the PNG company Oil Search said the policy change would 'help balance any potential influence from other nations that are prepared to provide material infrastructure funding to Pacific countries, often on a concessional basis'.[37]

In the short term, therefore, opportunistic local politicians and corporations stand to benefit from competition with China, but it carries serious
risks for Pacific island nations as a whole. Many of these nations are loose
federations, with domestic conflicts that could easily be exacerbated by geopolitics – I've already discussed the Solomon Islands as a case in point. In
Contest for the Indo-Pacific, Rory Medcalf embraces the trope of the 'Great
Game' to describe today's rivalries in the Indo-Pacific – invoking the contest that played out between the Russian and British empires in Central Asia
during the nineteenth century.[38] We would do well to remember, then, the
outcome of the Great Game for its primary playing field, Afghanistan. Long
conditioned to jump at Russian shadows, Britain's colonial impulse led it
to twice invade Afghanistan to install its preferred candidate for the Kabul
throne in the nineteenth century. Imperial rivalries continued to lay waste
to the country in the twentieth century and have contributed to drawing
out the two-decade long US-led occupation in the twenty-first.

The imperial instincts that drove the first Great Game are no thing
of the past. Australia and America warn of China's desire to militarise
the Pacific, but they are in the process of militarising it themselves via
the refurbished Manus Island naval base, a strategic window onto the
western Pacific. In the name of defending small Pacific nations from
China, Australia's foreign-policy establishment is debating blatantly neo-
colonial proposals to assume control of their affairs. In 2017, the Lowy
Institute's Greg Colton aired a proposal for compacts of 'free association' with Tuvalu, Kiribati and Nauru, offering their citizens the right to
work in Australia in return for exclusive military use of their territory
and 'consultation' on foreign policy. The move, he said, would 'extend
and deepen the second island chain formed by the US Free Compact
States [such as Palau] and enhance Australia's alliance with the US'.[39] In
2019, Kevin Rudd voiced his support for just such a 'constitutional condominium' as a response to climate change. Rudd was rebuked by Tuvalu's
prime minister, Enele Sopoaga, for his 'imperial thinking', but ANU's John
Blaxland picked up the baton, dismissing Sopoaga's criticisms as 'superficial'. Insisting that 'Australia is not an imperialist nation', in a 2020 senate
hearing he touted the 'benefits of peace, security and stability that would
accrue from having these states integrally connected with Australia'. In a
piece of imperial logic straight from the Great Game playbook, Blaxland

claimed that this diminution of sovereignty would in fact 'guarantee sovereignty' for Pacific nations. At the same senate hearing, DFAT officials confirmed that they were studying the proposal.[40]

*

There's nothing specifically Australian about all this. It's the logic of interstate competition that drives it to behave this way. The same logic may eventually induce China to respond in kind, with policies to push Australia out of parts of the Pacific, or to establish a military presence of its own. None of these developments is out of the question. Recognising this dynamic, some circle back to the question of regime type: it's preferable, they argue, for a democracy like Australia to play the role of hegemon than for China to. But if we're worried about someone 'exporting authoritarianism' to the Pacific, we're better off looking in the mirror. This is what we've literally done, in Papua New Guinea and Nauru, by exporting to these countries harsh detention facilities for people claiming their right to asylum. Particularly in Nauru, the country's role as a subcontractor for Australia's punitive refugee policy has been a catalyst for increasing corruption and authoritarianism in local politics.[41]

Standing up for the interests of small, impoverished nations bullied by their large neighbours is a worthy cause. So too is defending international institutions against the notion that might makes right, and fostering democratic governance and the rule of law. But upholding such principles in Australia has to begin at home, with a critique of Australia's role in the world. We certainly won't uphold them by escalating a rivalry with China, the purpose of which is to maintain Australia's ability to flout these principles when it suits its interests.

Yet with little public debate, Australia's support for the United States is locking us firmly into that rivalry. Since Obama announced the 'Pivot' in 2011, the US Marine Corps rotation in Darwin has risen to 2500. To Darwin's east, millions of dollars are being spent to upgrade port facilities that can accommodate American warships – with some advertising these facilities as a possible base for the US Navy's revived First Fleet. Three hundred kilometres to the south, at the Royal Australian Air Force base at Tindal, Morrison plans to spend A$1.1 billion to extend runways and enhance support capacity for US B-52s, transforming it into what commentator Paul Dibb excitedly calls 'the most potent military base south of Guam'.[42] Roughly $1 billion will also go towards purchasing Lockheed Martin anti-ship missiles, and defence hawks are lobbying for Australia to either acquire, or permit America to install, intermediate-range ballistic missiles in the Northern Territory. With a range of 3000–5500 kilometres, such missiles would be capable of hitting the southern provinces of China.

Beyond the tit-for-tat diplomatic exchanges that drive the news cycle, these are the hard realities of Australia's positioning today. Amid a deep post-COVID recession, Australia will direct $270 billion into military spending in the coming decade, shedding all pretence that this is not aimed at China. The 2020 meeting of the Australia–United States Ministerial Consultations (a forum known as AUSMIN) is said to have resulted in a 'secret defence plan' to counter China, but the basic plan is hardly a secret. By doubling down on Australia's historical role as an imperial sidekick in Asia, politicians of both major parties are pursuing policies designed to keep military options against China on the table and preserve America's role in the region. Guided by the expansive notion of 'security' that the architects of Australia's regional dominance operate within, these policies increase the likelihood of confrontation with the PRC and make ordinary Australians less safe. American military hardware and intelligence facilities on Australian soil, along with Australian ships and fighter jets embedded in US command structures across the Pacific, all but take the question that is most basic to any society – whether or not to go to war – out of Australian hands.

Currently there seems to be no appetite in the Australian parliament for considering the wisdom of the path the country is on, or what it might take to change course. That's not to say, though, that politicians will have no hesitations here. Only America can do the heavy lifting required to preserve the status quo, and not everyone is convinced that it will. Ongoing lobbying will be required to keep America's priorities aligned with Australia's. Outside parliament, elite voices warn of the folly of a pro-US alignment, or of the economic damage it will cause. These qualms and misgivings have yet to translate into significant public disquiet, but it's conceivable that they could. While polls show strong support for ANZUS, only one third of Australians endorse the idea of military action in Asia 'in accordance with our security alliance with the United States'. A majority of adults below thirty see relations with China as more important than relations with the United States.[43]

In any situation like this, there's a gap to be bridged between the ordinary, commonsense perceptions of security that inform the outlook of most Australians and the anxieties of defence strategists, which are liable to be triggered by geopolitical tectonic shifts far from the Australian continent. It's not as easy to do this as it once was. The old domino theory of communist expansion is gone, and none but the most imaginative security hawks can conceive of China ever invading Australia. The proposition that Beijing might choke off Australia's trade routes to its north is hardly persuasive either, since almost all of that trade is going to China. Why would China shut off trade with itself?

Still, a convincing rationale for confrontation with China has had to be found. In 2017, a curious phrase made its way into the introduction that Malcolm Turnbull penned to his foreign policy white paper. Australia's foreign policy, Turnbull wrote, was about 'resolutely resisting threats to our way of life'.[44] The choice of words in official texts like these is an exercise in precision: this wasn't a throwaway line. A single-minded focus on China in Australia's military thinking was now to be accompanied by claims that our very way of life was endangered by its rise. The enemy, we were being told, was already at the door.

4. INTERFERING WITH DEMOCRACY

The solidly bipartisan pro-American stance that informs Australian policy today makes it hard to imagine that Beijing has made much headway in infiltrating the nation's political system. Yet this is one of the key propositions that have animated Australia's China panic from the start. The message has been delivered from the top down, with the Australian Security Intelligence Organisation (ASIO) publicising warnings, from 2017 onwards, that espionage and foreign interference were occurring at an 'unprecedented scale'. In its 2017–18 report, ASIO said these intrusions constituted a 'serious threat to Australia's sovereignty and security and the integrity of our national institutions'. It now describes them as 'threats to our way of life'.[1]

Fresh from a stint working in the prime minister's office, John Garnaut reviewed the course of events that led to Australia's sharp turn on China in a *Foreign Affairs* article in February 2018: 'The process has involved security agencies communicating warnings to the public more clearly than before; journalists building on those warnings and drawing upon scholarly expertise; and politicians taking security agencies and credible media investigations seriously.'[2] This image of the fourth estate taking its cues from interventionist security agencies might not be everyone's idea of how the media should work in a liberal democracy. But it's an accurate picture of how the Australian media, or sections of it, have been operating in relation to China. The message from Australia's security agencies has simply been 'trust us', and many journalists have obliged, relaying warnings without critical scrutiny, and often attributing information to anonymous intelligence sources. The public can never be sure what credentials these sources have, or whether they even exist.

Often the most willing conduit for these security warnings has not been the conservative Murdoch press, but the ABC and Fairfax Media (now Nine), commonly thought of as the liberal wing of the Australian media. In June 2017, an ABC and Fairfax collaboration compiled a series of China-related stories for a *Four Corners* episode titled 'Power and Influence'. The exposé disclosed that ASIO had briefed both major parties on the risks of taking donations from businessmen with 'links' to the CCP. One of these businessmen, Australian citizen Chau Chak Wing, was also identified as an unindicted co-conspirator in an FBI investigation into a bribery case involving UN General Assembly president John Ashe. The episode examined claims that Chinese students were informing on fellow students to Chinese officials, along with the revolving door through which certain ex-politicians, such as Andrew Robb, had taken up consultancy jobs for Chinese corporations.

In the wake of the program, the well-resourced Chau Chak Wing took defamation action against ABC and Fairfax. Australia's defamation laws put defendants at a considerable disadvantage, requiring them to defend 'imputations' drawn up by the plaintiff before a judge decides whether they were actually conveyed. On the imputation that Chau had engaged in espionage for China, for example, Justice Rares rejected a defence of truth, concluding that the plaintiff's conduct was 'typical of a lobbyist', not a spy.[3] In his eventual verdict, the same judge determined that this imputation was *not* in fact conveyed by the program. Other imputations were, however – among them that Chau 'carries out the work of a secret lobbying arm of the Chinese Communist Party'. Justice Rares concluded that *Four Corners* had defamed Chau by depicting him as, 'in effect, a fifth columnist, and a man who paid bribes to Australian political parties and to Mr Ashe'.[4]

Chau's big win, to the tune of half a million dollars, renewed calls to implement the recommendations of state and territory attorneys-general to reform Australian defamation law. Their recommendations have the backing of the Media Entertainment and Arts Alliance, and I trust their call on this. It's debatable, though, whether more relaxed laws would've led to a different outcome in this case. Is the 'public interest' really served by stretching the evidence to portray Australian citizens as fifth columnists?

Critics of the court's decision also highlighted the impact the *Four Corners* episode had on Australian politics. This struck me as a strange line of defence – in and of itself, the impact of a piece of reportage is no guide to its quality. Still, impact it certainly did have. According to Malcolm Turnbull, it was ASIO's warnings of politically motivated donors with 'links' to the CCP that led him, in August 2017, to appoint John Garnaut as chair of an interagency inquiry into clandestine interference in Australian politics. While the inquiry's report remains classified, we can assume it contained some of the claims about Chinese party-state interference that would continue to filter into the media from this point on.[5]

Around the world, politics in like-minded countries was undergoing a similar shift. Australia's new discourse on foreign interference arose in the midst of American alarm about Putin's Russia and its role in the 2016 US elections, which was widely reported on and discussed in the Australian media. At the end of 2017, Malcolm Turnbull cited 'heavy Russian influence' in the United States as part of the justification for a package of new legislation he was introducing. 'Globally, Russia has been wreaking havoc across the democratic world,' he told the Australian Parliament, citing 'credible reports' that Russia had not just undermined the integrity of the US election but also the Brexit vote and the 2017 French presidential election.[6]

I was in the United States during the 2016 election and Trump's inauguration, and saw at first hand how vague 'links' to Russia were compiled into a narrative of collusion that quickly became an article of faith on the liberal wing of US politics. Night after night, anchors on cable news networks like MSNBC breathlessly described how the Trump campaign had enlisted Russian interference to win the election, that Trump was effectively Russia's Manchurian Candidate, and that the United States had lost its sovereignty to Vladimir Putin. In 2017, Republican senator John McCain stepped the rhetoric up a notch by describing Russian subversion of the elections as an 'act of war'.[7] In a Democratic Party debate in October 2019, two candidates made reference to a Russian 'invasion'. For former congressman Beto O'Rourke, the assault, and Trump's collusion with it, was ongoing: 'They are invading this democracy right now, as we speak, still at the invitation of this president.'[8]

This remarkable turn in US politics had a direct influence on Australia's thinking about China. In the middle of 2017, James Clapper, director of National Intelligence in the Obama administration, gave speeches in Canberra likening Chinese interference in Australian politics to Russian meddling in the 2016 elections, which he believed was a scandal 'bigger than Watergate' (which led to the resignation of Richard Nixon).[9] Hilary Clinton drew similar comparisons on her Australian speaking tour in May 2018.[10]

As Australia's own 'Chinagate' narrative consolidated in this climate, it was exported back to the United States; prominent voices – including Clive Hamilton and Garnaut himself – were invited to address US congressional committees and collaborate with North American think-tanks. Garnaut and Laura Rosenberger – now the senior director for China at the National Security Council – derived from this dialogue a generalised notion of 'authoritarian interference', which was best 'viewed through a single national-security lens'.[11] For participants in this exchange, America's 'Russiagate' naturally provided a something of a guide for Australia's response to China. In his 2018 *Foreign Affairs* piece, Garnaut encouraged Australian authorities to 'borrow from the playbook of special prosecutor Robert Mueller and use the prosecution process as an opportunity to advance public education.'[12]

At the time Garnaut was writing, it was still widely believed that the Mueller inquiry into Russian interference in the 2016 elections would reveal a deep vein of US collusion with that effort. In the end, though, there was no such exposé, and no one associated with the Trump campaign was linked to Russian meddling. Some two dozen Russians were indicted, none of whom will ever stand trial. Half of them were linked to a 'troll farm' that was responsible for some 3500 Facebook ads, not all of them anti-Clinton. The other half were linked to Russian military intelligence and indicted for phishing attacks that led to the hack of Democratic Party email servers. Many find this part of the Russiagate story persuasive, though the evidence that the Mueller investigation received from the CrowdStrike cybersecurity firm, the source of the accusation, was not entirely conclusive. Its president only testified that he had 'circumstantial evidence' of a hack occurring and had seen things 'consistent with activity we'd seen previously and had associated with the Russian Government'.[13]

To be sure, Mueller's investigation shed light on a murky world of influence peddling. Americans, some of whom were acting as lobbyists for foreign governments, were indicted for crimes such as lying to the FBI, identity theft and fraud. But the investigation did little to 'advance public education' on the question that first motivated it: collusion between the Trump campaign and Russia. Although the Mueller report found no hard evidence for the charge, a poll taken after its release found that 48 per cent of Americans still believed that 'Trump or someone from his campaign worked with Russia to influence the 2016 election'.[14]

Opinion in Australia remains similarly divided on this question, and the debate will likely go on. What is certain is that in much of the Trump–Russia discussion, the distinction between corruption and collusion became a blurry one. Given that the analogy with 'Russiagate' was drawn so vividly at the start of Australia's anti-foreign-interference campaign, we'd do well to avoid similar confusion.

Foreign Influence in Australia

China obviously has influence on Australia, which is exercised – from both the outside and the inside – in conventional ways. On many issues, Canberra politicians simply can't make decisions without weighing up how China might respond. Sometimes China communicates its preferences explicitly, particularly when it identifies its 'core' interests at stake. In 2018, for example, Beijing pressured Australia to call off talks with Taiwan on a new free-trade pact. In the absence of ministerial talks, the press conferences held by the PRC's Ministry of Foreign Affairs in Beijing have become keenly observed conduits for one-way missives. In Australia, Chinese diplomats and consular staff make the occasional, often clumsy, foray into public life – such as when they pressured a local council in Queensland to remove the image of a Taiwanese flag from the statue of a cow. The PRC's Ministry of State Security certainly has spies active in Australia (as Australia does in China), and bodies exist within the PLA that are capable of conducting work internationally. China's state-run media publishes in English, and some of this material ends up in the Australian press in the form of advertising inserts.

There's a hard edge to this, involving the monitoring, and sometimes intimidation, of citizens or ex-citizens of the PRC living in Australia. For those who are vulnerable to this kind of attention, it sets limits on their ability to take advantage of the freedoms of speech and association that the rest of us enjoy. China's not the only country to hound its dissidents in Australia – Cambodia and Ethiopia are among various other countries to have been in the news for this practice of late. Where it occurs, it needs to be exposed. Unfortunately, most of the pressure that people with family ties to China experience in Australia originates in China itself. If you're a Uyghur activist in Australia, for example, you risk getting a call telling you that you're putting your relatives at risk. It's a tragic situation – but, apart from telling China to stop, there's not a lot that the Australian government can do to prevent it.

China is sadly quite effective at this form of foreign influence. With many of the more standard techniques, though, it is struggling. Take, for example, overseas travel paid for by governments, companies and lobby groups, designed to inform and influence the recipients' policy views. From 2010 to 2018, federal politicians made sixty-three such trips to the PRC– making it second only to Israel (102 trips) in popularity.[15] Since 2018, though, they've all but come to a halt. From June 2018 to August 2020, federal politicians took twenty-four trips to Israel, seventeen to Taiwan (thanks to the Taipei Economic and Cultural Office), fourteen to the United States and only two to China.[16] These two were not initiated on the PRC side, but by the think-tank China Matters, whose efforts to facilitate a dialogue blew up when Andrew Hastie was denied a visa. The Liberal government then signalled its displeasure with these study tours by cutting funding to China Matters, and the Murdoch tabloids piled on, labelling it as 'a Beijing think-tank in China's grip'.[17]

The economy is where much of China's influence is said to lie, although untangling what counts as foreign influence and what counts as domestic influence is not always easy. Much of Australian policy in the past forty years, indeed the very shape of its political economy, has been *influenced* by decisions made in China. The restructuring of the Australian economy from the 1980s onwards was, in large part, a response to signals coming out of Beijing. But these reforms were obviously driven by Australian capital's sense of its own interests, to offshore production and seek profits in an emerging market. The primary beneficiaries of this shift were always going to be corporate actors, and their influence on policymaking outweighed that of unions and other sections of Australian society, for which the benefits of engagement with China were not so obvious.

There are two simple points to be made here, both of which often get lost. First, when figures from the business world pipe up in support of more China-friendly policies, they do so out of their own sense of where Australia's interests – or their individual interests – lie. Captains of industry who call for more accommodation of China – such as Andrew 'Twiggy' Forrest – are often misidentified as conduits for Chinese influence when they actually represent homegrown interests. The fact that China benefits from perspectives like Forrest's is an obvious corollary, but this is not his motivation. The second point to be made is that the ability of people like Forrest to actually influence policy again has nothing to do with China – it is a function of the skewed *domestic* distribution of political influence in Australia. Money buys influence in our system, and he has a lot of it.

It wasn't Beijing that decided to let the Australian economy rest on a handful of high-performing export sectors. And now that China is signalling its displeasure with Australian policies by buying less of these products, it's not Beijing that will decide how Australia responds. I don't want to downplay the wider significance of the trade surplus for Australia's wellbeing nor the impact that China's actions might have on ordinary Australians. But it's impossible to discuss the anxieties surrounding Australia's vulnerability to pressure on trade without reflecting more broadly on the enormous influence that the resource sector wields in Australian politics.

Whether or not restrictions on Australian coal give China leverage, for example, depends very much on what we think is the future of the coal industry in Australia. Instead of banging on China's door, or redirecting shipments elsewhere, we might also take China's actions as an opportunity to transition out of an unsustainable industry that is destroying the environment. Similarly, if we're worried about China using iron ore as a pressure point, why not prepare for that by taking steps to reduce the mining industry's influence on Australian policymaking? We could even nationalise the mines. The profits from selling to China would be more evenly distributed, and we'd be in a better position to weigh up options in the face of any future Chinese ban, without wealthy executives pressuring politicians behind the scenes.

Of course, if we took such a step, we would face resistance. Not from Chinese interests, though, but from the very large British and American interests which dominate the resources sector. A 2017 Australia Institute report found that 86 per cent of Australian mining was in foreign hands.[18] As much as we might imagine it to be otherwise, BHP and Rio Tinto are foreign corporations by Australian law. Should the sector one day exert pressure on Australia to ease off on China, it would be a case, largely speaking, of one foreign interest aligning with another. Direct investment gives these foreign companies a say in decisions that have an immediate impact on the lives of Australians: how and where production is to occur, for example, and what sort of jobs will be available. It gives companies an incentive to lobby for change to Australia's social, industrial and environmental policies, which they do via lobbyists or through membership in peak bodies such as the Minerals Council of Australia.

Of this kind of foreign influence, China has very little. Its outward investment in Australia is minuscule in comparison to that of the United States and the United Kingdom. Tracking precise amounts of foreign direct investment is difficult, but according to Treasury figures the city-state of Singapore still invests more in Australia than does China. After some notable rises at the beginning of the 2010s, Chinese investment declined significantly in 2018, totalling around A$8 billion. Despite the populist passions surrounding the foreign buy-up of Australian land, Chinese holdings of Australian agricultural land only comprise some 2.5 per cent of the country's farmland.

Given that the scale of Chinese investment has been so small to date (and is declining), conventional theories would tell us that China derives little influence from its financial stake in Australia. But here, the debate turns to questions of quality, not quantity. Chinese investment is different, we've been told, and must not be thought of in these terms. Treating all sources of foreign investment equally – as the Treasury and Foreign Investment Review Board commit to doing – is therefore misguided. When COVID-19 hit, the Foreign Investment Review Board set its screening threshold to $0, with much anxious talk of Chinese companies swooping in to buy-up the country. Citing the 'national interest', the treasurer has rejected Chinese bids for a Japanese-owned dairy, a South

African–owned construction company and a range of other enterprises not associated with critical infrastructure in any way.

The tendency to view Chinese investment as freighted with strategic implications is nowhere more evident than in Tasmania, with Greens Senator Nick McKim accusing Xi Jinping of coming to 'case the joint' on his visit there in 2014.[19] In 2018, controversy surrounding the Cambria Green development – a joint venture with a PRC company to build a luxury healthcare and tourist resort on the island's east coast – quickly escalated from issues of planning approval to talk of geopolitics, with China's ambitions for the South Pole a particular source of concern. Citing Tasmania's 'geographic importance as an essential stop on the air route from mainland China to the Antarctic continent', Greens MP Cassy O'Connor warned that the 3185-acre Cambria Green reflected 'a long-term strategic objective that clearly involves the land of Tasmania.'[20] University of Tasmania academic Mark Harrison envisaged a future PRC mining and trade hub in Antarctica that would draw Australia's southern states into its orbit, precipitating the 'pulling apart of the Commonwealth along the fissures of its federal system'.[21] In response, the director of the Australian Antarctic Division, Kim Ellis, took the unusual step of intervening publicly to deny that China had made any move to circumvent the Antarctic mining ban, and criticised what he saw as 'xenophobia ... focusing on China.'[22]

While Australia's trade minister has signed a Memorandum of Understanding (MOU) to collaborate with China on Belt and Road initiatives elsewhere in the world, domestically the stance has been wary. When Victoria's ALP premier Daniel Andrews signed two Belt and Road MOUs, it elicited an angry response from China hawks. Facing strong pressure, Andrews publicised the terms of the MOUs, which contained nothing more than standard boilerplate about welcoming the collaboration of Chinese and Victorian firms in the field of infrastructure. 'So vague [as] to be practically meaningless,' was how one analyst described the document.[23]

Yet for some, the lack of substance was itself evidence of their point: that the Belt and Road Initiative was primarily a political initiative, not an economic one. Invoking a military analogy, Clive Hamilton described the push into Victoria as reflecting 'Mao Zedong's tactic of "use the countryside to surround the city"'.[24] Worried that China was driving a wedge between Canberra and state governments, ASPI's Michael Shoebridge recommended, without noting any irony, that Australia take a lesson from China's highly centralised system: 'We need to see coordination between the Commonwealth and every state and territory that's on a par with what Beijing achieves with its other levels of government.'[25] Not for the first time, Australia was being encouraged to respond to the threat from authoritarian China by becoming more like China. Morrison was persuaded, and in 2020 he introduced a new foreign relations bill to give the foreign minister powers to scrutinise and veto (even retrospectively) any 'international arrangement' at state or local government level. To exercise the veto, the minister simply has to be satisfied that the partnership will 'adversely affect Australia's foreign relations or be inconsistent with Australia's foreign policy'. In the case of the Victorian MOUs, Marise Payne was so satisfied, and in April 2021 she announced a decision to scrap them.

The United Front and Dastyari's Downfall

The new claims of 'covert, coercive and corrupt' Chinese interference focus on an office within the CCP bureaucracy, the United Front Work Department (UFWD). Like much of CCP terminology, the term 'united front' has come a long way since its original coinage during the Russian Revolution. In Russia, the word referred to a temporary alliance of parties with a specific end in mind. In China in the 1920s, the term was extended to describe not a temporary alliance but the integration of the small CCP into the ranks of the larger Guomindang. This 'United Front' broke down in 1927 but was revived in 1937, when the CCP kidnapped Chiang Kai-shek and pressured him to collaborate in resisting the Japanese occupation. The party's ongoing quest to recruit friends and allies led to its founding of the UFWD in 1942, a mission of which was to establish and maintain the party's links with non-party organisations and individuals. The primary purpose of the UFWD is to win friends and insulate the party-state from those it identifies as domestic and foreign enemies.

Most of the UFWD's work is directed within China, where the UFWD runs China's civil society organisations, professional societies and liaison bodies engaging with Hong Kong, Macau and Taiwan. Only two of its twelve bureaus have responsibilities for work among the 'overseas Chinese'. The regulations governing this international work emphasise the cultivation of 'love of the motherland', and support for China's modernisation and 'national rejuvenation' among these communities, along with opposition to Taiwanese independence and ethnic separatism. On this basis, we can say that many, if not all, Chinese-Australian organisations potentially *fall within the scope* of United Front work. At a stretch, as Ryan Manuel has written, 'any overseas Chinese organisations could be described as being "linked to the United Front"'.[26] But this is not the same thing as saying that Chinese-Australian organisations are directed by, or take instructions from, the UFWD. In fact, the ability of the UFWD to orchestrate political work outside China is limited. It has relatively little clout within the party bureaucracy and no jurisdiction to direct activities internationally.

Chinese-Australian organisations come in all shapes and sizes, as all diasporic organisations do. Even among those that cultivate ties to the PRC, there is huge diversity. Many are business and community networks built on native-place associations, of a kind that has existed for centuries. They avail themselves of commercial opportunities between Australia and China, and cultivate friendly ties to officialdom in both countries. In China, this brings them into contact with local party offices, which have United Front work as part of their remit. Then there are organisations with a more direct connection to the political goals of the United Front, such as the Australian Council for the Promotion of Peaceful Reunification of China (ACPPRC). The first such organisation was established in New York in 1982, as an initiative to counter support for Taiwanese independence. A central council was set up in 1988, after which more bodies were established internationally, including in Australia. By 2004, these organisations had been brought within the UFWD. Here, then, is something that can be termed a 'United Front organisation'.

The ACPPRC is public in its mission to promote the 'reunification' of Taiwan with the People's Republic of China – it's right there in the name. On occasion, it has also held activities promoting a pro-PRC counter-narrative on Tibet. It organises fundraising and charity work, and cultural exchange with the PRC, as well as glitzy networking events designed to promote itself and win friends. In its early days, its honorary patrons included such luminaries as Malcolm Fraser, Bob Hawke and Gough Whitlam. Since then, it has become something of a rallying point for wealthy Chinese Australians with pro-PRC views, led by individuals with considerable influence in their own right. Its first, long-serving chairman was the Malaysian-born philanthropist William Chiu. He stepped down in 2014, to be replaced by a property developer from Shenzhen, Huang Xiangmo.

Huang was a big donor to both major parties, credited with gifts totalling A$2.7 million, which gave him entree to the highest circles of Australian political life. He exploited this to various ends: we know, for example, that in 2016 he paid a Liberal Party lobbyist for a meeting with immigration minister Peter Dutton, during which he pressed his case for favourable handling of his and his family's immigration status. Huang, though, was said to be unhappy with the return on his investment in Australian politics and complained that Chinese-Australian donors were simply seen as 'cash cows' by the major parties.[27] People like him got less bang for their buck, that is to say, than non-Chinese donors.

In July 2016, when the UNCLOS tribunal in The Hague decided that China's artificial islands in the South China Sea were not land features, Labor's response was divided. Opposition leader Bill Shorten joined the Liberal Party in calling on China to respect the ruling, but right-wing defence spokesperson Stephen Conroy went off message by urging Australia to follow the United States in carrying out 'freedom of naviga-tion exercises'. Speaking from Washington, where he was on a paid trip for a meeting of the Australian American Leadership Dialogue, Conroy criticised the Liberals for their reluctance to authorise the Australian Navy and Air Force to enter the twelve-nautical-mile zone around Chinese-claimed reefs and islands.[28] This came at a point when Huang Xiangmo had been waving a A$400,000 contribution in front of the Labor Party, and he threatened to withdraw it in response to Conroy's intervention. At the time, junior senator Sam Dastyari was the ALP's 'party bagman', in charge of managing relations with donors. The position made Dastyari cosy with people like Huang, cosy enough for the businessman to have picked up some of his bills. The day after Conroy's speech, to keep Huang onside, Dastyari went before a small scrum of Chinese-language media to tell them that 'the Chinese integrity of its borders is a matter for China', and that 'the role that Australia should be playing as a friend is to know that we see several thousand years of history, thousands of years of his-tory, where it is and isn't our place to be involved'.[29]

It was a ridiculous, dishonest performance, but there was an element of charade about the whole affair. Conroy's bravado on freedom of navigation operations was a typical case of ALP point-scoring from opposition, designed to impress his American hosts. Dastyari's pandering to PRC sensibilities was 'narrow-casting' to a particular audience. Different wings of the party were saying different things to keep various constituencies onside and the cash rolling in – not an unusual phenomenon. In terms of any actual effort to shift ALP policy on the South China Sea, Conroy's speech had much more impact than Dastyari's press conference, which he deliberately hid from the public eye. It was a deceitful act, to be sure, but was it exceptional by the low standards of New South Wales politics?

When the full picture of this secretive event emerged in 2017, immigration minister Peter Dutton let fly with accusations that Dastyari was a 'shady figure' working for Beijing. Soon, the espionage angle was heightened by a follow-up story, that Dastyari had met Huang Xiangmo at his home and invited him to turn off his phone during their conversation. There was nothing particularly surprising about this: it was public knowledge that Huang was being surveilled by ASIO. But the escalating scandal left Shorten little choice but to ask for Dastyari's resignation. Huang himself soon became the primary focus of espionage talk.

Should an affair like this be considered a case of 'foreign' interference? The mission of the ACPPRC is no secret: it exists to promote a pillar of China's foreign policy. Obviously, members like Huang can be expected to make use of available avenues to pursue that objective, be they public lobbying or private influence-peddling. It has organisational ties to the CCP, but it's hard to imagine the party having the will or capacity to micromanage ACPPRC affairs to the point of telling Huang what to do with one of his many donations to Australian politics. Certainly no evidence of this was ever provided. It's just as plausible that Huang was acting to salvage his own reputation: to be seen funding the ALP when it was moving in a hawkish direction on the South China Sea would have been a bad look for the chairman of the ACPPRC.

No one should mourn Dastyari's downfall, but the case raised questions of principle that were lost amid the furore. The first is whether Chinese Australians who hold pro-Beijing views, and who express those views by involving themselves in organisations with ties to China, have the right to participate in the Australian political system on the same terms as anyone else. Sordid as it was, no one involved in this dalliance broke any laws. Huang was buying influence the same way many wealthy, politically interested donors do on a regular basis. A second, and very different, question is whether the political system should allow wealthy donors to buy influence in this way. My answers to these two questions would be yes to the first, no to the second. The government's response has embodied the opposite approach.

Any time concerns arise involving political donations, there's always an option available to us: comprehensive limits and strict reporting requirements. When you consider that donations were at the centre of ASIO warnings that foreign interference threatened our 'way of life', it's strange to think we wouldn't do this. It seems negligent, even cynical, not to plug the conduit for such threats. But the fact is, the reforms introduced to Australian electoral law in 2018 did nothing to prohibit the kind of political donations that featured in the Dastyari saga. Chau's and Huang's donations could still be made today – anonymously, even, if they were broken into chunks below the $14,300 reporting threshold. Instead of reforms that would genuinely enhance the workings of Australian democracy, the government chose to preserve an easily corruptible system intact and embark on a campaign to exclude Chinese actors from it through new, selectively enforced, legislation.

Foreign-Interference Laws

A warning from ASIO that espionage and foreign interference was occurring at an 'unprecedented scale', reports that the agency had briefed Australian politicians on donors with 'links' to the CCP, and the Dastyari scandal: this was the information available to the public on 5 December 2017, when Prime Minister Malcolm Turnbull unveiled a package of new laws to uphold the 'sovereignty of Australians to make their own decisions'.[30] Almost immediately, a new set of stories hit the press. One was an anonymous account that PRC security chief Meng Jianzhu had tried to bully the ALP into supporting ratification of an extradition treaty with China by threatening to tell Chinese Australians that the party was anti-China (the ALP continued to oppose ratification, and as far as we know, no such message was sent). Then, ASIO tipped off *The Weekend Australian* that it had identified ten candidates for political office in Australia who had suspicious 'links' to China.[31]

Turnbull's announcement was made in the midst of a tense by-election campaign in the northern Sydney electorate of Bennelong, home to a large Chinese-Australian community. On the campaign trail, he fingered Dastyari as a subversive who had 'betrayed his country'. Hitting back, Labor's candidate, Kristina Keneally, spoke for those in her electorate who saw Turnbull as gripped by 'China-phobia'.[32] Within days, Bennelong itself became the story, when a letter in Chinese was discovered circulating on WeChat, encouraging people to vote Labor and deprive the Coalition of their one-seat majority in parliament. The letter described the Liberal Party's policies as anti-immigrant and anti-China, and advertised Labor as the party of multiculturalism and Australia–China friendship. Its authors were anonymous, but among those circulating it online was a vice-president of the ACPPRC – enough of a 'link' to trigger talk of foreign interference. Liberal MP Dave Sharma speculated that China was engaged in 'active measures' – a Russian term for the subversive activities of the Soviet security services that entered the Cold War lexicon – to swing the election to Labor.[33] The assumption that the letter was in some way linked to Beijing became confirmed in the retelling. Within a few months, Clive Hamilton was opining that it 'seems likely that … the consulate was instrumental in organising it'.[34] No evidence was ever provided for this claim.

Turnbull's new laws comprised a package of legislation. The first was the National Security Legislation Amendment (Espionage and Foreign Interference) Bill 2017 (the EFI Bill), which was designed to update a series of offences in the *Criminal Code*. Second was a new Foreign Influence Transparency Scheme (FITS) to create a register of lobbyists, with requirements on individuals and groups to disclose their relationship to foreign 'principals'. Finally, the Electoral Legislation Amendment (Electoral Funding and Disclosure Reform) Bill 2017 would prohibit donations from foreign governments and state-owned corporations, and extend the electoral law's party registration regime to civil society organisations, imposing new regulatory obligations on them. For this, it became known as the 'Anti-GetUp Bill'. This was a major shake-up of Australia's security laws, with considerable implications for free speech and civil liberties. Hoping to rush the laws through with a minimum of debate, Attorney-General Christian Porter referred the EFI Bill to the Joint Parliamentary Committee on Intelligence and Security for only a fortnight of consultation, but opposition soon grew as its terms became known, and the bill was delayed.

The centrepiece of the EFI Bill was the invention of a new category of offence: 'foreign interference'. What exactly is this? In Chau Chak Wing's defamation suit, ABC and Fairfax at first tried to justify the imputation that Chau was engaged in 'espionage' by putting forward a definition of 'espionage' (which is a crime) that included 'attempting to advance the United Front Strategy and the interests of the CCP' through 'conduct which achieves or is intended to achieve, or is intended to make possible, influencing and/or subverting and/or otherwise interfering with, covertly and/or deceptively (in the sense that the Agent's role as such Agent is not disclosed), the policies of foreign governments and/or the political and democratic processes of foreign countries'. The judge found this to be an 'embarrassing' definition of espionage: 'It seeks to expand that well known everyday word to encompass vague and imprecise concepts so that the activity can also be what the respondents call "espionage" because the person has not disclosed his or her connection to China'.[35]

To criminalise the kind of conduct that ABC and Fairfax believed Chau to be engaged in, a new offence was therefore necessary. The 'foreign interference' clauses of the EFI Bill were written to fill this gap. Without going into a full dissection of these clauses, let me quote a definition given by the attorney-general's office: foreign interference 'includes covert, deceptive and coercive activities intended to affect an Australian political or governmental process that are directed, subsidised or undertaken by (or on behalf of) foreign actors to advance their interests or objectives'.[36] To give an example, if an Australia citizen consults with a foreign actor, then tries to exert some influence on Australian politics without disclosing that prior consultation, they are now committing foreign interference and liable for prosecution.

The EFI Bill also contained a range of reforms to espionage laws, including a new category of 'inherently harmful information', the disclosure of which would constitute a crime, irrespective of whether doing so resulted in any harm. It introduced an expansive definition of 'national security', encompassing Australia's 'political, military or economic relations with another country or other countries'. Conduct that will 'prejudice Australia's national security' therefore includes any activities that might complicate Australia's relationship with a foreign country – an incredibly wide scope. As a corollary, conduct that may 'advantage the national security of a foreign country' (for example, by opposing a war against it) is also criminalised. 'Dealing' with information which 'concerns Australia's national security' (the act of 'dealing' can be as simple as receiving or obtaining information) was also made an offence, regardless of whether the information was classified or already in the public domain.

The scope of the FITS Bill was equally troubling. Knowing who is lobbying for whom is obviously a public good, and Australia has been lax on this front. Yet while the FITS Public Register is modelled on America's FARA (*Foreign Agents Registration Act*) register, Australia's definition of 'foreign principal' is much wider than FARA's, encompassing not just governments and government-related entities, but also foreign political organisations. These include political parties but also any 'foreign organisation that exists primarily to pursue political objectives'. Registrable activities include not only lobbying in its restricted sense of persuading politicians but all 'communications activity' designed to shift public opinion on any issue of the day. The threshold for acting 'on behalf' of the foreign principal can simply be 'under an arrangement' with them. The upshot is that anyone coordinating with a foreign organisation to campaign in Australia is technically required to register and comply with the Act's disclosure requirements, or else face fines and/or a jail sentence. At the same time, the FITS Bill deliberately excluded subsidiaries of foreign corporations from its purview, meaning that lobbyists for such subsidiaries have no obligation to declare themselves. Facebook's recent efforts to stymie the government's News Media Bargaining Code, for example, do not count as foreign influence under the terms of the FITS.

The bills provoked considerable disquiet. Media organisations and unions warned that they would criminalise ordinary journalism; law bodies pointed out the implications for civil liberties'; and charities and civil society groups complained of new restrictions on their activities. A group of academics who work on China and the Chinese diaspora, myself included, made a submission arguing that exaggerated claims of

PRC influence had poisoned the political climate, and also that the laws might endanger academic freedom.[37]

In response, the attorney-general reduced the penalties for some offenses, restricted the scope of certain key terms, and introduced a set of new defences and exemptions – for journalists, for example. In the face of Senate crossbench efforts to refer the legislation for more consultation, Porter insisted that the laws were needed in advance of an upcoming round of by-elections, which he implied would otherwise be at risk from Chinese interference: 'Even in the time that it has taken to consider the Espionage and Foreign Interference Bill, the threat environment has changed and become more acute.'[38] Having invoked the spectre of electoral interference to pass the laws, the attorney-general then did the same to hasten their implementation. With a federal election approaching, Porter announced that new requirements to register a relationship with a foreign principal would take effect from 10 December 2018. On that day, the attorney-general also acquired the power under the FITS Act to issue a 'transparency notice' designating someone a foreign agent.

The Hunt for Manchurian Candidates

Was there foreign meddling in the 2019 federal election? Anticipating an ALP victory, *The New York Times* depicted Labor as a party that put Australia at risk with its pro-China proclivities: 'Bill Shorten Wants Australia to Embrace China. But at What Cost?' Shorten's election, according to this article, would 'signify a crack in the united front' that Donald Trump was building against China. 'Connections to China run deep in the Labor Party', the article continued, claiming that Bob Carr had 'essentially become one of the Chinese government's most effective spokesmen.'[39] China had taken a position on the election, *The New York Times* claimed: 'It's clear which leader Chinese officials prefer.' The evidence for this claim was an academic study of official PRC social media accounts, many of which were critical of the Liberals and Prime Minister Scott Morrison. But was this evidence of a pro-Labor push from Beijing? Given that the Liberals had by now held government for two terms, why wouldn't PRC critics of Australian policies focus their fire on them? Would we argue that someone criticising Trump without also attacking the out-of-office

Democrats was thereby displaying a partisan preference? One of the study's authors explicitly contradicted *The New York Times*' interpretation, noting that this critical trend was long in evidence and had nothing to do with the election.[40] Arguably, *The New York Times* article had more influence on the 2019 poll than anything China was shown to be doing.

The foreign-interference legislation has given considerable ammunition to those hoping to prosecute 'agents of influence' in Australian society, but so far their primary effect has been to create suspicion of Chinese Australians involved with community organisations deemed pro-Beijing. This has become a feature of the political landscape in Australia. Instead of taking these associations as evidence of a candidate's *politics*, they've come to be seen as evidence of a candidate's *loyalties*.

An early flare-up came in Tasmania, where the Greens cited 'extremely credible evidence' that Beijing intended to interfere in the 2018 Hobart council elections, pointing the finger at independent candidate Yongbei Tang. Tang had held positions in the Multicultural Council of Tasmania and the Chinese Cultural Society of Tasmania, and edited a monthly Chinese-language magazine. She had also been a member of the ACPPRC and done volunteer work for the local PRC consulate. On this basis, critics insinuated that she was an 'operative' for the United Front, although the only concrete act of 'interference' they pointed to was that Tang encouraged non-citizen residents to enrol to vote – something they are entitled to do at the local level in Tasmania. For informing people of their rights, Tang was accused by a rival candidate of 'exploit[ing] an electoral loophole'.[41] Greens leader Cassy O'Connor also attacked her for an article making the observation that 'Australia is a society dominated by white people' and expressing her desire 'to see a powerful Chinese community'.[42]

In the midst of all this, Clive Hamilton flew down to deliver a lecture on the risks to the 'independence of the Tasmanian community' from 'a concerted campaign ... to extend the Chinese Communist Party's political influence in Tasmania'.[43] Calling it a 'matter of respect for Australian values', the Hobart *Mercury* took the unusual step of publishing an anonymous letter from a group of Chinese Australians stating that Tang 'does not represent the majority of the Chinese community in Hobart' – probably right as it turns out.[44] In the election itself, on the eve of which her signs were defaced by racist slurs, Tang received a paltry 1.12 per cent of the vote. Even if we assume (which we can't) that this entire vote came from Hobart's small contingent of voting non-citizens, it would still represent less than half of that constituency.

Both major parties still practise a fairly crude, transactional form of engagement with immigrant communities, often plucking out candidates less on the basis of their politics than on their ability to mobilise communities en bloc and attract donations. In the 2019 race for the seat of Chisholm in Melbourne, both parties fielded Chinese-Australian candidates – Hong Kong–born Gladys Liu versus the Taiwanese Jennifer Yang – with the Liberal Party's Liu claiming a narrow victory. Both Yang and Liu had links to groups that the media was by now collapsing into the single category of 'United Front organisations', and these became the focus of commentary surrounding the election. In a typical gotcha interview with right-wing commentator Andrew Bolt, Liu made a mess of his questions about her honorary role with the China Overseas Exchange Association, a branch of the PRC's Overseas Chinese Affairs Office. On the ABC's *Insiders* program, Phil Coorey described the Overseas Exchange Association as a 'particularly nefarious organisation'.[45]

In his interview with Liu, Bolt put a question to her that Chinese Australians have now come to expect on entering politics: would she denounce the PRC (more stridently than anyone else would be expected to)? He pressed her for her views on 'China stealing the South China Sea' and whether or not Xi Jinping was a 'dictator' – claims that not even Morrison would be willing to endorse. Hamilton weighed in, suggesting that Liu's election might be invalidated by section 44 of the Australian Constitution, which prohibits candidates from holding 'allegiance, obedience, or adherence to a foreign power'.[46]

Morrison rebuffed the attacks on Liu as racist, but so far politicians of both parties have done a poor job of explaining precisely why such attacks *are* racist, let alone displaying consistency on the issue. Not only have the major parties seen advantage in attacking Chinese-Australian rivals for their United Front 'links', but factions have exploited the same line of attack against members of their own parties.

In the case of Malaysian-born Jing Lee, a Liberal member of the South Australian Legislative Council, it was not only Labor, but three senior Liberals who questioned her suitability to hold office on national-security grounds. The Lee case centred on her involvement with the Xinjiang Association of South Australia – an organisation that liaises with the local Chinese consulate and exists in part to combat the lobbying efforts of the local pro-independence East Turkistan Australian Association. Anyone taking such a stance on Xinjiang can expect to face questions; to support an organisation that whitewashes Beijing's policies in the region reflects poorly on Lee. But when filtered through the national-security lens, the politics of the Xinjiang issue fell out of the story, which was dominated by less substantial, but more sensational, hints of a PRC influence operation.

The idea that Beijing is grooming individuals to run for office as part of a long-term strategy to influence Australian politics has given rise to some unlikely theories. One involved Nick Zhao, a car dealer and member of the Liberal Party in Chisholm, who is said to have told ASIO that a Chinese-Australian businessman had offered to finance his preselection campaign. When the story broke, Liberal MP Andrew Hastie described Zhao as a 'perfect target' and claimed the case represented 'a state-sponsored attempt to infiltrate our parliament'.[47] The skulduggery angle was reinforced by Zhao's mysterious death in March 2019, though police eventually ruled this a suicide. Zhao, it was disclosed, had been in custody for fraud during the 2018 Liberal Party preselection and was facing serious criminal charges when he spoke to ASIO. Could Beijing officials have really imagined him a suitable vehicle for their interests?

The Australian media's credulity towards narratives like this has contributed to a climate in which any Chinese-Australian candidate must now expect special questioning, not to mention online abuse. Australian politics remains overwhelmingly white – with only 4 per cent of members of the federal parliament coming from non-European backgrounds – and these attacks will only dissuade more Chinese Australians from participating.[48] Li Zhang, a candidate in Victoria's 2020 council elections, said she found the abuse so disturbing she gave up her ambition to win a seat.[49] And it's not only Chinese Australians who are vulnerable. Before the 2020 election in the Australian Capital Territory, Liberal candidate Elizabeth Lee, a Korean Australian, described the racist attacks she had been receiving: "'Go back to your country, you're a Chinese spy.' I've gotten that quite a bit.'[50] I will explore the wider consequences of this discourse for Asian Australians in the final chapter of the book.

Looking for Scalps

The new foreign-interference panic can't be thought of solely in terms of its domestic impact. Australia's policies towards China must always be seen in the context of a strategy to maintain the US–Australia alliance by showing Australia's relevance to US interests and catalysing a wider US-led response to China. In a recent speech, George Brandis – Australia's former attorney-general and current high commissioner in London – informs us that the new laws 'were developed by Australia explicitly as a Five Eyes project, in consultation with the four other governments [Canada, New Zealand, the United Kingdom and the United States], so as to produce a world's best practice model, which could be readily adopted by others'.[51] The full extent of this collaboration has never been fully disclosed, but John Garnaut described one element of it in a 2018 talk at the Hoover Institution: 'We did a lot of learning from the US, and took back what the FBI wished they had.'[52]

Having implemented this FBI wish list, Australia has gone on to advertise its new foreign-interference laws to the world, and encouraged US allies to follow suit. As Hamilton describes it, Australia has received 'a steady stream of visitors from Western civil services, intelligence agencies, think-tanks, universities and parliaments, all interested in one thing: what measures had Australia taken to protect its institutions from interference and infiltration by the Chinese state? Experts have been explaining over and over what Australia has done and the circumstances that turned this country into the global leader pushing back against the Chinese Communist Party's interference.'[53]

But are these laws really the 'world's best practice'? The rollout of the government's FITS has been tentative, even slightly farcical. Among the earliest to register themselves was a 9/11 conspiracy theorist. Responding to an ALP tip-off, the attorney-general's first request for information was from Andrew Cooper, the organiser of a Sydney conference of the right-wing American Conservative Political Action Committee. Cooper was required to submit a wide range of information on the organisation of his conference, its participants and even what was said at the event. For his participation, Tony Abbott was likewise asked why he had not registered on the FITS Public Register. The former prime minister was enraged and expressed his intention to defy the intrusive request.

Porter sheepishly advised his subordinates to 'focus on the most serious instances of noncompliance' – that is, to keep the focus on China.

Kevin Rudd has recently highlighted the wide scope of the FITS, after receiving advice that interviews with foreign media organisations may constitute registrable foreign influence. The question is a genuine one. During the 2019 parliamentary inquiry into press freedom, it was revealed that the attorney-general's office had written to the Nine Network, asking them to consider whether their joint investigation with Qatar-based Al Jazeera into One Nation made it an act of foreign influence. During the inquiry, ASIO cautioned against any giving journalists special protections or exemptions from the new laws, citing once again the 'unprecedented threat' from foreign actors.

So far, the chief application of the foreign-interference laws has been to summarily expel non-citizens from the country. Unsurprisingly, the first such action was taken against Huang Xiangmo, bête noire of journalists on the hunt for PRC influence. Following the introduction of the new laws, Huang was punished on pre-emptive grounds, not on the basis of any crime he had committed. ASIO is said to have told Dutton that Huang was 'amenable to conducting acts of foreign interference' and had in the past shown a 'willingness' to engage in such actions. On this basis, Dutton decided that Huang failed the 'character test' of section 501 of the *Migration Act*; his application for Australian citizenship was rejected and his permanent residency revoked.

We'll never know exactly what information ASIO had on Huang, but this mode of enforcement flies in the face of one of the four 'pillars' of Turnbull's counter-interference strategy: 'sunlight'. Little sunlight will ever shine on a ministerial decision to terminate someone's residency rights. The law affords no right to examine, let alone test, the advice on which such a decision is made, or to challenge the merits of the decision in any way.

Taking Huang's scalp emboldened the security agencies for a more ambitious operation: the June 2020 dawn raid on New South Wales MP Shaoquett Moselmane and some of his Chinese acquaintances. Thanks to a tip-off to the media, the raids on the houses of Moselmane and his former policy adviser John Zhang were well publicised. What the public didn't know at the time was that ASIO and the federal police were also raiding the houses of four Chinese journalists and preparing advice to Dutton to revoke the visas of two PRC scholars of Australian literature, Chen Hong and Li Jianjun.

Interest in these raids centred on their possible role in provoking retaliation from China, which led to the Australian media's last representatives in China departing the country. It's troubling to think that ASIO might exert that kind of influence on Australia–China relations, but we shouldn't lose sight of the implications of the case here in Australia. In booting out Chen and Li, Australia has become a country that, like China, bans foreign academics on suspicion of ties to foreign conspiracies. As far as can be ascertained from court filings, the basis for the warrant against John Zhang was suspicion that he was trying to influence Moselmane via a private WeChat group, without revealing that he was collaborating with a United Front organisation. He is now challenging this warrant on free speech grounds, which will be an important test case. So too will the upcoming trial of Sunny Duong – a separate case and the first actual charge under the new legislation. Duong, a Melbourne community figure, faces up to a decade behind bars for the crime of 'preparing to commit an act of foreign interference'.

The raids also offer a case study in the chilling effect such actions can have on political life. Moselmane's views on China have never been any secret – he admires the party's poverty-reduction efforts and is optimistic about China's international role. He has written articles and given speeches praising the Chinese government's response to the COVID-19 crisis. In April 2020, two months before the raids, Dutton cited this fact to call for Moselmane's resignation. 'You can't have an allegiance to another country and pretend to have an allegiance to this country at the same time ... To be talking from the talking points of the Chinese Communist Party is completely unacceptable, and he must resign.'[54] The June raids only entrenched this stigmatising framing of Moselmane's views – and his engagement with PRC nationals who hold the same views – as potentially criminal. After the raids, Moselmane's ALP colleagues joined the campaign to ostracise the pro-China Moselmane by immediately suspending his party membership.

The specialist in Australian literature Chen Hong had also been publicly critical of Australia's post-2017 hawkish turn, and like John Zhang was a member of Moselmane's 'Fair Dinkum' WeChat group. Rendering someone like him persona non grata has sent a warning to all Chinese in Australia not to be too vocal in their criticisms of government policy. Lest anyone doubt that political views were a factor in the decision to take action here, witness Dutton's comments in response to a question on the raids on Chinese journalists: 'If people are here as journalists, and they're reporting fairly on the news, then that's fine. But if they're here providing a slanted view to a particular community, then we have concern with that.'[55]

So far, a degree of criticism has been levelled at the selective enforcement of these laws against Chinese people. It's a valid point, but we need to insist that Australia's foreign-interference laws criminalise things that should not be criminal. There are many organisations active in Australian public life with links to foreign governments and political parties. The Zionist Federation of Australia, for example, proudly advertises the fact that it consults with the government of Israel. The Hindu Swayamsevak Sangh – the international branch of the Hindu Rashtriya Swayamsevak Sangh, from which Modi's Bharatiya Janata Party springs – is active in Australia. The list could go on. You don't have to like the politics of such groups, but that's a different question from whether their activities should be criminalised.

Let me use one of these non-Chinese examples to spell out the significance of the foreign-interference laws. Say, for example, that the Zionist Federation holds a meeting with officials from Israel's Ministry of Strategic Affairs and Public Diplomacy to discuss plans to combat the international boycott of Israel – the Boycott, Divestment, Sanctions campaign. Then, in the course of lobbying against the boycott here in Australia, they fail to mention that they've had such meetings. This is probably newsworthy. We're better off knowing the full extent of such international links. But current legislation would now deem this as 'covert' and therefore an act of 'intentional foreign interference', punishable by up to twenty years in jail.

These laws are not the 'world's best practice' – they are draconian and dangerous. And without wider exposure and critique, they risk providing a new paradigm for the ongoing expansion of the Australian security state. The Law Council of Australia observes that Australia has adopted over fifty pieces of anti-terror legislation since 9/11, many of which 'run contrary to established notions of criminal justice'.[56] 'Foreign interference' is now replacing terrorism as the primary justification for new security laws, with similar implications. If enacted, for example, the draft Australian Security Intelligence Organisation Amendment Bill will extend ASIO's authority to conduct compulsory questioning in terrorism investigations to its investigations of 'foreign interference', and increase the agency's ability to surveil and track individuals without warrant.

There are calls for new laws too. As early as 2017, Clive Hamilton and ASPI analyst Alex Joske worried that Turnbull's laws did not capture the sweep of 'foreign-interference operations that are being undertaken by the PRC in Australia'.[57] John Lee, a former adviser to Julie Bishop, has written that 'the countering of Beijing's United Front operations needs to be taken seriously ... Legislation prohibiting such activities ought to be passed.'[58] Lee's recommendation was vague, but it implied the possibility of simply proscribing certain Chinese-Australian organisations. At times, the proposals have been too radical for even the security agencies themselves. When Peter Hartcher argued in his 2019 Quarterly Essay, *Red Flag*, that ASIO should be empowered to vet candidates for public office, ASIO immediately came out and distanced itself from the idea.[59]

The entire approach here has been misguided from the start. History yields up no examples of liberal democratic institutions being strengthened by a country continuously granting new powers to its security agencies. Unlike the US Congress, Australia's parliament has no oversight of the operations of the nation's intelligence agencies, and ASIO to this day remains a highly secretive organisation. It has a history of politicisation and an institutional self-interest in stoking public anxiety towards hidden enemies. It simply cannot be seen as an ally in the defence of democratic rights. Should we continue to entertain that fantasy, today's China panic will erode civil liberties in just the same way that 9/11 and the War on Terror did in the 2000s.

5. COLD-WAR CAMPUS

Outside the political sphere, much of Australia's China panic centres on university campuses. This is hardly surprising, given the deep connections of the Australian higher-education sector to China. In 2019, before the COVID-19 pandemic hit, higher education brought in some A$12 billion in export revenue, most of it from China. With more than 150,000 Chinese international students enrolled, some institutions relied on that single revenue stream to make up a quarter of their total budget before the current drop-off. Mandarin is the second language of campus life in most universities these days; Confucius Institutes have been established at thirteen universities; partnerships and MOUs with Chinese universities proliferate in many fields. Australian academics now collaborate more with colleagues in China than in any other foreign country: one report found that an incredible 16.2 per cent of scientific papers by Australian researchers – almost one in six – were co-authored with researchers in China, with papers in the fields of materials science, chemical engineering and energy topping the list.[1]

Having been among the most enthusiastic participants in the China boom, universities are now bearing the brunt of the political backlash. The public has been presented with a grim picture of the consequences of all of this China engagement. Financial dependency, it's claimed, has engendered political subservience. Critical discussion of China is falling silent, while administrations subcontract their core business to PRC state agencies and pursue partnerships that put Australia's national security at risk. It's a picture replete with martial imagery. Andrew Hastie talks of universities as 'modern battlegrounds of covert influence and interference'. Journalist Rowan Callick warns of a 'war being waged by Chinese international students against "politically incorrect" lecturers'. 'A military-academic onslaught' is how Alex Joske describes China's approach to international scientific collaboration.[2]

How accurate is this picture? As a critic of Australian universities, I'd never argue that all is healthy within the sector, including in its dealings with China. But as universities have become a microcosm for the wider China debate, it's important that we characterise that debate correctly. In many ways, we face the same choice here as we do in the political sphere: to remedy the erosion of Australian institutions, or to join in a campaign to isolate and exclude Chinese actors from them. At the same time, there are ethical and political questions specific to the university context that administrators and academics alike face. In tackling them, though, we have to remain conscious of the various ways in which university autonomy and academic freedom can be compromised, including of course by the intrusion of domestic political influences. The language of war that now envelops campuses has, in my opinion, laid the basis for domestic government interventions that present more of a risk to universities' autonomy and independence than anything China is doing.

As they do in the political sphere, openings for undue influence exist in universities. However, China is far from the only actor taking advantage of what are self-inflicted wounds. The basic crisis is the inexorable decline in public funding. At 0.7 per cent of GDP, public investment in Australian higher education already sits well below the OECD average and will continue its downward slide thanks to recent reforms. This long-term transformation has put universities at risk from private philanthropists and foreign lobbying ventures alike, wheeling all sorts of ideological barrows into the halls of learning. As governing bodies reshape themselves along corporate lines and restrict the participation of academics in decision-making, transparency is eroded, and the attraction of get-rich-quick schemes only increases.

Universities have been put on the back foot in the current political climate. On the one hand, as public institutions they can hardly avoid the impact of the changing winds of political opinion on China. Yet at the same time, universities have in practice been all but privatised, with many vice-chancellors enriching themselves to the tune of more than a million dollars annually. Any effort to criticise the direction of Australian policy can easily be met with accusations that they have a pecuniary interest in the question. It's a simple fact that they do. In August 2020, when the senate announced it would be conducting an inquiry into 'national security risks affecting the Australian higher-education and research sector', federal MP Bob Katter railed against universities that had their 'snouts ... well and truly in the trough' and had 'gone from selling visas to selling their souls'.[3] Having long encouraged universities to find funding elsewhere, politicians now home in on their ties to China to argue that they've lost their way, engendering a hostile public mood that blunts criticism of ongoing funding cuts.

What this highlights, I think, is the need for a perspective that's independent of both the government and the corporate university, one that's able to make the necessary criticisms of universities as institutions and international actors, without falling into uncritical subservience to the government's foreign-policy objectives. This is not the first time that universities have had to face this challenge. During the first Cold War, through both enticements and pressure, Western universities were encouraged to align their work with the state's diplomatic and military interests. The conditions then were not conducive to free, critical inquiry, and they're not likely to be a second time around either.

Talking about China at Australian Universities

University administrators clearly can't be trusted to get everything right on China. Just before I arrived at the University of Sydney in 2013, a talk by the Dalai Lama was mysteriously relocated off campus – at the request, it seems, of the vice-chancellor himself. The organisers demanded an explanation, but as is often the case, the university avoided clarifying the precise course of events that led to the change. At the time, Sydney was engaged in a push into China, reinventing itself as a leading centre for studying and collaborating with the country. A new 'China strategy' was in the works; a China Studies Centre was being set up, and a companion centre was planned for the city of Suzhou; the university had just inked a contract bringing a Confucius Institute to campus. It wasn't difficult to imagine a speech by the Dalai Lama causing undesired complications for university administrators.

We don't know how much, if any, pressure was applied for the university to take this decision. But the sad fact is it would not have taken much. Universities these days are run by ban-happy administrators, keen to control damage and avoid controversy on any range of issues. In 2019, one of the biggest 'foreign interference' stories at Sydney University didn't involve China, but Morocco. In September, a Sahrawi activist from Moroccan-occupied Western Sahara was scheduled to talk at the Law School. The Moroccan consulate inquired about the nature of the event, and it ended up being cancelled. The university's explanation was that the activist had previously spoken elsewhere on campus; the 'second event appeared to be a duplication, or too similar, to justify being hosted at the same university', was the official line.[4] The actual worry seems to have been that the university might be perceived as having an official stance on the Western Sahara conflict. This was entirely unsatisfactory: the idea that discussing a sensitive topic might reflect an institutional position on that topic would chill intellectual life on campus.

Contrary to the popular conservative talking point, it is most often minority and progressive groups whose activities are stifled by overly sensitive university administrators. In 2014, Michael Spence prevented the University of Sydney's Muslim Students' Association from holding an event with Uthman Badar, spokesperson for the Islamic political party Hizb ut-Tahrir. In 2015, Spence unilaterally revoked a booking for a socialist organisation to hold an anti-war meeting on Anzac Day. Responding to a recent independent review of free speech in the Australian higher-education sector, the university has strengthened its commitment to academic freedom, pledging that it 'shall not refuse permission for the use of its land or facilities by an external visiting speaker or invited visiting speaker ... solely on the basis of the content of the proposed speech by the visitor.'[5] But in the two cases I mention above, the university cited vague security concerns as grounds for its decisions, and there is nothing to stop it doing the same again.

When universities cave in on issues involving China, it needs to be seen in this wider context: as a systemic failing, not the sign of a particular obeisance to Beijing. For the most part, critical discussion of China is alive and well at the University of Sydney. In 2019 alone, the university's flagship public talks program, Sydney Ideas, held a large public forum on Xinjiang, featuring Erkin Sidick, a Uyghur dissident from the United States. The same program hosted a discussion of China's May Fourth movement, Tiananmen and the state of student activism in China today (at its end, the audience was invited to join a solidarity photograph for detained labour activists in south China). Uyghur activists also organised their own talks and film screenings; Chinese democracy activists held a day-long conference. Multiple public events and a loud rally in the centre of campus were held in support of Hong Kong. I was involved in many of these activities: they went off without a hitch or interference from any direction.

Successful events, of course, are not as newsworthy as those that get disrupted or administratively nixed, so they tend not to make the press. The only time the public hears about China-related events at universities is when something goes wrong, and a one-sided narrative grows. A bit of perspective, then, is helpful. We can certainly put to rest claims such as those made by Anastasia Lin, a Canadian-Chinese activist and visiting scholar at the Centre for Independent Studies think-tank, that 'academics don't even have freedom to even talk about Uyghurs or Tibet on Australian soil'.[6] We certainly do. In my eight years as a specialist in Uyghur history at the University of Sydney, I've never experienced the slightest pressure, on or off campus, to modify what I say about China.

I wish I could say the same about my views on Palestine. In 2015, I gave an interview to *The Australian* about my support for the boycott of Israeli universities, part of the solidarity campaign known as BDS (Boycott, Divestment, Sanctions). Within a week, a representative of one of New South Wales's pro-Israel organisations was in my department chair's office with a complaint: according to him, a Jewish PhD candidate studying the Israel–Palestine conflict was worried that my politics might bias me against her in the administrative role I was performing at the time. After the meeting, my chair and I scoured the enrolment lists and consulted colleagues, but could find no such PhD candidate. We came to the conclusion that the story was made up, designed to intimidate me out of public commentary on Israel.

This, unfortunately, was not a one-off experience. For helping to promote a rally to commemorate the expulsion and flight of half the population of Palestine in 1948 – the *Nakba*, Arabic for 'catastrophe' – the

university investigated a complaint from off campus that I was supporting terrorism. Many colleagues around the country have similar stories.
While we don't keep statistics in Australia, in 2020 the independent
organisation Palestine Legal responded to 213 incidents of suppression
of Palestine advocacy in the United States. Of these incidents, 80 per cent
targeted students and scholars at sixty-eight different universities.[7] On
more than one occasion in the last decade, North American administrators have intervened to rescind job offers to academics critical of Israel.

The point here can be made a little more strongly. All things considered, there are upsides in the West for scholars who are publicly critical
of China. As much as it might draw attacks, speaking out against Chinese
policies also draws considerable plaudits. Having expertise on a sensitive
topic like Xinjiang or Hong Kong also attracts press coverage, something
universities increasingly require of their academics, and can only help in
landing competitive grants and publishing opportunities.

Of course, in China the story is different. There, any foreigner who
works on sensitive topics will, at some point, confront the party-state's
techniques for guiding and controlling academic discourse. On one trip to
Ürümchi a decade ago, I found myself taken out to lunch by people who
claimed to work for a think-tank, but who were almost certainly linked
to the security services. They wanted to know what Xinjiang scholars in
the West were up to and why we spent so much time focusing on negative sides of Xinjiang's history. If China forms the view that someone is
involved in activities that threaten it – such as collaboration with foreign
intelligence agencies – that person may face a ban on entering the country.
Risks like these weigh on people's minds, particularly if they are just starting out in the field. Even if foreign scholars are not directly targeted by the
party-state, they have to weigh up their ethical obligations to colleagues
and interlocutors inside China. Sadly, in some circumstances cutting off
contact is the only way to ensure their safety.

Internationally minded institutions have to take the good with the
bad: by opening up to China, they can't escape the effects of deteriorating
academic freedom there. They need to be sensitive to the pressure on staff
and students, particularly those who are Chinese citizens themselves, or
who have family in the country. Along with causing trauma, political
conditions at home may well inhibit these scholars from publishing freely

or participating in conferences to the extent they'd like. Universities have to make allowance for this, and recognise the many and varied contributions these scholars can still make to teaching and learning.

'Self-censorship' is a term that gets thrown around when China scholars fail to meet expectations to publicly criticise the PRC, but I find this term too reductive and ill-defined to capture the complexity of the situation. The varying responses we see from China scholars to the issues of the day reflect a range of factors. One is simply politics. There are some Sinologists whose mission in life is to bring down the CCP, some who are strongly pro-CCP and many with viewpoints somewhere in between. We also have to take into account the fact that not every scholar conceives of their role, particularly their public role, in the same way: some are collectively minded activists, some are reclusive. An apolitical withdrawal is common among academics in all disciplines. Obviously, I don't believe that the ethical choices of China scholars should be above criticism. I'd think less, for instance, of a colleague in Xinjiang studies who thought it appropriate to carry on normal academic exchange with China at this time. Without setting up rigid expectations about who and what China knowledge is for, and how it should be produced and disseminated, we should aim to foster a field that is aware of and responsive to issues of injustice and oppression in China. But we can do that without the hasty accusations of cowardice or complicity that often accompany the term 'self-censorship'.

Collaborations and Confucius Institutes

There's a tension in the idea of the public university. On the one hand, universities describe their aspirations in universalist terms: to advance human knowledge, meet scientific and social challenges, and improve public well-being. Academics tend to see themselves as contributing to international fields and aim for the widest possible dissemination of their work. Society recognises that for universities to do their jobs effectively, free of distorting influences, they need to be autonomous from the political interests of the day. These ideals can run up against competing claims, however, that as recipients of government funding, universities should serve the 'national interest', something that usually gets defined elsewhere. Such claims justify the calibration of university activity with the imperatives of foreign and defence policy, and allow national-security considerations to infringe on normal principles of academic work. Taken to their logical conclusion, they require universities to have friends and enemies.

This debate has been a tug of war since the Middle Ages, and universities have been losing it of late. In 2018, the Department of Defence sought to radically revise the *Defence Trade Controls Act* to effectively allow officials to veto any technological exchange between Australia and the outside world, and to enforce compliance with warrantless search and seizure powers. Although Defence did not name any particular country as a source of concern, the spectre of Chinese influence obviously lay behind this push. Universities resisted the power grab, but the notion that *any* scientific research with China is a potential risk has informed much of the debate since then.

Although universities insist that they fully comply with all of their security obligations, critics charge that they lack the specific knowledge to gauge the risks of collaborating with Chinese universities, and fail to appreciate the nature of China's 'civil–military fusion'. In 2019, ASPI's Alex Joske received funding from the US State Department to set up the 'China Defence Universities Tracker', a register of institutional ties between China's universities and its military. This site has served as the basis of much criticism of academic collaboration with China. One source claims it also 'heavily influenced' Donald Trump's decision in 2020 to revoke the visas of some 3000 Chinese postgraduate students and researchers with current or past associations with Chinese universities linked to the PLA.[8] A second report by Joske, in 2020, led *The Australian* to publish the names and faces of thirty scientists, most of them Chinese, who it claimed were participants in the PRC's 'Thousand Talents' program, which seeks to reverse China's longstanding brain drain by recruiting foreign scientists. The story's author, Sharri Markson, cited FBI director Christopher Wray's description of the program as 'economic espionage', but her sole evidence to back this up was the unsurprising fact that China retains the intellectual property rights to any research it funds.[9]

In any wide-ranging research entanglement, such as Australia's with China, it's natural for the occasional conflict of interest to arise. There have been cases of double dipping on grants, and some academics fail to disclose all of their affiliations. It is hard to say how serious this problem is, though, because the only research ties being examined are those involving China: we have no data on research ties with other countries. Still, despite the intense focus on collaborations with China, not a single breach of the *Defence Trade Controls Act* has been discovered, and many specific accusations have been refuted. The CSIRO, for example, hit back at *The Australian* for its 'alarmist and irresponsible reporting' on a collaboration between a Qingdao laboratory and CSIRO's Centre for Southern Hemisphere Oceans Research.[10]

It's true that basic scientific research can have military applications and may contribute to tools of domestic repression. There are boundaries here that universities, with their humanistic mission, can and should observe. The fact is, though, that the boundaries between basic and military research have all but vanished at Australian universities, as they've willingly embedded themselves with Australian, American and private multinational defence interests.

Universities now have dedicated staff whose job it is to court collaboration with the Department of Defence on priority initiatives, either via portals such as the Defence Innovation Hub and the NSW Defence Innovation Network, or by directly engaging with bodies such as the department's Information Warfare Division. Australian academics are also encouraged to work with the American military by bidding for contracts with the US Defense Advanced Research Projects Agency and the Office of Naval Research Global, or by applying to the Australia–US Multidisciplinary University Research Initiative.

Private collaborations with defence companies such as Lockheed Martin and Raytheon also abound, and these companies have representation in university governance. The chancellor of the University of Sydney, for example, is the board chair of the Australian subsidiary of French weapons manufacturer Thales. This state of affairs puts the reputation of Australian universities at serious risk. In 2021, for instance, the World Health Organization and the International Agency for Research on Cancer expressed reluctance to collaborate with the University of Melbourne because of its partnership with Lockheed Martin, explaining that 'WHO and IARC do not engage with the arms industry or non-state actors that work to further the interests of the arms industry'.[11]

While basic research with China, published in ordinary academic journals, is being stigmatised, universities have never been so committed to helping Australia and its allies improve their military capacity. This is Australia's version of the very thing it accuses China of: a 'civil–military fusion'. Considering this state of affairs, China might well conclude that by collaborating with Australia it runs the risk of having its science appropriated for military purposes. It's obviously impossible to make sense of this stance in terms of any principled opposition to academic work having military applications. It's slightly easier to comprehend, I think, when we realise that those warning against institutional ties with China – primarily ASPI – are less concerned about the nature of the ties than about their scale. For Peter Jennings, cutting ties with Chinese universities – like decoupling the Australian and Chinese economies – is a worthwhile end in itself. As a necessary part of 'strategic distancing', he believes Australia will have to 'review and reduce the many hundreds of research connections between Australian and Chinese institutions'.[12]

This push for disengagement is the wider context for specific controversies such as that surrounding Confucius Institutes. Part of a government-directed cultural promotion initiative, the institutes occasioned considerable unease in Australia's Chinese-studies community when they arrived here. Affiliated with China's Ministry of Education, the Hanban office (also known as the Confucius Institute Headquarters) includes senior party officials among its staff and clearly has a mission to burnish China's international image. While most centres serve as a link between Australian and Chinese universities, some also support Chinese-language programs at schools – the 'Confucius Classrooms'. In America and elsewhere, many have now been shut down in response to US government pressure or at the insistence of faculty who believe the partnerships cross a line. Anthropologist Marshall Sahlins, who led the campaign against Confucius Institutes at the University of Chicago, describes them as 'peripheral propaganda branches of the Chinese party-state'.[13] In Australia, Kevin Carrico calls them 'arms of the Chinese Communist Party'.[14]

Public discussion often depicts universities as outsourcing their core business to Confucius Institutes. Clive Hamilton complains they teach 'Chinese language and culture as essential components of the academic environment'.[15] Swinburne University's John Fitzgerald holds that 'a number of Australian universities that are keen to expand their Chinese language and studies offerings have undermined their academic integrity, autonomy and freedom by ceding control over staffing and content to a donor'.[16] It's true that some administrators were initially open to doing this. At the University of Sydney, the draft contract would have consigned undergraduate language teaching to Confucius Institute staff. But thanks to the timely intervention of faculty members, it was kept physically and intellectually at arm's length from the undergraduate curriculum.

To my knowledge, no university in Australia has ceded control of its undergraduate teaching on China to PRC interests. In one case I'm aware of, Victoria University let faculty from Beijing's University of International Business and Economics co-design and co-teach a few units in its Business School – not a particularly unusual form of scholarly exchange. At the University of Queensland, the Confucius Institute provided small start-up grants for courses on China, but without any say in their design or the appointment of staff (similar to grants provided by the Japan Foundation).

Clearly a financial relationship sets up a possible conduit for wider influence on the university. Confucius Institutes are integrated into universities in ways that institutions like Germany's Goethe-Instituts or France's Alliance Française centres are not. The distinction here is not completely black and white, though. In Adelaide, for example, the Alliance Française has signed an MOU with the University of South Australia. The partnership has obvious political and commercial motivations, and a media release notes there will be a focus on 'the emerging defence relationship between the two countries'. Alliance Française is itself a subcontractor of French defence manufacturer Naval Group's Attack-class submarine program in Adelaide, and it sponsors French Day at UniSA, where students can find out about 'careers and student exchange with French Defence Companies'.[17]

There's clearly a need for vigilance in such situations; however, as far as Confucius Institutes go, faculty (but not necessarily administrators) have been on guard. The University of Sydney's Confucius Institute runs language courses open to anyone from the public at its Centre for Continuing Education, where Chinese is taught from American textbooks, along with calligraphy and tai chi. As a vehicle for political influence on campus or in wider society, it simply cannot compare with the university's United States Studies Centre. Partially funded by the Murdoch family's American Australian Association, the centre was explicitly conceived of as a vehicle to revive popular support for the US alliance when this eroded in the wake of the invasion of Iraq. While the Confucius Institute sits in a single, hard-to-find office, the US Studies Centre occupies some of Sydney University's best real estate and offers a smorgasbord of undergraduate courses, which it advertises widely. Alongside its teaching, it plays a prominent role in public debate on US–Australia relations.

In response to concerns that the US Studies Centre was straying from its original mission, University of Queensland chancellor Peter Varghese and diplomat David Ritchie led a review of the centre's operations in 2017, which found that 'disseminating an appreciation of the importance to Australia's national interests of the US alliance' had to be a key objective of the centre, one that should be impressed on all staff.[18] Consistent with these recommendations, in 2019 the centre entered into a collaboration with the US State Department to offer seminars on 'Indo-Pacific Strategic Futures', the aims of which included the promotion of 'support for the rules-based order' and 'a commitment to countering malign influence'. The seminars were intended to influence Australian policymaking and produce a 'small but well-informed cohort of "next generation leaders" who will … become leading voices within the alliance and partner network'. We can only imagine the outrage that would (rightly) ensue if the university's China Studies Centre were to join with Beijing's Ministry of Foreign Affairs to promote Xi Jinping's vision of 'win-win cooperation' and set out to influence Australian policymaking.

What we see here is that universities are not so much outliers when it comes to China as they are mirrors of Australia as a whole. While reliant on China financially, universities remain politically tied to the prevailing alliance orthodoxy. As a source of pressure, this orthodoxy is just as capable of compromising their institutional autonomy as anything else. A university centre dedicated to the study of the United States should be a forum for the freest possible debate on the costs and benefits of the ANZUS alliance. For it to adopt a partisan standpoint in that debate severely compromises the independence of the institution.

Australia's policy response to foreign interference on campuses

exemplifies the contradictions in its approach to the issue more generally. While politicians claim that they are applying principles to ensure
the integrity of the system, for practical purposes their focus is entirely
on China. It's hard to maintain that state of affairs without its inconsis-
tency and arbitrariness eventually becoming obvious. The outcome has
been something of a good-cop-bad-cop approach, as ostensibly country-
blind consultative methods give way to more hardline measures to sever
ties with China.

In August 2019, the Australian education minister launched the
University Foreign Interference Taskforce, which brought university
officials and bodies such as Universities Australia into a collaborative
relationship with Home Affairs, ASIO and other government agencies.
The same year, the taskforce issued a set of voluntary guidelines to counter
foreign influence. Universities have since been busy reviewing their partnerships with China and responding to inquiries as to whether Confucius
Institutes should sign up to the FITS Public Register. The same universities then found themselves 'blindsided' when, without any warning or
consultation, Morrison announced his 2020 Foreign Relations Bill. Soon
enacted into law, this empowers the foreign minister to simply scrap
international collaborations, including collaborations entered into by universities, which are state institutions. Its intended scope is not simply the
hard sciences, where much of the immediate anxiety lies. In his speech
outlining the bill, Morrison complained more broadly that scholars were
able to enter into 'cultural collaboration ... without having to inform the
Commonwealth'. Confucius Institutes have been listed among the partnerships that are now vulnerable to cancellation by ministerial fiat.

Interestingly, the *Foreign Relations Act* won't apply to all partnerships
with all foreign universities, only those that the foreign minister decides
'do not have substantial autonomy'. A memorandum accompanying the
bill explained that 'a lack of institutional autonomy may include a government or a political party exerting control or influence over the university
management, leadership, curriculum and/or research activities'. Clearly,
the point here is to restrict the law's focus to China and similar countries.
The irony, though, is that government 'control or influence' of research
activities is precisely what the Act prescribes. Given that a minister can
now cancel international research collaborations with the stroke of a pen,

and without providing any justification, would Australian universities themselves qualify as having substantial autonomy?

Campus Politics

Universities have marketed themselves aggressively as a destination for Chinese undergraduates, and Australia is now home, temporarily at least, to some 160,000 students who are citizens of the PRC. Some are rich kids who pursue business interests alongside their studies. Some struggle to make ends meet, finding themselves vulnerable to exploitative landlords and work conditions. Most of them, like their local peers, are relatively apolitical. Some involve themselves in progressive activism, some network with conservatives. Some hold strong patriotic views, some are dissidents. There are CCP members among them, who hope to one day climb their way up the bureaucratic ranks back home. The Chinese Students and Scholars Association, one of the organisations that support this diverse group, liaises on occasion with the PRC's consular network, which sees this work as part of its pastoral care brief.

Among young Chinese living abroad, a new-found confidence to voice opinions can bring sensitive politics into the classroom. In the digital age, minor incidents can blow up into social-media campaigns, and recent times have seen a steady trickle of such episodes. In 2017, one lecturer was rebuked for using a map that represented a disputed territory in the Himalayas as belonging to India; another was criticised for using materials that referred to Taiwan as a 'country'. In 2020, an online campaign resulted in the University of New South Wales taking down an article published on the Law School's website, which called for international pressure on China to end its crackdown in Hong Kong.[19]

Within the Chinese student body itself, peer pressure exists to hold certain political opinions. Given that most intend to eventually return to China, there's a risk that becoming known for contrary views will have consequences for an individual's future or for their family. Documented instances of retribution for things said in the classroom are rare, but they have occurred, and universities should do what they can to prevent them occurring again. This might involve updating their codes of conduct, for example, to take such eventualities into account.

The situation requires a firm institutional stance on the principles of academic freedom and free speech, and reflection on techniques to either defuse or debate sensitivities. There are thorny pedagogical questions in play here too. How exactly do you teach journalism, for example, to a student whose ambition is to return to the PRC to work in China's highly censored media industry? When international students found themselves stuck in China thanks to COVID-related travel restrictions, it raised a new issue: how safe is it for them to remain there while accessing course materials that might be considered politically sensitive? Some have come up with ad-hoc solutions – warnings, or modifications to their units – but the situation strikes me as ultimately untenable, and it shouldn't be allowed to persist post-COVID.

Some of Australia's public discussion on these questions has been enlightening, but some of it less so. When considering the way the politics of China can enter the classroom, we need also to acknowledge the way that media discourse here is contributing to an embattled defensiveness among temporary Chinese residents. By the middle of 2017, John Garnaut was warning Australians that Beijing was exporting 'racial chauvinism' to universities. The same year, Merriden Varrall wrote in *The New York Times* that 'many of the 150,000 visiting Chinese students are import-ing a pro-Beijing approach to the classroom that is stifling debate and openness'. How many is 'many', though? Such claims were reinforced by pointed, public injunctions from both the foreign minister and the sec-retary of DFAT for international students to respect freedom of speech.[20]

The *Four Corners* episode 'Power and Influence' had an important role in triggering such interventions. That episode included an interview with the president of the Chinese Students and Scholars Association at the University of Canberra, an organisation it depicted as a proxy for the Chinese embassy's efforts to monitor anti-China rallies on campus. Subsequently, a defamation suit brought to light the full recording of her interview, showing that she had denied on three occasions that she would feel any obligation to report such activities to the consulate. *Four Corners*, which had edited these denials out, quickly settled out of court.[21] One Chinese student at Canberra University at the time recalled the atmo-sphere as tense: 'The media was constantly targeting ... the Canberra CSSA ... People from all the other clubs kept pointing at them and saying,

"Isn't what you're doing a bit suspicious, aren't you spies?" and whatever. I actually think that the mainstream media in Australia didn't handle it very [well], they manipulated the debate just like the media in China do."[22]

In 2019, *Four Corners* featured a segment on student elections at my own university in a follow-up episode, 'Red Flags', which was billed as an investigation of 'the infiltration of Australia's universities by the Chinese Communist Party'. There are of course students with patriotic pro-China views at Sydney. For a time, their electoral vehicle was the 'Panda' ticket, which ran apolitical, services-centred campaigns in alliance with the Liberals. Chinese international students have never been a single bloc, though. In 2018–19, the more progressive Advance, allied with the left, vied with Panda for their vote. The rivalry was fierce at times – for instance, when Advance members put a motion to the Students' Representative Council to support the anti-ELAB campaign in Hong Kong (the campaign against the Extradition Law Amendment Bill), Panda left the room to pull quorum. But still, the rivalry was evidence of what we'd hope to see in this situation: participation leading to political differentiation on a range of issues – from transport card concessions to Chinese politics. This is healthy, something to be encouraged, and we won't do that by depicting these students as 'infiltrators'.

Of course, we can't excuse instances of nationalist bullying in the classroom, but reported examples of such aggression are often more complicated than the media narrative allows. In one case, Chinese students at the Australian National University took offence when their lecturer put up a slide in Chinese and English which told the class not to cheat. They interpreted him as saying that (a) the Chinese students in the classroom were most likely to cheat, and (b) their English was substandard. In a second case, students complained about a quiz that contained a joke about Chinese officials only telling the truth when they were 'drunk or careless'. In a third, they took offence at an assignment on the 'Chinese (Wuhan) COVID-19 virus outbreak'. In a climate in which loose talk of the 'Chinese virus' was stoking racism, it's not too hard to see why such language provoked a reaction.[23]

Sometimes media stories simply stretch the evidence too far. In *The New York Times*, an article on 'Chinese nationalism' in 2017 reported that a Monash lecturer was met with an 'icy silence' when he asked his

Chinese students a question about individual rights during the Qin dynasty (221–206 BCE). Eventually two students voiced their opinion that human rights were not relevant to a discussion of ancient history.[24] I can only sympathise with a colleague whose discussion questions fell flat. We've all had that experience. But was this awkward silence, broken by the expression of a valid opinion, really evidence of the deleterious effect of Chinese nationalism on Australian universities?

When we consider pro-PRC nationalism in Australia, we have to remember that nationalism within a diaspora is never quite the same thing as nationalism at home, and that the mainstream framing of, and response to, such sentiments can significantly influence the dynamics. The narrative that developed at this time, of PRC students as mindless patriots, was but one dimension of an environment that was becoming increasingly unwelcoming for them in Australia. In 2017 racist anti-Chinese graffiti and postering was seen on multiple campuses, and some Chinese students fell victim to physical assaults.

The question of how to navigate this situation became particularly pressing during the Hong Kong mobilisations of 2019, which I was involved in at the University of Sydney. By August of that year, as second semester commenced and patriotic mobilisations were organised in response to small pro-Hong Kong events, it was obvious that the situation on campus was becoming volatile. A series of evening rallies in Melbourne drew hecklers and occasionally descended into pushing and shoving. Similar scenes occurred at the University of Adelaide and the University of Queensland, where it kicked off a long-running saga involving student-activist Drew Pavlou. Pavlou was right to stand alongside his Hong Kong peers in the face of pro-PRC backlash, but he did nothing to help the situation by antagonising PRC nationals on social media in the week leading up to the clash. During the confrontation itself, one of his Chinese-speaking allies taunted the pro-PRC contingent as 'Shina pigs' – invoking the derogatory language of the Japanese occupation. Right-wing figures from off campus were soon circling around; Andrew Cooper, organiser of Australia's Conservative Political Action Conference, was among the invitees to a follow-up rally against the Confucius Institute. While they had stood up to the nationalist counter-rally the first time around, the university's Greens and socialist organisations recognised

the dangerous dynamics and issued a call for the second rally to be cancelled – a call I eventually joined.

None of these complexities made it into the media coverage, fixated as
it was on the figure of the angry Chinese patriot. But this fixation, giving
international students a sense that they were besieged by negative media
portrayals, was part of what motivated them to continue rallying behind
the PRC flag. 'Stop provoking Chinese international students,' was a slogan I observed on a large banner at a pro-Beijing rally in Sydney's Belmore
Park. In a perverse way, the media's obsession with Chinese nationalists
actually created incentives for confrontation. When we held a rally in
solidarity with Hong Kong at the University of Sydney, a huge gaggle of
media turned up, no doubt anticipating similar scenes to the University
of Queensland. The only sign of hostilities came while I was speaking on
behalf of my union, the NTEU, and a Chinese student paused to give me
the finger before going on his way. The media set off after him, but he
didn't oblige them with any more outbursts. In the end, our noisy march
through the middle of campus went off without a hitch and, unsurprisingly, received no media coverage at all. Some of the Hong Kong students
concluded, logically enough, that if they wanted publicity for their cause
they would need to get into a fight.

Thankfully, the university environment provided opportunities to
direct this energy towards more positive ends. As wary as they were, many
Hong Kong students were keen to engage with and debate their mainland peers. As they recognised, they had an opportunity to talk to them
directly in Australia in a way that they could not in China. Crucially, too,
there were mainlanders willing to listen. Sympathetic to the cause, they
were also worried at the collective image PRC students were acquiring
in the Australian media, and saw a need to defuse the hostility and find
some common ground.

Working alongside such students at the University of Sydney, we put
on a Chinese-language forum simply titled 'Let's Talk About Hong Kong'.
The conversation required us to step away from mainstream narratives
and establish a different starting point: recognising the risks that Hong
Kongers were taking to speak out, but not dismissing mainlanders who
had criticisms of the anti-ELAB campaign as unthinking victims of party
propaganda. We acknowledged instances of violence perpetrated not only

by police but also by protesters, as well as the media's distortions and the hypocrisy of Western politicians; in doing so we dispelled many of the distractions that were impeding discussion of the issue. The ensuing debate was lively, passionate at times, but always respectful. The students clearly appreciated having space to air their views: after an hour and a half, the room was still full. At the end of the forum, we invited them to write messages on Post-it notes for a Lennon Wall. Most of the audience, the majority of whom were of PRC background, did so. My collaborators were thrilled at the way they'd broken down the Hong Kong–mainland divide and, along with that, the stereotype of Chinese international students.

Of course, this was only a single event, but it provided a template that was applicable elsewhere. As the Hong Kong campaign wore on, friends at the University of Melbourne organised reading groups and webinars along similar lines. In 2020, I found myself in New York, working with postgraduates on a 'Let's Talk About Hong Kong' event at Columbia University. Some 150 participants took over an entire floor of Hamilton Hall for small-group discussions and all-in debate, again without any of the hostilities that were marring events elsewhere. This may have been partly down to luck, but I think not entirely. Most Hong Kong–related events at Western universities were pitched to a Western audience and linked the issue to wider public anxieties towards China. Such framings can feed into views that mainland students are part of the problem – a disruptive, threatening presence that needs to be kept at bay. Our events, by contrast, engaged the students as potential allies. They weren't premised on an essential difference between Chinese and Western political culture, and they situated Hong Kong within a critique of anti-democratic politics everywhere. It really wasn't hard to do this: the same evening we met at Columbia, the New York police were shutting down a Black Lives Matter rally in the neighbouring suburb of Harlem.

In Australia we enjoy political freedoms that people in China don't, which puts an onus on us to use those freedoms effectively. As I see it, one of the most valuable things we can do at Australia's universities right now is provide a platform for debate and exchange among those most invested in China's future – the citizens of the country themselves. Without more sympathy for their cause among ordinary Chinese, it's hard to see a better future for the Hong Kongers or the Uyghurs.

Unfortunately, some of the more attention-grabbing forms of anti-CCP activism on campus have inhibited this kind of exchange. Pavlou's campaign against Chinese influence at the University of Queensland has won him immense media attention but has polarised the campus – and indeed the wider discussion of China in Australia – in an unproductive way. I've met Drew Pavlou and believe him to be sincere in his left-wing commitments, but his rise to celebrity exemplifies the way that those commitments are liable to fall by the wayside when China is involved.

To applause from the right of Australian politics, Pavlou has combined on-campus stunts (including posing outside the Confucius Institute in a hazmat suit during the COVID-19 pandemic) with relentless denunciations of China 'apologists' on Twitter. For his efforts, pundits such as Andrew Bolt, Chris Kenny and Alan Jones have welcomed him onto their Sky News talk shows. While not a defender of Donald Trump, Pavlou has closely aligned himself with something of the Australian version: the pro-gun, anti–marriage equality, Islamophobic 'maverick' Bob Katter. In 2017, Katter called for a ban on immigrants from 'North Africa and the countries between Greece and India', excluding religious minorities – that is to say, a Trump-style ban on Muslims. In 2018, he expressed his '1000 per cent support' for a speech by Fraser Anning (at the time a member of Katter's Australia Party) that called for a 'final solution' to Muslim immigration.[25] Surely better allies can be found for a campaign in solidarity with the majority Muslim Uyghurs?

The University of Queensland administration certainly didn't help the situation by investigating and suspending Pavlou from his studies. Vague and selectively enforced codes of conduct endanger intellectual freedom at Australian universities – of that there's no doubt. I was among those who called on the university to drop the case, which eventually saw Pavlou suspended for a semester and dismissed from the university senate, to which he'd been elected on a pro–Hong Kong, anti–Confucius Institute platform.

It's plausible, though impossible to prove, that revenue considerations influenced the university to pursue this case with such vigour. So far, freedom-of-information requests have revealed no evidence of direct Chinese pressure. We don't really need such proof to explain the course of events, though. The pursuit of Pavlou was a typically nervous

reaction to controversy that we see all too often among university officials, who can be very quick to pull the trigger in response to complaints.
Hyperbolic claims that the university's vice-chancellor, Peter Hoy, and
chancellor, Peter Varghese, are pawns of the CCP are unjustified. But
that's not to say we can trust such people to uphold academic freedom,
either. As I mentioned earlier, it was Varghese who led the 2017 review of
Sydney University's US Studies Centre and who claimed – seemingly in all
seriousness – that requiring the centre to advocate for the US–Australia
alliance was not in conflict with the principle of academic freedom.

Destroying the Universities to Save Them

The government's ongoing withdrawal of higher-education funding – and
its neglect for the welfare of the international students whose fees make
up the shortfall – has long been a brewing crisis. With the onset of the
COVID-19 pandemic, the storm broke earlier than expected. Universities
scrambled to stem the drop-off in enrolments by moving their teaching online, but in 2020 international commencements fell by some 22
per cent from 2019 levels (with a 13 per cent decrease in Chinese student commencements).[26] That decline, and the Liberal Party's failure to
extend temporary welfare measures to universities, has led to mass lay-
offs around the country. Vulnerable casual staff were first in the firing
line, forcing an entire generation of young academics to look elsewhere
for work. Aggressive restructuring, much of it already in the pipeline, was
brought forward by administrators, and pandemic conditions offered staff
unions little chance to mobilise in response. To date, hiring freezes and
redundancies – both voluntary and involuntary – have depleted universities of some 13 per cent of their staff.

International students who did make it into Australia were bluntly
told by the prime minister to 'go home' if they were experiencing hard-
ship. Many students from China reported heightened racism, from verbal
abuse to physical attacks. Morrison and his ministers were quick to dismiss as 'rubbish' and 'disinformation' Beijing's warnings that Australia
was becoming unsafe, but by and large the picture was substantiated by a
survey of international students published in September 2020.[27] As well
as financial stress and a sense of neglect, the survey found that more than

half of its Chinese respondents had experienced some form of abuse or shunning because of their appearance. Three out of four said they were less likely to recommend Australia as a place of study. With China's own higher-education system expanding rapidly, it was predictable that the attractions of an Australian degree would eventually diminish for young Chinese. Today's climate only increases the likelihood that they won't be back on the scale of the pre-COVID boom.

Secure employment is the best guarantee of intellectual freedom at universities, and it is drying up; around two-thirds of university work is now in the form of casual or fixed-term contracts. The situation will be made worse by the Liberal Party's 2020 reforms to higher-education funding, which reduce the government's contribution to the cost of an average degree by 15 per cent and hike average student fees by 7 per cent. Classrooms, already brimful, will squeeze more students in, staff work-loads will intensify, and the quality of teaching and learning will suffer. At the same time, the decline in revenue will only increase pressure on universities to sell their integrity to the highest bidder.

As long as China is not involved, it seems, politicians are happy for them to do that. Witness, for example, the strong support in the Liberal Party for the Ramsay Centre for Western Civilisation. The Paul Ramsay Foundation, established by the late healthcare billionaire, held out millions in funding to universities in return for a say in the design and delivery of an entire humanities degree. Those denouncing PRC influence on campus were often the most vocal in calling on universities to get into bed with this conservative off-campus lobby. Similarly, as universities reel from the impact of COVID-19 austerity, voices from the think-tank world now hold out the carrot of restored funding should universities deepen their ties with the national-security world and thereby render themselves 'Five-Eyes–friendly'.[28]

For all the talk of academic freedom and free speech, today's policy responses to 'foreign interference' effectively increase outside intervention into the operations of universities. A single-minded vigilance towards China is going hand in hand with the increasing integration of universities with Western military institutions, hardly a recipe for institutional integrity. We're not yet back in the days of McCarthyism, but the spirit of the 1950s can be felt in the way hawks decry an 'intellectual failure' in the confrontation with China, which clearly spells dissatisfaction with the direction of Chinese studies in Australia. Already, the debate has seen discriminatory proposals such as Euan Graham's recommendation that universities refrain from hiring experts in Chinese politics who were trained in China.[29] Ironically, if this principle were applied, some of our leading Chinese Australian dissident voices would be blacklisted.

It's imperative that Australian universities resist such pressures. At a time when the national debate surrounding China is so crucial, they cannot afford to simply fall into line with a foreign policy shift that positions China as Australia's enemy. But in the hands of the small cohort of administrators who currently run them, there is every chance that they will. Having put up precious little resistance to the trend towards privatisation, with all its deleterious effects on the independence of our universities, officials cannot be relied on to resist the political pressures now pulling them in a different direction.

What the situation calls for, I believe, is for the university community itself – the staff and students who compose it – to reassert themselves as the voice of the institution. Their role is necessary, first of all, to pressure the government to restore public funding, the precondition of institutional autonomy. But it is also necessary to take up questions that cannot be left to politicians or executives: ethical questions such as whom the university should collaborate with, and on what basis. When given the opportunity, faculty have shown themselves capable of grappling with these questions in the past. A revival of the all-but-lost principle of faculty governance at Australian universities will show that again. But crucially, those questions must be dealt with on the basis of principle, not foreign policy partisanship. Universities' dealings with China are but one, small part of the picture; it must be widened to include the many and varied threats to their integrity, including those originating from Canberra.

6. HUMAN RIGHTS AND XINJIANG

That Beijing is clamping down on the freedoms of its citizens is evident across Chinese society today, but just how far it's willing to go to inoculate itself against dissent is clearest in the far north-western region of Xinjiang – a region some Uyghurs prefer to call Eastern Turkistan. The heightened repression in the Xinjiang Uyghur Autonomous Region (to give it its full, official name) and the mass detention of its Muslim, Turkic-speaking population, most of them Uyghur, has coincided with – and exacerbated – the downturn in Sino–Western diplomacy. The once obscure territory has come to replace Tibet, or the Falun Gong, as the most talked-about case of domestic repression in China. In almost any public discussion to do with China today – be it on trade policy or tech – the conversation is likely to turn to Xinjiang at some point. Many of these issues are implicated in the Xinjiang crisis directly; it casts a weighty moral shadow across the rest. Australian media has given the crisis wide coverage, with a moving *Four Corners* episode highlighting its impact on Australia's Uyghur population. ASPI's Xinjiang Data Project, using open-source data and satellite imagery, has produced a series of reports that have influenced policymaking worldwide.

Xinjiang is the part of China I am most familiar with, since I first began visiting and studying the region some twenty years ago. I've never known it to be a particularly happy place. Even two decades ago, to ask Uyghurs there about politics was to be met with an awkward laugh – as if we'd talk about that. But when I visited in 2017, before news of the 're-education' camps had broken, the stark change was obvious: new police stations at every major intersection, ubiquitous checkpoints on all main streets, public buildings ringed with razor wire, and flags and surveillance cameras everywhere. Even in outlying villages, loudspeaker broadcasts could be heard exhorting the Uyghurs to love the CCP and study Mandarin. In Kashgar, I saw elderly men and women trudging through the streets on anti-terror drills, and police holding up young men to check their phones for state-mandated spyware. In the city's main mosque, a portrait of Xi Jinping hung in the direction of Mecca. On a busy weekday, the city went into lockdown as a column of military vehicles and PLA soldiers reminded locals of their presence. It felt like a military occupation.

Human rights remains the dominant moral language of our time but has particular purchase in relation to China, where it serves as shorthand for all of the infringements on liberty that the CCP commits. Rights to freedom of expression and religion, freedom of movement, freedom from slavery and torture – these and more were part of the 1948 Universal Declaration of Human Rights. All are being violated to some degree in the CCP's ongoing efforts to mould the Uyghurs into loyal, reliable Chinese citizens.

We might also use other language to discuss Xinjiang. For Uyghurs, the deteriorating situation remains part of a story that has long centred on *national* rights. Inside China, space to make good the limited provisions of China's system of national autonomy has all but disappeared. But outside China, in the Uyghur diaspora, national rights remain part of the debate. I don't believe it's necessary for outsiders to take a position on what the best outcome for Xinjiang is – be it independence, genuine autonomy or simply equality in a more democratic China. But we should defend the right of Uyghurs to formulate solutions in these national terms – this is the meaning of the right to national self-determination.

For the time being, though, Uyghurs are worried about survival. Questions have been raised about whether certain dimensions of China's campaign qualify as genocide or crimes against humanity. There is clearly an intent to dilute, maybe even erase, key components of Uyghur cultural and religious identity. The charge of physical genocide centres on coercive policies to reduce the birthrate among non-Han groups. China claims this is a poverty-reduction measure, but as we know in Australia, welfare orthodoxies can have devastating consequences when applied to vulnerable groups. Although international lawyers at the State Department saw insufficient evidence, on the eve of his departure from office, secretary of state Mike Pompeo made a determination that China's policy was one of genocide. So far, the Biden administration has maintained this position.

China's own view of human rights has evolved considerably since the Maoist period, when it rejected the term as a tool of capitalist privilege and a pretext for the West's ongoing intervention in the decolonising world. The PRC committed to the Universal Declaration of Human Rights in 1971, though this was hardly meaningful amid the turmoil of the Cultural Revolution. Since the 1980s, China has developed its own language of human rights, attempting to shift international debate away from civil and political liberties, and towards economic rights, such as the 'right to subsistence'. In Xinjiang today, advancing the 'right to development' is one of Beijing's justifications for its actions. In the 1990s, China allied with other authoritarians in Asia to reframe human rights in terms of distinctive national conditions, or 'Asian values'. At the same time, it was beginning to engage with international human-rights institutions by signing UN conventions and joining bodies such as the UN Human Rights Commission (UNHRC). China is now one of the most active participants in human-rights horsetrading at the UN, where it lobbies for its non-interventionist approach.

Political boundaries should not impede the basic human instinct to support victims of state repression. But in a world of interstate rivalries, human rights becomes a scene of vexed debates on moral standing and the efficacy of different responses. The debate sometimes turns on abstract questions of moral superiority, but it need not. Despite our lack of formal human-rights provisions, it's true that Australians on the whole have more freedom than people in the PRC. That includes the freedom to advocate for people elsewhere, which we should take advantage of. But it's perfectly possible to do this while remaining conscious of Australia's grievous historical and ongoing abuse of human rights.

It's when human-rights advocacy navigates its relationship to a suite of other, often competing, foreign-policy priorities that things get complicated. One long-running debate centres on the merits of quiet 'backdoor' diplomacy versus the pressure of the megaphone. But the deeper issue is the way human-rights idealism intersects with the preponderant economic and security interests that drive foreign policy. This intersection gives rise to a wicked conundrum in relation to China. On the one hand, it's obvious that the perceived economic benefits of ties with China have at times militated against seriously pressuring China on the issue of human-rights violations. In the 1990s, Beijing correctly concluded that these interests outweighed the West's commitment to civil and political liberties in China. Now that relations have become conflicted, firmer measures become thinkable – but the very fact that they are only thinkable at such times can very easily dilute the impact of those measures. China is well aware that the West's interest in human rights is selective, and blows hot and cold. It views the West's criticisms as made in bad faith, still motivated by its own interests, which are now no longer economic but focused on isolating and shaming China internationally. We need to confront this conundrum and think our way through it.

Human rights emerged as a distinct sphere of Australian engagement with China following the Tiananmen crackdown in 1989, although Canberra made some awkward forays into this territory earlier that decade. In the 1990s, setting aside some short-lived sanctions, Australia positioned itself firmly on the side of a non-confrontational approach to China, hoping to quietly coax it towards liberalisation. In the United States, that decade saw a long-running debate on whether to make China's 'most favoured nation' trade privileges conditional on its progress on human rights; Australia was among those that lobbied against the move. For a time, Australia joined America in sponsoring resolutions against China at the UN Human Rights Commission, but in 1997 the Howard government shifted its focus to dialogue and 'human rights technical cooperation' activities.

In return for this milder stance, Australia was invited to send delegations to Tibet in 1991 and Xinjiang in 1992, and to partake in a series of human-rights dialogues that continued until 2014. Some participants believe these exchanges provided genuine support to China's embattled human-rights activists. A visitor to Xinjiang in 1992 came away feeling that they had had 'an enormous capacity to make contact and pursue matters away from the official meeting environment'.[1] But today, this softly-softly approach stands accused of providing a moral alibi for a self-interested trade policy. In parliament itself, human rights in China remained a niche concern. One study found that a single politician – the ALP's Michael Danby – did more to raise and document the issue than the rest of the 2004–07 parliament combined.[2]

The approach is different now, but how different exactly? Australia regularly issues public criticisms of China's human-rights violations, vowing to 'hold it to account'. Other than calling for UN investigations, though, the Liberal government tends to leave unsaid just how it intends to do that. For all its declaratory noise, the government has shown little interest in a responding to the plight of the Uyghurs at the policy level.

The conflicted Australia–China relationship has given Australia's few thousand Uyghurs a better hearing than they've ever had, but it's hard to conclude that Australia is now prioritising their wellbeing in its dealings with China. The multidimensional nature of the conflict – with headline-grabbing stories from the military and trade spheres – can still leave them well down the agenda. I was struck by this last August, when China's deputy ambassador to Australia, Cheng Jingye, addressed the National Press Club. This was an ideal opportunity for Australia's journalists to press him on Xinjiang (or Hong Kong), but none of them did, preferring instead to pepper him with questions on the Australian trade minister's inability to reach Beijing by phone. While public knowledge of the Uyghurs' plight has risen exponentially, in many way it still struggles to attract engagement.

We can and should do more. But what exactly? There is low-hanging fruit among our options: we can make sure Uyghurs have refugee protections, and we can extend these protections to people living elsewhere in the world at risk of deportation to China. In the case of Uyghurs who hold Australian citizenship but are stuck in China, we should push Beijing to let them leave. We also need to do what we can to ensure that Uyghurs in Australia can advocate for their cause freely, without risk to their family members back home. Asking China to play nice is not a very promising strategy, though, and while certain concessions might be winnable in a state of improved relations, Uyghur activists are wary of any return to 'business as usual' with China. It's perfectly understandable – they look at the history and think the West will go soft on China again.

The fact is, neither the 'dialogue' nor the 'shaming' paradigms of human-rights activism have done much to improve the situation in China. It's this fact that drives some activists into alliance with more right-wing, pro-regime-change circles in Western countries. There, waiting for them with open arms, are people such as Michael Pillsbury, who have long held that those 'who champion the Dalai Lama should ally with US defense experts who promote spending for the Pentagon's AirSea Battle program'.[3] But this is no solution either. Genuine, effective action on human rights, I believe, will never be achieved as part a wider campaign of economic and military pressure on the PRC. If there's one kind of 'decoupling' we should be seeking, it's to decouple the pursuit of human freedom from the politics of interstate rivalries.

China's Colonial Frontier

Most Australians still have, at best, a hazy grasp of the history and peoples of Xinjiang, so I'll begin there. Scholars in the Chinese academy today must comply with CCP dogma, according to which Xinjiang has long been part of China, but few dynasties had much influence, let alone control, in the vast territory south of the Tianshan, known as the Tarim Basin. Only in brief windows at the height of the Han and the Tang – more than two millennia and one millennium ago respectively – did imperial China directly administer parts of the region. Those periods contributed to its cultural complexity, but the sediments they left were overlaid by more dominant trends from the end of the Tang dynasty onwards: the influx of people speaking Turkic languages and the conversion of the region to Islam. These two transformations made the Tarim Basin part of a wider Central Asian world, one that eventually became known as Turkistan. The term is taboo in China today, and dismissed as a foreign invention, but locals embraced it well before the arrival of modern nationalism. For one author in the 1740s, the oasis town of Yarkand was the 'capital of Turkistan'.[4]

The story of Beijing's rule in Xinjiang – indeed the birth of Xinjiang as a defined territory – begins with the Qing empire's invasion of the 1750s. This took place around the same time as the British East India Company secured its foothold in India by defeating France in war. Both were acts of imperial expansion, but of different kinds. It was not commercial greed, a thirst for resources or missionary zeal that drove the Qing armies into the north-west, but a desire for security. The reigning Qianlong emperor's ambition was to rid his empire of its last-remaining rivals on the steppe, the Buddhist Junghar Mongols. Having all but wiped them out, the Qing then laid claim to the entirety of their domains, including the Muslim society of the Tarim Basin.

Security remains China's prevailing imperative in the region. Notwithstanding Xinjiang's deeper integration into the national and global economy today, and its significant natural resource deposits, the territory has never been a profitable possession for China. Beijing subsidises the province's economy to preserve it as a secure frontier zone and transport corridor to continental Eurasia.[5]

Qing rule in Xinjiang was indirect at first, leaving much authority in the hands of Muslim elites. Like many of the world's monarchies, the Qing was a dynastic state with an ethnically diverse ruling elite, to which local Muslim aristocrats came to belong. The chief challenge to this structure came in the form of militant Sufi networks, whose charismatic shaykhs rallied support for periodic incursions.

In the 1860s, many believed the Qing had lost control of Xinjiang for good, when a military man by the name of Yaqub Beg took advantage of the empire's crises to establish an emirate in Kashgar. Yaqub Beg's emirate was not a national state. By many accounts, it wasn't even particularly popular among locals. But by forging ties with the Ottoman Empire it encouraged some in Xinjiang to imagine themselves as part of a wider 'Islamic world'. For a brief time, the fate of Kashgar became a cause célèbre in political circles in Istanbul. The question some ask today – whether Muslims outside China will come to the aid of Muslims in China – was raised for the first time in the 1870s.

Then, as now, the response was disappointing. The Qing retook Xinjiang without much of a fight, and from the 1880s onwards it implemented a more deliberate colonial policy: to administer the territory as a Chinese province, populate it with Chinese migrants and bring natives into the fold of Chinese civilisation. There's no precedent for the scale and coercive force of today's policies, but this turn-of-the-century effort to sinify Muslim children in Chinese-language schools was similarly a point at which the policy pendulum swung in the direction of assimilation. Not surprisingly, complaints against the policies of this period have a contemporary ring to them. As one man from the town of Kucha put it in 1910, 'The population are thankful for the government's efforts to promote education, but they're troubled by the fact that they can't study their mother tongue or the precepts of their religion in these schools, and many are leaving their country as a result.'[6]

These late-Qing policies failed on their own terms, but they ensured Xinjiang remained part of China when the dynasty fell in 1912; Tibet and Mongolia, by contrast, made bids for independence. For a brief window, collaboration between Chinese republicans and modern-minded Muslims seemed a possibility, but, as occurred elsewhere in China, the radicals who led the anti-Qing revolution were sidelined by a conservative old guard. In a sense, Xinjiang was independent during much of the Republic of China period (1912–49), but independent in the hands of Chinese war lords. Locals with aspirations for self-rule or a state of their own went into exile, either to the Soviet Union or the Middle East.

It was in the Soviet Union in the 1920s that the intellectual reimagining of Xinjiang's Turkic past combined with revolutionary ambitions for its future, producing a new sense of Uyghur national identity. Uyghur communists came close to achieving an 'Uyghuristan' in 1921, when the Bolsheviks debated, but ultimately rejected, a proposal from the Comintern to carry the Russian revolution into Xinjiang.

By the 1930s, with the Stalinist chill setting in, some in Xinjiang still held out hope for support from Moscow, but others were bitterly hostile to Soviet communism. This explains the nature of the two Eastern Turkistan Republics in this period. The first of these republics, in Kashgar in 1933–34, had an Islamic constitution, comparable in some ways to the reform-minded monarchy of neighbouring Afghanistan, and was firmly anti-communist. The second republic, in the Ili district in 1944, was the product of a Soviet-instigated uprising, designed to gain leverage against the Chinese Nationalist government. The rebels took much of Xinjiang's north and could have pressed their advantage, but on Stalin's instructions they entered into a coalition with the Nationalists in Ürümchi. It was with Xinjiang in this divided state that the PLA entered Xinjiang in 1949.

These brief experiences of self-rule are highpoints of political history from the Uyghur point of view. Today, many Uyghurs still prefer the name 'Eastern Turkistan' to the colonial-sounding 'Xinjiang', and the crescent-moon flag flown by both republics remains the symbol of the Uyghur nation. Although Xinjiang's incorporation into the PRC took national independence off the table, in the 1950s some tried to negotiate a more robust form of national autonomy – something like a Soviet Republic of Uyghuristan – and were disappointed when the CCP delivered only an autonomous region, one that still bore the name 'Xinjiang'. Others, meanwhile, went into exile, seeking to work the fault lines of the Cold War to win foreign support for the cause.

Although they offer non-Han peoples certain affirmative-action measures, China's 'autonomous regions' have never been autonomous in the sense we might imagine. All local policy variations require the centre's approval. Beijing's abiding security sensitivities were reflected in the formation of the Xinjiang Production and Construction Corps in 1954, a paramilitary organisation that commands a major presence in the local economy to this day.

From the 1960s to the 1990s, these security sensitivities centred on the possibility of Soviet intervention. Such was the level of Soviet influence in the region that most Australian politicians seem to have mistakenly believed the Soviets were actually in control of Xinjiang. Multiple parliamentary speeches from the 1950s refer to 'Russian possession' of the province. This helps explain why in 1964, on a visit to Moscow, Australia's virulently anti-CCP foreign minister Paul Hasluck all but encouraged Moscow to enforce its claim to the region, asking whether his Soviet counterpart Andrei Gromyko believed the Chinese had any right to Xinjiang, 'which they claimed to be a part of China'.[7]

When Australia flipped its position on the Sino–Soviet rivalry in the 1970s, Xinjiang remained of interest primarily as a strategic hotspot. On a visit in 1976, Malcolm Fraser was hoping to see firsthand the heavy artillery that China had pointed at the Soviet Union. Instead he got the usual tourist fare: a trip to the mountains, and a show of local singing and dancing.[8] The *Bulletin* journalist who accompanied Fraser made note of the fact that Xinjiang's chairman, Saifuddin Azizi, was Uyghur, likening the situation to South Australian premier Don Dunstan's appointment of an Indigenous Australian, Douglas Nicholls, as governor of the state. It's hard to say exactly what he intended by the comparison: were both appointments signs of progress or tokenism? I happened to be in Ürümchi when ex-chairman Saifuddin died in 2003, and I saw much of the city's Uyghur neighbourhood line the streets as his hearse drove by. He was clearly held in great respect, but it was the sort of respect enjoyed by someone who'd tried their best amid tight constraints.

Certain of these constraints were lifted in the 1980s, a period of relative optimism about the direction of nationality policy in China. With a softening on the cultural front, Uyghurs took the opportunity to test China's political boundaries. In Beijing, Ürümchi and elsewhere, student demonstrators raised slogans against nuclear testing (which was conducted at the Lop Nur site), and in support of political and cultural rights. More militant forms of resistance emerged in the south, with a serious clash occurring in the village of Baren in 1990 – a friend of mine from the region once described it to me as a 'revolution'. The trends were enough to spook the party and push it back towards more hardline policies.

Since that time, large-scale 'Western development' schemes to integrate the region economically have gone hand in hand with 'strike hard' security crackdowns. These crackdowns laid the foundation for China to quickly adapt to the new international environment after the 9/11 attacks in New York, when America sought Beijing's acquiescence in the invasions of Afghanistan and Iraq. In return for this, US deputy secretary of state Richard Armitage listed the 'East Turkistan Islamic Movement' as a terrorist organisation. The movement was then an obscure group, with no obvious presence inside China, but in the global climate of that period, talk of subversive Muslim networks was met with credulity. Beijing took full advantage of the situation to shift its security discourse in Xinjiang away from a traditional focus on separatism, redefining its actions as part of an international struggle against terrorism.

Deliberate attacks on civilians, while rare, have occurred in Xinjiang, but China's definition of terrorism extends beyond this to encompass almost any violent incident. On that basis, its most recent defence white paper cites 'thousands of terrorist attacks' in Xinjiang from 1990 to 2016.[9] This rhetoric hides a far more complex reality: a degree of ideologically motivated violence, to be sure, but also invasive security measures, land grabs and relocation policies that push Uyghurs into conflict with the state, in addition to local conflicts surrounding resources that spark communal tensions.

A 'poverty-reduction' scheme that remains in place today – to transfer Uyghurs to factories in the Chinese interior – was behind major riots in

Ürümchi in 2009. When two Uyghurs working in a southern Chinese factory were killed in a brawl, Ürümchi residents demanded a public response from the government of the autonomous region. Failing to obtain one, they took to the streets. After police dispersed the march, violence broke out that evening, which claimed the lives of almost 200 people, mostly Han. The Han population replied with vigilante violence of its own, and an unknown number of Uyghurs were imprisoned. That November, I was in Ürümchi and saw the lockdown for myself. Gun-toting police lined the main streets, and patrols of soldiers bellowing slogans kept the city awake at night. Communication in and out of Xinjiang was severed for twelve months.

After a car ploughed into pedestrians in Tiananmen Square in 2013, a spate of incidents in 2014 triggered a major escalation of Beijing's counterterrorism campaign. March saw a group of Uyghurs go on a stabbing spree in Kunming in China's south. During Xi Jinping's visit to Ürümchi in April, an improvised bomb went off in the city's train station. The following month, two cars rammed an outdoor market before their occupants set off explosives. In July, a loyal pro-government imam in Kashgar was assassinated. Around the same time, an attack on police and government offices in Yarkand left dozens dead.

Meanwhile, reports were also emerging of Uyghurs joining Islamist militias in Syria and Iraq, including the anti-Assad alliance Jabhat al-Nusra and the Islamic State (ISIS). China has a chokehold on Xinjiang's entry and exit points, so any direct 'blowback' from the Syria conflict was unlikely, but the presence there of an estimated 3000 to 5000 Uyghur fighters have sustained propaganda claims that Xinjiang was on the verge of becoming 'a second Syria'.[10]

The party's call in 2014 for a 'People's War on Terror' had a distinctively CCP flavour to it, but Xi Jinping also encouraged his officials to study the lessons of the US-led war on terror elsewhere. As the crackdown expanded in Xinjiang, it claimed a high-profile victim in Beijing. Ilham Tohti, a CCP member and economist who was critical of the marginalisation of Uyghurs, was sentenced to life in prison on charges of promoting separatism in September 2014. In 2016, the party secretary of Tibet, Chen Quanguo, was appointed secretary in Xinjiang, bringing with him policing techniques from his previous appointment and a mandate for a new experiment in mass counterterrorism.

The Camps Crisis

China's policy turn in 2016 reflects a radicalisation of its official discourse on both religion and nationality. Its view of Islam as potentially dangerous has evolved – in line with the West – from a 'counterterrorism' philosophy to a much more all-encompassing 'anti-radicalisation' approach, which seeks to identify individuals on a 'pathway' to radicalism and to preemptively intervene. The guiding principle is a deeply Islamophobic one, which deems displays of religious piety – be it mosque attendance, religious dress or simply refraining from alcohol – as a proxy measure of someone's inclination towards violence. Muslim Uyghurs have been given hefty jail sentences for as little as encouraging their peers to observe their faith.

At the same time, Islamophobia in Xinjiang is inseparable from questions of national identity. For a decade now, academics and policy advisers in China have criticised the nation's existing system of national (or *minzu*) autonomy, arguing for measures that promote assimilation and diminish the political salience of national or – as they prefer it – 'ethnic' difference. Although this critique is often presented in a liberal guise, the basic proposition here is that an overly strong sense of non-Chinese identity has national-security implications. While the party has refrained from major constitutional reforms, this line of thinking continues to gain ground amid the wider crackdown in Xinjiang.

It's important to recognise the way that the recent focus on Islam intersects with pre-existing racism and discrimination towards Uyghurs in China, where they have long been vilified as backward, criminal, and recalcitrant towards the CCP's nation-building enterprise. Twenty years ago, I saw 'Han only' job advertisements in Xinjiang and listened to Han taxi drivers complain about how lazy Uyghurs were. In the same way that Western Islamophobia will not impact a white convert in the way it impacts Muslim migrants from Africa, nationality still plays a role in determining the impact of China's policies towards Islam. Islamophobia, as I use the term here, is not something distinct from racism: it is racism, but a form of racism in which negative views of Islam serve as the key mobilising discourse for the state's oppressive practices. Alongside the Uyghurs, other majority-Muslim communities in Xinjiang have also been hard hit. Much of what is known about the camps derives from Kazakh ex-detainees who fled to neighbouring Kazakhstan; often it was their ties to that country that led to their detention in the first place. In New York, I met a traumatised young Hui man (a Chinese-speaking Muslim), who spent months in a filtering facility for little more than acting up at school.

When people in Xinjiang began severing contact with relatives outside the region, it was one of the earliest indications of China's new internment policy. Before long, well-known intellectuals and artists were going missing. By 2018, online sources were posting evidence of the camp-construction boom. In phone interviews with officials, activists extracted some rough data on the scale of internment. Periodic leaks and satellite imagery have fleshed out the picture, and we now have a large body of individual testimonies describing the facilities. While China has offered sanitised images of the camps, most testimonies describe prison-like conditions, and some include accounts of torture and rape. Extrapolating to some degree, estimates of the detainee population range from the hundreds of thousands up to more than a million. China's own statistics indicate that some 40 per cent of school-aged children in Xinjiang study in boarding schools, with many growing up in state orphanages.[11] The all-encompassing nature of the policy, and its impact on families, is easily detectable outside the country, where many Uyghurs, Kazakhs and others still live with the trauma of not knowing the fate of their relatives.

When first questioned at the UN's Committee on the Elimination of Racial Discrimination in August 2018, China denied the camps existed. When that became untenable, it introduced new 'de-extremification' regulations to legalise its actions. These regulations ban public expressions of religiosity, such as veiling, and call for religion to be made compatible with 'socialist society'. They also emphasise the practical, 'vocational' training that detainees receive in some camps, which is designed to instil factory discipline into Xinjiang's rural population. This rhetorical shift coincided with an intensification of non-voluntary labour programs sending young men and women to the Chinese interior for work, in some cases in factories connected to supply chains of Western corporations. By late 2019, Xinjiang officials were claiming that most detainees had finished their term of 'study' and returned home, yet some 'graduates' now face work assignments in which they have little choice. Other camp detainees have been redirected to the formal criminal justice system, with Xinjiang witnessing a surge in incarcerations.

After the 2018 confrontation at the Committee on the Elimination of Racial Discrimination, the United Nations became a scene of duelling letters for and against China's policies. In 2019, Australia was among twenty-two signatories to a letter to the UN Human Rights Committee criticising China. China responded by mobilising thirty-seven countries to defend its actions. In 2020, the score was thirty-nine to forty-five. The blocs shifted to an extent – some signatories to the 2019 letter in defence of China withdrew from the second letter in 2020 – but the basic divide on the issue persisted. While Western nations and Japan have taken a firm stance, China has been able to enlist the support of Russia and much of the developing world, including many Muslim-majority countries. These alliances present a challenge for anyone who wants to apply international pressure on China: it is not isolated.

Islamic solidarity with the Uyghurs has been visible at the popular level, in countries such as Indonesia and Bangladesh, but the failure of governments in Muslim-majority countries to criticise China has disappointed many. In fact, at the most recent meeting of foreign ministers of the Organisation of Islamic Cooperation, they went so far as to 'commend the efforts of the People's Republic of China in providing care to its Muslim citizens' – an appalling stance.[12] Political and economic ties are obviously influencing factors, but many of these countries also share an interest with China in stifling human-rights criticism. Some insight into the situation can be gained from WikiLeaks cables from 2009, which show how, in the wake of the Ürümchi riots, 'PRC officials scrambled ... to head off potential anti-Chinese reactions in the Muslim world'. One Egyptian official accounted for his country's decision to side with China in terms of its 'own internal political concerns that resemble the problems in Xinjiang'. The cables also show a basic ignorance of Xinjiang in these countries: 'Many in the Middle East were only beginning to learn about and form opinions on China.'[13]

Activists can take some encouragement from this evidence that China is sensitive to international opinion: it has no desire to gain a reputation as anti-Muslim. And while many of the factors inhibiting a high-level political response from the Muslim world remain in place, we have to remember that few of its governments really represent the will of their people in any way. The Palestinian Authority, which subcontracts Israel's occupation in the West Bank, was a signatory to the pro-China letter, but a 2020 opinion poll shows that 83 per cent of Palestinians believe they should stand in solidarity with the Uyghurs, and 80 per cent believe Palestinians should condemn China's policies if media reports of repression are true.[14]

Public shaming in the world's media has no doubt had some effect on the direction of policy in Xinjiang, but just how much is hard to say. Inevitably, speculation about more concrete action has mostly centred on Washington. America's interest in Xinjiang is still yet to rise to the level of its engagement on Tibet, which Congress described in the 1990s as an occupied country with the right to self-determination. It was not until the early 2000s that Washington's human-rights wing took much interest in the Uyghur cause, possibly to compensate for America's emerging counterterrorism collaboration with China. Financed primarily by the US Congress, the National Endowment for Democracy gives grants to the Uyghur American Association and the Uyghur Human Rights Project, and it also helped to set up the World Uyghur Congress in Munich in 2004. Until 2017 the charismatic entrepreneur Rebiya Kadeer raised the profile of the World Uyghur Congress as its president. Today, Dolkun Isa holds the position, a man with activist credentials going back to the 1980s in Xinjiang.

It's perfectly understandable that Uyghur activists might want this kind of support; without it, they'd have little platform internationally. But for those looking for opportunities to deflect the focus from China, the National Endowment for Democracy serves as a lightning rod for criticism. A product of Ronald Reagan's Cold War 'crusade for freedom', it concentrates its support for democracy and human-rights activism on countries that lie outside Washington's sphere of influence. Regime change has been part of its portfolio in the past, particularly in Latin America, where its trainees have destabilised governments such as the Sandinistas. Reliance on American patronage might be understandable, therefore, but it is problematic. Similar criticisms can be levelled at organisations such as Human Rights Watch, which is closely intertwined with the US foreign-policy establishment. The effect this has on China's perceptions is predictable enough, particularly when US-aligned Uyghur groups adopt militant pro-independence rhetoric, as they occasionally do.

Still these entanglements shouldn't distract us from the basic issue. Just imagine if China were funding African-American racial-justice activists: this would probably complicate the politics around movements such as Black Lives Matter, but it wouldn't be an excuse to ignore or discredit the injustices taking place in the United States. Too often, sceptics put the cart before the horse and use the political alliances that China calls into being to downplay or even dismiss claims of repression in Xinjiang. It's wrong in and of itself, but it's having a corrosive effect on progressive principles more generally. Defenders of China's policies end up sounding much like defenders of the West's war on terror, endorsing a 'de-radicalisation' paradigm that has done huge damage to Muslim communities worldwide.

Linking human rights to trade negotiations has been one course of action considered in Washington, but it was only an outside possibility during the tenure of Donald Trump, who took no interest in the issue and by one account even encouraged Xi Jinping to get on with building his camps. A second option has been sanctions: a series of Chinese tech companies are now on the 'entity list' due to their connections to the camps, and bans have been applied to a list of Chinese officials deemed complicit in the repression in Xinjiang. Finally, early in 2020, and after much delay, Congress enacted the *Uyghur Human Rights Policy Act*, which prescribes more sanctions, new resources to monitor the situation in Xinjiang and in diaspora communities in the United States, and a special coordinator for Xinjiang, modelled on a similar position that was established for Tibet (which is only intermittently filled these days). So far, the most hard-hitting sanctions have been applied to the Xinjiang Production and Construction Corps and its subsidiaries, which prohibit all transactions with the paramilitary body.

The United States' current focus on supply chains and corporate due diligence represents its chief departure from earlier tactics. In an effort to pressure China to cease its coercive labour practices – both inside and outside the re-education camps – trade unions, fair-trade groups and Uyghur organisations have pressed companies to scrutinise their supply chains or pull out of Xinjiang. While pleading innocent to charges of complicity, companies such as H&M and Patagonia have since cut ties to the region.

US Customs and Border Protection initially enforced bans on imports from specific Chinese companies and factories, imports worth an estimated US$200 million. A more drastic move to ban all cotton and cotton products originating in the Xinjiang Production and Construction Corps then effectively blacklisted around 40 per cent of Xinjiang's cotton, and a third of China's total cotton. More hard-hitting again, if the Uyghur Forced Labor Prevention Bill becomes law, it will impose a presumption of forced labour on *all* products from Xinjiang. Since it would be hard to show conclusive proof that supply chains are not tainted in some way, this would equate to an effective embargo on Xinjiang.

Australia is yet to take any similar steps. The idea of introducing laws facilitating 'Magnitsky' sanctions on individuals has been debated for some time. Australia's autonomous-sanctions law in fact gives government the ability to sanction individuals, as it did in 2018, when it applied sanctions on Burmese generals deemed responsible for violence against the Rohingya. The Law Council of Australia has criticised the government's selective, politicised use of such sanctions – defined by law as a measure to influence foreign entities in accordance with government policy – and questions whether it is capable of responding to 'violations by powerful persons in states on which Australia depends to achieve broader economic, trade or foreign policy outcomes'.[15]

While the letter of any Magnitsky law may be different, the rhetoric around this legislation has had the same defect, depicting it exclusively as a tool for use against non-Western offenders. Human rights lawyers Geoffrey Robertson and Chris Rummery argue that if 'all advanced democracies ... adopted such laws, the pleasures available to the cruel and corrupt would be considerably diminished'.[16] Obviously, though, some of the world's 'cruel and corrupt' already reside in the advanced democracies. What do we propose doing to them? Preventing Chinese officials from retiring to a comfortable life in Australia after a tour of duty persecuting Uyghurs in Xinjiang seems a worthwhile measure, but to do so without considering similar action against Western war criminals will likely have little effect on China's policy.

Australian law lags well behind America's on the question of forced labour, but the Xinjiang crisis is an opportunity to improve it. Australia's 2018 *Modern Slavery Act* only requires companies with an annual turnover of A$100 million or more to report on the risks of forced labour in their operations and supply chains. Both the Australian Council of Trade Unions and Human Rights Watch have pointed out certain obvious deficiencies in this legislation: the reporting threshold is too high, there are no penalties for non-compliance, and there is no independent watchdog.[17] An effective response to China's coercive 'proletarianisation' of the Uyghurs should begin with a prohibition on the import of *all* products of forced labour (as exists in the United States), with penalties that are genuine deterrents, and an independent commissioner capable of responding to complaints and carrying out investigations. Australia's response would also be strengthened by ratifying the International Labour Organization's 2014 Forced Labour Protocol, which has been signed by forty-five countries so far. Only when Australia affirms its own adherence to international standards on the issue can it pressure China to do the same.

I imagine almost all Australians would support measures to prevent companies profiting from gross violations of labour rights, but we shouldn't underestimate the ability of corporate lobbies to resist such efforts. During the 1990s, Human Rights Watch founder Aryeh Neier all but gave up on China. 'It is clear,' he said, 'that taking on trade, except with countries where the economic stakes are paltry, is beyond the capacity of the human-rights movement.'[18] America's conflict minerals rule, introduced in 2012, is in many ways the model for the supply-chain due-diligence approach towards Xinjiang. The goal was to force companies to disclose any connection to forced labour in African diamond mining. Since it came into effect, though, companies have lobbied against the rule's disclosure requirements on First Amendment, 'free-speech' grounds, and in 2017 a Securities and Exchange Commission ruling rendered it null and void.

Corporate America is likewise lobbying against the Forced Labor Prevention Bill – but, for the time being, those in Washington pushing for a hardline response on Xinjiang have some wind in their sails. As corporate social-responsibility measures evolve towards more hard-hitting sanctions, though, the usual questions surrounding sanctions will apply. How will the 'pain' caused by sanctions be distributed in China? And will the sanctions have any effect on policymaking? For instance, will a crippled Xinjiang Production and Construction Corps pull strings in Beijing to modify a security policy the CCP clearly sees as non-negotiable – a policy the CCP has already paid a large reputational price for? The party's calculations on this will be informed by its wider view of the developing situation. In light of Washington's declared intention to engage in long-term, wide-spectrum great-power competition, China can rationally anticipate ongoing conflict, irrespective of any softening of its policy on Xinjiang. That will make it less likely to back down, and more likely to write off human-rights sanctions as one more front in a campaign of economic pressure. Where will the United States go then?

Ending the Global War on Terror

The language of human rights may be adequate to describe the impact of China's policies in Xinjiang, but it's not specific enough to name and challenge what is driving those policies. The situation in Xinjiang can be thought of in terms of colonial exploitation, or a Chinese-style civilising mission, but time and again China justifies its actions in terms of counterterrorism and anti-extremism. In a global climate of Islamophobia, which normalises the repression of Muslims, this framing influences international perceptions of the issue. The Australian ex-diplomat Gregory Clark, for example, recently wrote that the 'binding attraction' of Islam is too strong for Beijing's 'mere proselytising' to erode, and China therefore has little choice but to go hard to avoid Xinjiang becoming 'another Chechnya'.[19] On his *Friendlyjordies* podcast, ALP-aligned pundit Jordan Shanks explained that 'the reason the Uyghur population is detained is because they're causing trouble'. 'What, like, old-school Islamic trouble?' his co-presenter queried. 'Yeah, yeah, yes it is,' a third presenter chimed in.[20] The religious identity of the Uyghurs is still a liability for them in winning international support.

It's possible to look at this and think that China is simply being opportunistic in its framing of its policies. In a study of late-Qing periodicals, Haruka Nomura shows that during Zuo Zongtang's reconquest of Xinjiang in the 1870s, Chinese commentators in the treaty-port press drew on a narrative of Islam's incompatibility with Western civilisation to justify the Qing's brutal pacification campaign.[21] At times, something similar seems to be going on in the punditry of outlets such as the *Global Times*. But the links today between China and the West's anti-Muslim policies are far from merely discursive. China's alignment with the US war on terror wasn't just window-dressing. The new American paradigm genuinely influenced the shape of China's attitudes to Muslims – both inside and outside the CCP. There are anti-CCP liberals in China who are as virulently Islamophobic as any party official you're likely to find.

Counterterrorism also became a field of international collaboration for China. As recently as 2017, the UK Foreign Office sponsored the Royal United Services Institute to run a 'Track 2 Dialogue' in Xinjiang's capital of Ürümchi, the purpose of which was 'to demonstrate the effectiveness of UK best practice in CVE [Countering Violent Extremism] and identify ways this can be adopted in China'.[22] Around the same time, the Australian Federal Police signed a statement of intent with Beijing, one element of which was counterterrorist collaboration. Chinese security specialists and 'terrorism experts' have travelled the world to study and synthesise the lessons of counterterrorism elsewhere. I met a pair of them one day in Sydney, visitors from the People's Public Security University in Beijing. We sat down for coffee to exchange views, but I soon raised the case of Ilham Tohti, and the conversation quickly came to an end.

Everyone watching the issue of Xinjiang recognises that George W. Bush's decision to list the 'East Turkistan Islamic Movement' as a terrorist organisation legitimised China's stance. In 2020, when Trump removed the organisation from the list, some claimed this would deprive China of the ability to justify its actions in Xinjiang. The fact is, though, the synergy between the West and China draws on much more than a single name on a list. To this day, Beijing presents itself as engaged in, and learning from, the same anti-terrorism campaign the West is engaged in; many people inside China see things this way, as do many outside it. While the scale of repression in Xinjiang is not replicated in any domestic counterterrorism campaign anywhere in the world, the basic philosophical principles clearly are. We're yet to fully grapple with the strategic implications of this.

Many Western countries, Australia included, have gone to excess in their domestic policing of terrorism, but the most stark example today is in France. In discussing policies in Xinjiang, Chinese analysts often refer to French precedents of bans on religious dress, a 'deradicalisation centre' and a plan (never implemented) to pre-emptively detain thousands of people on a government watchlist. Today, President Emmanuel Macron sounds every bit like Xi Jinping when he calls for a 'society of vigilance' capable of resisting 'Islamist separatism'. Macron describes Islam as a religion 'in crisis' which must be brought into line with republican values through state supervision of mosques and Islamic associations.[23]

Civil society organisations that campaign against Islamophobia have been proscribed.

When Macron's provocative stance ignited a global backlash, some Uyghurs were bemused that Muslim-majority countries would be so enraged at France's actions but not China's. It's an understandable sentiment, but it would be wrong, morally and tactically, to dismiss this criticism of France. After all, when a liberal democracy such as France intensifies its crackdown on Islam, it only eases the pressure on China. The lesson we need to take from these divergent international responses is that there is still much work to be done to link campaigns against Islamophobia in the West with something similar directed towards China. It's this kind of campaign that I believe offers the best chance of actually exposing and confronting the political rationale for Beijing's actions in Xinjiang.

An orientation like this is necessary, I believe, because in the absence of a wider framing of the issue, counterproductive alternatives can easily fill the gap. Azeem Ibrahim, co-author of a recent Newlines Institute report that upholds the genocide charge, is among those who discuss advocacy for the Uyghurs as part of a campaign to contain China. 'If the international community responds robustly to the Uighur genocide,' he writes, 'this may be the moment when China's global ascendency is stopped in its tracks.'[24] This kind of language only gives Beijing the ammunition it needs to depict Western human rights criticism as motivated by geopolitics.

A better approach, as I see it, is to situate this advocacy within a wider campaign to end the war on terror, both domestically and internationally. This would, I believe, improve our chances of having some impact on the situation. It's crucial that we can make a convincing case to ordinary Chinese that outrage towards the situation in Xinjiang reflects a commitment to anti-racism and justice for all. It's also important to strengthen alliances with Muslim communities, whose scepticism of America's intentions can blunt their criticism of China. A genuine commitment to end the war on terror internationally would immediately create the possibility of bringing more Muslim-majority countries onside. China, as I've discussed, is anxious to avoid being seen by the outside world as anti-Muslim. Withdrawing Western troops from Afghanistan will be a good start, but to truly disrupt the global counterterrorism paradigm and the 'securitocracy' it has given rise to we will have to work toward ending small wars and military collaborations across the globe. (According to one study, the United States engages in counterterrorism in some 40 per cent of the world's nations.)[25] Most importantly, a campaign centred on opposition to the war on terror would undermine the basic propositions by which China legitimates its actions in Xinjiang, and the accusations of 'double standards' that it flings back when criticised.

In any such solution, I readily admit, Australians can only play a small role, but we still have choices to make about where we put our energies and what we call on our politicians to do. If the West is capable of fighting a 'global' war on terror, why should it not be able to organise a similarly global campaign to undo the damage that war has done, be it in Australia, Afghanistan or China?

Twenty years on, it's well past time for us to recognise that counter-terrorism and the abuse of human rights have always been two sides of the same coin. In a 2017 report entitled *Leaving the War on Terror*, the Transnational Institute describes how British counterterrorism policies 'ratcheted up the powers available to the police and intelligence agencies, creating a shadow criminal justice system in which legal principles applicable in other spheres were dispensed with; ... the use of surveillance and propaganda was expanded and deepened; military force and extra-judicial killing as counterterrorist methods became routine; and complicity with torturers was normalised.'[26] Whether as a *casus belli* or domestic policing practice, 'counterterrorism' applies a distorting lens to political realities and justifies gross excesses of violence and infringement on freedoms.

Muslims in Australia, still the most maligned minority in the country, have been telling us for a long time about the suspicions and hostility they have experienced since 9/11. A recent study found that 80 per cent of Australian soldiers believe that 'the Muslim religion promotes violence and terrorism'.[27] This is the Islamophobic climate that incubated not just the war crimes enumerated in the Brereton Report, but the violence of the Christchurch massacre. No, Australia doesn't detain Muslims in mind-numbing 're-education' camps, but that shouldn't blind us to the similarities of the philosophies of counterterrorism that prevail in both countries, and the terrible impact this has had on members of the Australian community.

I've tried to show in this book that effective responses to China are those that at the same time strengthen Australian democracy, and this is a case in point.

Of course, a wider campaign to roll back the effects of the war on terror internationally is not a substitute for the basic, necessary work, of exposing, criticising and, where possible, taking action against China's repression in Xinjiang. The various initiatives that exist today – to name and shame companies with links to coercive labour practices, to apply pressure on Beijing during its hosting of the 2022 Winter Olympics, to publicise the plight of individual detainees, or simply to preserve and promote Uyghur culture in the diaspora – these all deserve support. What I'm outlining here is a perspective that can guide us as we do that. The alternative, as I see it, is an untenable one: to say to China that our war on terror is good but yours is bad. I just don't think that's going to work.

In Australia, we've recently seen what governments can do when they're able to portray foreign criticism of their policies as made in bad faith. Having long insisted that Australia should butt out of its internal affairs, China has now begun responding in kind to Australian criticism. In December 2020, foreign ministry spokesperson Zhao Lijian tweeted out a digital artwork attacking Australia for its war crimes in Afghanistan. Instead of taking the criticism on the chin, Morrison seized the opportunity to shoot the messenger and inflame nationalist passions. His angry response outweighed anything he had said about the Brereton Report itself, and gave him political cover to reject the report's recommendation to strip an SAS unit of its service awards. Just as China has done in the face of criticism on Xinjiang, Australia rallied international support to denounce what it bizarrely referred to as a 'fake image'. Britain, Canada and the United States all described Zhao's tweet as 'disinformation', seeming to cast doubt on the veracity of the killings it referred to.[28] Right-wing commentators laid into the Brereton Report for giving China an opening to attack Australia.

For all Australia's talk of reckoning with its crimes in Afghanistan – after a long delayed inquiry, police raids on journalists and the prosecution of whistleblowing soldiers – the combined effect of this furore was to make it less likely that we really will take serious action on the issue. If politicians in a country such as Australia can manipulate foreign criticism in this way, it shouldn't surprise us that Beijing is capable of doing the same.

I couldn't help feeling a sense of historical irony in the way Afghanistan stood at the centre of last year's war of words between Morrison and the 'wolf warrior' artist whose satirical image irritated him so effectively. The exposure of the Australian military's killing of innocent civilians in Afghanistan – a country bordering on Xinjiang – was a chance for us to reflect on the devastating impact that the war on terror has had all across Central Asia. It was in Afghanistan, after all, that the global war on terror first got going in 2001. Two decades on, that war continues to ravage communities around the world, with the Muslims of Xinjiang among the worst affected. It's well past time that we declared an end to it.

7. THE BATTLE FOR HONG KONG

From the middle of 2019, Australians watched with a mixture of admiration and trepidation as millions of Hong Kong residents threw themselves into a defiant struggle against local authorities and Beijing. A campaign to fend off an unpopular extradition bill soon widened into a fight to preserve the democratic rights that define Hong Kong's precarious self-rule. In mass demonstrations, and hit-and-run street battles that pitted a militant minority against the reviled Hong Kong Police Force, the 'anti-ELAB' movement sustained itself for an impressive six months, reaching something of a crescendo in its desperate defence of Hong Kong's besieged universities and the resounding victory of pro-democracy candidates in local elections in November 2019. All along, though, a sense of impending doom pervaded the confrontation. Beijing held many, if not all, of the cards, but was slow to play them. A violent showdown – the second Tiananmen that some anticipated – never arrived, but the energy of activists had to eventually wane. Early in 2020, the COVID-19 pandemic gave Hong Kong's chief executive Carrie Lam the opportunity she needed to restrict the scope of opposition activity, before Beijing finally intervened, announcing new national-security legislation that has triggered a major, ongoing crackdown on Hong Kong's dissidents.

Home to around 100,000 Australian citizens, and host to many more who pass through on tourism and shopping trips, Hong Kong is a much more recognisable setting for Australians than Xinjiang is. By the same token, almost 100,000 Australian citizens were born in Hong Kong, and some 10,000 Hong Kong citizens reside here on study and work visas. Despite its small size, the city rates highly as a destination for Australian exports and investments, and is the site of the largest Australian Chamber of Commerce in the world. In return, Australia receives more foreign direct investment from Hong Kong than from the rest of China combined. These facts haven't just bred familiarity, they've given Australia a vested interest in Hong Kong's status quo for the last two decades: a freewheeling capitalist economy with a relatively independent judiciary and civil liberties, but only a semblance of democracy.

The huge Western media presence in Hong Kong also ensures it a prominent place in Australian thinking on China. In the 1990s, much of the world's media made it their base for reporting on the PRC and the rest of Asia. Press freedom survived the transition to CCP rule relatively intact: as recently as 2016, Hong Kong sat above Japan on Reporters without Borders' World Press Freedom Index. That standing is now in steep decline, though, and the large cohort of foreign and local journalists who provided extensive coverage of the anti-ELAB campaign often had to brave police violence to do so.

The eruption of struggle in Hong Kong was the product of local political dynamics, the end point of a slow working out of a political contradiction: local aspirations to make good the heavily circumscribed democracy they inherited from British colonial rule, and Beijing's determination to limit, and on some fronts roll back, the city's freedoms. But the fight, coinciding as it did with a major rupture in China's relationship with the West, could not avoid taking on international dimensions. Hoping that outside pressure might help resolve the impasse, Hong Kong activists were often drawn to conservative 'Cold Warriors', who seemed the most willing and able to take action against Beijing. Others saw the Hong Kong mobilisation as part of a wave of global uprisings of disenfranchised youth. Sometimes, the activists made direct links with other protest movements, such as Thailand's 2020 rebellion against military rule, which brought into being a pan-Asian 'Milk Tea Alliance'. Sometimes the dialogue was more tentative – as with Black Lives Matter in the United States.

I didn't see any of Hong Kong's uprising firsthand, but the situation reminded me of scenes I'd once witnessed in Moscow. In the wake of Putin's re-election in 2012, anti-Putin gatherings known as 'people's walks' sprang up in different locations across the city from week to week. They were small, but represented a wide political spectrum. In post-communist Russia, the opposition is divided between those who think that Russia has embraced far too much capitalism, and those who think it's still not capitalist enough. I remember one particular meeting in a park. On one side, the right was holding forth and attracting most of the media: the liberal-nationalist Aleksei Navalny and chess-champion dissident Garry Kasparov. Opposite them, small groups of socialists and anarchists mingled nervously.

I could see something similar going on in Hong Kong, as people with divergent political sympathies, and social positions, united against a common enemy in Carrie Lam and the CCP. You'll probably find this type of dynamic in any society outside the Western 'democratic' camp, but particularly one in confrontation with 'communism'. For some Westerners on the left, this was too hard to think through. Seeing their political enemies latch onto Hong Kong as a platform, they became sceptical of, even hostile to, the Hong Kong movement.

We need not adopt a simplistic East–West framing of the conflict to sympathise with Hong Kong's activists. The exaggerated images of Hong Kong residents that circulated in the West – either as anti-communist freedom fighters or pro-Western subversives – often obscured the reality of the city's politics. In saying this, I don't wish to downplay the attraction that the imagined possibilities of a Sino–US stand-off still holds for many Hong Kong residents. But events themselves have already exposed the many limitations of that framing.

From Annexation to Anti-ELAB

Born out of the punitive terms that the British Empire imposed on the Qing at the end of the First Opium War, the colony of Hong Kong Island was expanded by the acquisition of its hinterland in the late nineteenth century, and took on the form it has today. As the prototypical treaty port, the city was riven by racial and class divides: a small Chinese elite found a niche collaborating with the foreign banks and import–export firms that dominated Hong Kong's economy, but they were still excluded from whites-only clubs and vacation reserves until as late as the 1940s.

China's 'Father of the Nation', Sun Yat-sen, was educated in Hong Kong, and the fall of the Qing saw nationalist agitation develop there. Rickshaw drivers and dockworkers went on strike against repressive colonial laws in the nineteenth century, and in the 1920s the city's labour militancy linked it to mass movements across southern China. But while Hong Kong would remain a site of both Guomindang and CCP activism, neither party had the strength or inclination for a major confrontation with British rule in the colony. Sheltered from much of China's twentieth-century political turmoil, the city evolved its own conservative, apolitical culture and a distinct identity.

As World War II drew to a close, many anticipated that Hong Kong would revert to Beijing's control, but the CCP did not object when British officials retook the city from its Japanese occupiers and ran up the Union Jack. Mao saw advantage in preserving the anomalous status quo: improved relations with Britain (one of the first Western countries to offer the PRC diplomatic recognition) and an economic lifeline across the US Cold War blockade. Beijing declared it was willing to wait until 1997, when London's ninety-nine-year lease on the Kowloon Peninsula would expire, to retake possession.

As the reconstructed colonial regime negotiated its accommodation with the anti-colonial PRC, Hong Kong also became a place of refuge for those escaping the bruising campaigns and persecutions of Maoist China. Under the watchful eye of the colonial police, clandestine CCP members and a wider circle of sympathisers vied for influence with operatives of Nationalist Taiwan. Liberals and dissident leftists defined themselves against both authoritarian camps and critiqued the absence of political freedoms in Hong Kong itself.

The issues that animate Hong Kong politics today were as glaring during British rule, if not more so. The right to demonstrate, the right to form political parties that advocate freely for their positions, and the right to elect representatives to the colony's governing bodies: city residents enjoyed none of these. The cost of living was high and social services non-existent, which aroused opposition too. In the late 1960s, labour disputes set off a wave of rioting and attacks on police, resulting in some fifty deaths. Communist-aligned unions had a leading hand in these events, and for the British this highlighted Hong Kong's precarious position on the PRC's doorstep.

Obviously, Britain couldn't afford to adopt the same counterinsurgency techniques in Hong Kong that it was applying to 'Communist

Terrorists' in Malaya and Singapore. Luckily for London, though, Beijing was also wary of confrontation and reined in the city's Maoists. From then on, London's gambit was to pump up Hong Kong's newly industrialised economy to ensure Beijing continued to benefit from the status quo. It was also at this time that Britain permitted Hong Kong to join international organisations in its own right, giving it the appearance of an independent, state-like actor in the economic sphere, if not the political.

While most city residents still thought of themselves as very much Chinese, by the 1970s a new sense of Hong Kong Chinese identity was perceptible, often drawing on a sense of superiority to the mainland that derived from the city's colonial institutions. Pro-Beijing leftists tried to combat this tendency with cultural campaigns encouraging people to get to know, and identify more closely with, mainland China. As communication increased in the 1980s, exchange with the mainland took on many forms. Hong Kong films and music were widely enjoyed throughout the rest of China. When natural disasters struck China, Hong Kong residents fundraised for relief efforts. The city's activists followed the rise, fall and rise again of the democracy movement in China as if it were their own.

As the 1997 deadline for the handover came into view, Britain initially held out hope for some role in the city's post-transition governance. Prime Minister Margaret Thatcher was herself reluctant to let go of Britain's last colony in Asia, rejecting China's claims of sovereignty. In the end, though, London saw little alternative but to comply with Beijing's insistence that it would retake full sovereignty. Beijing raised the slogan 'Hong Kongers should govern Hong Kong', but made little effort to rouse the anti-colonial sentiments of the population, preferring to liaise behind the scenes with the same wealthy Hong Kong Chinese who had served as loyal intermediaries for the British. Local critics realised that the CCP's rhetoric had less to do with democracy than elite networking, but their response was not to oppose the handover, it was to call for more popular participation in setting the terms of Hong Kong's future as part of China. Some on the left imagined that the meeting of mainland welfare provisions with the freer political culture of Hong Kong might create political synergies that would be salutary for both sides.

The relative optimism towards the PRC's political trajectory in the 1980s was dispelled by the crushing of the 1989 Tiananmen rebellion, in memory of which Hong Kong still holds annual rallies. But by that time, Britain had signed off on the Sino-British Joint Declaration, and a committee in Beijing was finalising the Basic Law, Hong Kong's 'mini-constitution'. This document satisfied China by preserving the colonial system as it stood in the middle of the 1980s: a dominant executive alongside a legislative council with very limited authority. At the same time, the Basic Law offered hope to those envisaging a more thoroughgoing democratisation of Hong Kong, by holding out the promise of 'universal suffrage' at some unspecified time – interpreted as a 'one resident, one vote' system for both the legislative council and chief executive positions. Belatedly, and more than a little cynically, Britain's last colonial governor, Chris Patten, further democratised the legislative council before the transition. The last-minute modifications, along with Patten's efforts to recruit international support for them, enraged officials in Beijing.

Since 1997, the Standing Committee of the National People's Congress of the PRC (NPCSC) has reserved the exclusive right to interpret the Basic Law. The nomination and election of the chief executive remains in the hands of an electoral committee representing only a tiny minority of Hong Kong's population. At times, there have been multiple nominees for the position – an 'opposition' figure even made the list once – but there have also been instances of a single candidate being nominated. Prising open this system to 'civic' nomination was a longstanding objective of Hong Kong's democrats, as was reform to the constituency voting system. Beijing, for its part, firmly opposed any structure in which an anti-CCP candidate might rise to the top and only offered limited concessions. The result was a long-running arm wrestle. While the business-heavy functional constituencies ensured a pro-Beijing majority in the legislative council, the pro-democracy camp traditionally won enough of the remaining seats to hold a veto over constitutional change. At times of low mobilisation, some democrats reconciled themselves to Beijing's halfway-house proposals. At other times, they left the table and took to the streets.

Hong Kong entered the PRC on the understanding that for the next fifty years there would be no change to the 'one country, two systems' model, but some elements of that model remained undefined. Article 23 of the Basic Law, for example, required Hong Kong's officials to pass their own national-security laws. This they tried to do in 2003, sparking a ten-month opposition campaign that culminated in a massive demonstration on 1 July, the anniversary of the handover. The bill was shelved, and 1 July has seen anti-Beijing rallies ever since.

Beijing's response to these events was to accelerate Hong Kong's economic integration with the mainland, opening it up to tourism, investment and limited migration. Along with mainland capital came campaigns to promote the Mandarin language, and increasingly direct interventions into the city's politics. After peaking in 2008, local trust in the Chinese government fell rapidly; by the time of the 2012 elections, anxiety towards 'reddening' or 'mainlandification' was a feature of the city's politics. The elections took place amid renewed mobilisations against a new 'moral and national education' curriculum, which was designed to inculcate pro-China patriotism in Hong Kong's high schools. High-schoolers led the opposition to the change, an indication of the new generation's growing sense of estrangement from, and even hostility towards, the mainland.

The opposition's victory in the 'national education' campaign led to a renewed push for electoral reform in 2014. This commenced with a small occupation of the CBD and an unofficial poll of city residents on various alternatives to the prevailing system. In August, the NPCSC in Beijing disappointed activists by unveiling a model of 'universal suffrage' elections for the chief executive that retained a strict political filter on nominees. In response to this, the Hong Kong Federation of Students led residents back into the streets for a seventy-nine-day occupation. Protesters unfolded umbrellas to ward off the pepper spray that police fired at them, and the name 'Umbrella Movement' stuck. Yet as Beijing held its ground, divides emerged around tactical questions. Should they escalate the confrontation or make a tactical withdrawal? Should they maintain a common front (the 'Big Stage') or engage in more decentralised actions? Questions such as these split and gradually demobilised the movement, fuelling recriminations once the police had taken back the city streets.

Reflecting a widely felt impatience with negotiations with Beijing, and a newly politicised sense of Hong Kong identity, alternative political voices were now challenging the traditional monopoly on opposition held by the liberal 'pan-democrats'. These included student organisations like Scholarism, led by Joshua Wong, which evolved into the self-described social-democratic party Demosisto. Wong and his collaborators sat at the moderate end of a wide 'localist' spectrum of opinion, which sees self-determination, or even independence, as the solution to Hong Kong's predicament. At the other end of this spectrum, more xenophobic, nativist voices were also emerging, expressing fierce hostility to all things associated with the mainland, including ordinary mainland immigrants.

In the 2019 anti-ELAB uprising, localist slogans like 'Reclaim Hong Kong, Revolution of Our Times' would inspire many, but their attraction lay partly in their imprecision. What exactly would a self-determining Hong Kong revolution look like? In the absence of any thought-out strategy, localism often taps into pop-economic theories of mainland China's coming collapse, with a crisis in Hong Kong sometimes imagined as a trigger. This sentiment came to be expressed in the doctrine of *laam chau*, or 'mutual destruction'. Naturally, some right-wing nativists also engage in fantasies of America charging in, Napoleon-style, to impose freedom on China by force of arms. In its extreme forms, Hong Kong nativism can exhibit some of the nihilism and glorification of violence we associate with the far right in the West, but it remains an essentially Hong Kong product.

Hong Kong's Last Hurrah?

My last visit to Hong Kong was in 2018, at which time I sensed a pessimistic mood among local academic colleagues. Some were toying with the idea of leaving, but the city's fraught relationship to the mainland also generated a certain intellectual energy, which was enough to hold them for the time being. Activists on the city's small anti-CCP left were still talking about a strike at the docks in 2013 as the main highlight of an otherwise dull period. Trends in electoral politics were uninspiring from their point of view. Localists had made a splash in the 2016 legislative council elections. Some of the candidates had been pre-emptively disqualified, and six of those who actually got elected were expelled for abusing protocol at the swearing-in ceremony. Interestingly, though, in the ensuing by-elections, pro-Beijing candidates won back two of the vacancies. My friends saw this as a sign of political fragmentation and passivity; they didn't hold out much hope for the revival of mass opposition any time soon.

Within just a few months, they'd be proven seriously wrong. In February 2019, Lam announced an extradition bill that would allow anyone deemed a criminal fugitive to be returned to mainland China. The pretext was the case of a Hong Kong man who had killed his girlfriend in Taiwan before fleeing home. Authorities also pointed to the need to close off Hong Kong as a bolthole for corporate criminals from the mainland. But like Article 23, extradition provisions had long been on the to-do list of Hong Kong authorities, and critics feared it could legalise the rendering up of Hong Kong dissidents. Something like this had already been going on clandestinely. The Causeway Bay Books case was still fresh in people's minds: five booksellers had vanished from various locations, including Hong Kong, before eventually turning up on mainland television in confession videos. The campaign against the Extradition Law Amendment Bill is known as anti-ELAB in English, but its purpose is made more explicit if we translate its Chinese name literally: 'oppose extradition to China'.

After an early round of large demonstrations did nothing to deter Lam, activists stepped up their efforts at the start of June, bringing two million people into the streets by the middle of the month. This represented something approaching one in four Hong Kong residents, a display of popular will that is rarely seen anywhere in the world today. Some rallies were met with serious police violence, so when Lam announced the suspension of the bill on 15 June, residents not only insisted it be formally withdrawn but also demanded redress for the attacks. This would require an independent investigation into police violence, the withdrawal of any accusation that those protesting were 'rioters' and amnesty for demonstrators who were already detained. Hong Kong's pan-democrats were reluctant to resurrect the Umbrella Movement's main slogan of 'universal suffrage', knowing what a drawn-out struggle it would entail. But these instinctive negotiators were losing the initiative to more radical elements in the pro-democracy camp. When militants broke into the legislative council on 1 July and graffitied its halls and corridors, 'universal suffrage' consolidated its position as the fifth of the protester's 'five demands'.

It was an ambitious escalation. The city's small left also tried to inject questions of social inequality into the debate, while nativists raised pro-independence slogans. But all along, the space for politics

was constrained by an ethos of unity. The principle was to 'not sit separately' – that is, to not damage relations by criticising fellow activists.
This principle applied to tactics as much as it did to ideology. For security, but also to maintain their freedom of action, activists eschewed
representation or deliberative bodies, coordinating among themselves
via online forums and the Telegram chat app. On the streets, a recognisable division of labour prevailed between the mass of peaceful
demonstrators and the black-clad front-liners, who harried the police
with their mobile, flash mob–style actions.

The police themselves had become a unifying focus of hostility for the
anti-ELAB campaign, setting in motion a dynamic of violent action and
counteraction. One key incident came on 21 July, when demonstrators
returning from a rally at the central government's Liaison Office were set
upon by a pro-Beijing gang in the suburb of Yuen Long, obviously in collusion with police and local officials.

At times, it seemed as if the movement's direct-action tactics might
backfire: the shutdown of Hong Kong's airport in August was widely criticised internationally. But despite going on a propaganda offensive, Hong
Kong authorities found it impossible to drive a wedge between the militant minority and their wider base of support in the 'yellow' camp. A week
after the airport debacle, mass demonstrations resumed, and a human
chain organised by high-schoolers linked arms defiantly across the city.

Strike action was one obvious way to escalate the campaign, but
options here were limited by the pro-Beijing stance of Hong Kong's main
union body, the Federation of Trade Unions. Industrial action in support
of the five demands was only a possibility in a few sectors, such as aviation, where the rival Confederation of Trade Unions had a presence. On 5
August, some 350,000 people took part in an impressive half-day political
strike, but the retaliation was severe, and a lack of experience and organisation saw momentum on this front lost.

A humiliated Lam eventually withdrew the extradition bill, and went
partway to meeting a second of the five demands, by inviting foreign officials to convene an investigatory body into the violence. All concessions
were met with the same response: five demands, not one less. By now, a
gritty ethos of fighting to the end pervaded the front lines. In the eyes of
many, anything short of victory would be the demise of Hong Kong once

and for all. Lam needed to realise that she was playing with fire: if we burn, you'll burn with us. Moreover, had negotiations been possible, it is hard to say who exactly they might have been with. Celebrities such as Joshua Wong, often imagined to be a guiding hand in the movement, were far less influential than they had been in previous campaigns.

The longevity of the anti-ELAB campaign rested in large part on its mobility – the 'be water' strategy to provoke and discredit the Hong Kong police, while avoiding a major showdown. Then, in November, there was a change in direction: militants converged first on the Chinese University of Hong Kong and then the Hong Kong Polytechnic University. It was natural that the university campuses would serve as a base of resistance, but the activists soon found themselves ringed by a police siege, and nights of fighting ensued. The anti-ELAB diehards shot arrows and threw Molotov cocktails to keep the riot police at bay, but the outcome was never in doubt. Drivers and motorcyclists rallied to shuttle militants away from the Polytechnic; others escaped via the sewerage system. But in the end, more than a thousand were detained. Hong Kong's street-fighting opposition had suffered a serious reversal, and would not re-emerge with the same strength again.

Still, the basic fact of Lam's immense unpopularity was not changed in any way by these events. This was amply confirmed in the district council elections that took place a fortnight after the campus conflagrations, which returned a decisive win for the anti-Beijing camp. The moral victory was also a shot across the bows in advance of the scheduled 2020 legislative council elections.

It was in high spirits, then, but without an obvious way forward, that the Hong Kong opposition entered the new year. Union organising again became a focus, this time in a more deliberate fashion. Some of the new unions that came into being were small, intended mainly as vehicles to participate in the chief executive elections. Some were more serious, including the Hospital Authority Employee Alliance (HAEA), whose members were immediately thrust into the spotlight as news of the COVID-19 pandemic filtered into the city. Radicalised by the anti-ELAB campaign, the healthcare workers raised their own five demands, calling for support and decisive action against the pandemic – including the closure of the border with mainland China. The debate over border closures as a health measure was taking place around the world, but it was imbued with distinct significance in Hong Kong. In a concrete way, the question represented the basic motivating force of the anti-ELAB movement – the wish of Hong Kong residents to determine for themselves their relationship with the rest of China.

COVID-19 was nothing short of a godsend for Lam, who invoked health risks to tighten restrictions on public gatherings and, eventually, to postpone the forthcoming legislative council elections. With the annual demonstrations in June and July in doubt, the NPCSC in Beijing now made its move, bypassing the Hong Kong legislature to approve new national-security legislation. The laws did what the Hong Kong Special Administrative Region had so far been unable to, and filled the blank space left in the Basic Law's Article 23. National-security offences of secession, subversion, terrorism and collusion with foreign forces were defined broadly enough to apply to many of the actions and slogans seen during the anti-ELAB demonstrations, and they were to be applied retroactively, with heavy penalties.

The manoeuvre was constitutionally questionable. Beijing sidestepped Hong Kong's legislative mechanisms and Article 23's requirement for Hong Kong to self-legislate by claiming that the national-security offences fell within the scope of Article 6, which gives the central government authority over foreign affairs and defence. The chief of the central government's Liaison Office in Hong Kong now sits on a new Committee for Safeguarding National Security, and serious national-security cases can be tried in mainland courts. The laws also met a second longstanding objective of the Hong Kong authorities by imposing 'national-security education' on Hong Kong schools.

On 4 June, against expectations, thousands did in fact defy the authorities to commemorate the Tiananmen crackdown. But the newly empowered authorities would not cede the initiative and immediately began a wave of arrests. Some of these arrests, such as that of Hong Kong Council of Trade Unions chairman Lee Cheuk Yan, were made under the colonial-era Public Order Ordinance, which gives police the right to prosecute participants in anything they deem to be an 'unauthorised assembly'. Joshua Wong and Agnes Chow, a popular figure in Japan, have received thirteen- and eight-month sentences for such offences respectively, but

Chow may also face trial for the more serious national-security charge of secession. Others detained for national-security offences include the owner of the *Apple Daily* tabloid Jimmy Lai, who held well-publicised meetings with Mike Pompeo during the anti-ELAB campaign. Warrants were issued for activists who were already abroad or able to get away, including one US citizen. Some desperate Hong Kongers whose passports had been confiscated tried to flee the city in speedboats. A dozen escapees were caught by the Chinese coastguard and taken to face trial on the mainland.

As I write, the ongoing police round-up is continuing to thin the ranks of the opposition. The first national-security legislation trial is underway: the case of a man who rode a motorbike into police officers while carrying a 'Liberate Hong Kong, Revolution of Our Times' flag. The flag was enough to attract a charge of secession, while the injury to police has been deemed terrorism – both charges carry maximum penalties of life in prison. Hong Kong's Court of First Instance has clarified that it still interprets national-security legislation within Hong Kong's common-law tradition, and will 'give a generous interpretation to the constitutional guarantee of rights and a narrow interpretation to statutory provisions which impair liberty or restrict fundamental rights'.[1] It would be wrong, therefore, to say that the rule of law has been completely abolished, or that Hong Kong's judicial system is now fully assimilated to that of the mainland. But the authorities clearly intend to make use of the wide scope of national-security legislation to silence dissent. In January, fifty-three members of the opposition were arrested for the offence of participating in an unofficial primary election, forty-seven of whom have now been charged with conspiring to subvert state power.

The International Front

All along, Hong Kongers knew full well they couldn't 'reclaim Hong Kong' from Beijing by relying on their own strength alone. Much hope was invested in the 'international front': the battle for global public opinion and the direct lobbying of foreign governments, particularly the United States, to apply pressure on Beijing. Naturally, it was the most pro-US activists who were drawn to this tactic. Images of small groups flying the

Stars and Stripes and calling on Trump to 'liberate Hong Kong' were seen around the world, and were seized on to both promote the cause and attack it. Opposition politicians, pop stars and trade unionists toured Western democracies, each finding distinct constituencies for their message. In these same countries, the Hong Kong diaspora itself mobilised – sometimes by itself, sometimes in an alliance of groups on China's periphery, including the Uyghurs and Tibetans, and sometimes with wider allies from both the right and the left. It was often within this diaspora activism that political divisions that were considered of secondary importance in Hong Kong came to the fore and were clarified.

The rhetoric of Hong Kong solidarity varied. It was naturally tempting for activists to position their cause on the front lines of a global confrontation between authoritarianism and democracy. This was Hong Kong as a besieged West Berlin, the 'fall' of which would embolden an expansionist China to continue on its destructive path. The message was tailor-made for the neo-Reaganite right in the United States – including such figures as senators Marco Rubio and Tom Cotton. Less ideological rhetoric emphasised principles of human rights and rule of law. One popular strategy was to point out how Beijing's intervention undermined Hong Kong's standing as a safe and reliable hub for international business. The assumption behind this rhetorical gambit is that Beijing still depends on Hong Kong as a conduit for foreign capital and might be deterred by a foreign exodus and capital flight.

Hong Kong's small left-wing diaspora rejected this idealisation of their city in Cold War and capitalist terms. Networks such as the Lausan Collective pitched the uprising to the international left by emphasising collaboration between Chinese and Western elites, not conflict. 'Competing and successive imperial regimes have subordinated Hong Kong to their capitalist interests,' they argue, 'constraining Hong Kong's ability to build [its] own political futures.'[2] In their interventions, they pointed to the social grievances – poorly articulated, but nonetheless genuine – that had driven the city's youth into rebellion, and they sought common cause with other struggles for autonomy and against state repression.

In Hong Kong itself, where the 'left' is synonymous for many people with capital-C Communism and the mainland, this framing was unlikely to ever win wide acceptance. More surprising was the resistance it encountered from members of the international left, some of whom took Beijing's side and tried to discredit the campaign as a conspiracy to destabilise China. This line of attack came from relics of the pro-China Old Left, but also from anti-war organisations, whose focus on opposing the United States inclines them to see Washington's hand everywhere, as well a newer cohort of extremely online 'anti-imperialist' media pundits. These voices drew on and amplified many of the same narratives fuelling the nationalist backlash in China: that the five demands hid the pro-democracy movement's true goal of seceding from the PRC; that the movement was resourced and coordinated by American actors; and that the presence of xenophobic, anti-mainland voices within the campaign was evidence enough to characterise the whole as a right-wing, even fascist, insurgency.

To some extent, the polarisation was a function of the hypocrisy of Western politicians, whose gushing enthusiasm for popular militancy in Hong Kong stood in stark contrast to their hostility towards it at home. Similarly, the Western media's coverage of the Hong Kong rebellion was strikingly more favourable than, say, its coverage of the simultaneous Yellow Vest uprising in France. The inconsistencies were obvious; online, you could see them gradually pushing some people in a pro-Beijing direction. But the abiding fact of Western double standards is a poor excuse to side with police repression.

That certain Hong Kong activists were liaising with American diplomats, parastatal 'pro-democracy' organisations, such as the National Endowment for Democracy, and possibly even intelligence agencies was not in doubt – just as it was undeniable that some members of the Uyghur diaspora were doing the same. It would have been a dereliction of duty if the CIA had *not* had its people in Hong Kong. In Western think-tanks, pushing on the Hong Kong pressure point was a topic of open discussion. In 2019, my own university's US Studies Centre organised a 'US–Australia Deterrence Dialogue', which discussed 'the exploitation of Beijing's anxieties about foreign influence in places like Hong Kong and Taiwan' as a possible pushback measure against China.[3] It was a frank and, in my opinion, irresponsible admission of Western interest in stirring things up in Hong Kong. China was always going to exploit any sign of foreign interference, and by sanctioning the National Endowment for Democracy and a range of American NGOs it tried to strengthen this narrative. Still, the idea that organisations such as these could summon into being and direct a struggle on the scale of anti-ELAB was always a ludicrous proposition. To entertain it only discredited the left and confirmed the suspicions of Hong Kong activists that their best friends were on the right.

Members of Trump's inner sanctum such as Pence and Pompeo would often hold forth on the situation in Hong Kong, but the president himself took no noticeable interest in it. Indeed, at one point he more or less endorsed Beijing's view of the movement, stating that Hong Kong had experienced 'riots for a long period of time', which China would have to 'deal with' itself.[4] The focus of Hong Kong lobbying in the United States was naturally the US Congress, the body that has usually been most willing to antagonise China. Within Congress, a coalition emerged around the *Hong Kong Human Rights and Democracy Act*, which eventually passed both houses with a large enough majority to make it immune to presidential veto. Alongside clauses relating to reporting on Hong Kong and sanctioning officials, one controversial provision recommended that Washington determine whether Hong Kong was still sufficiently autonomous to justify the distinctive trade rules and visa privileges that the city enjoyed in relation to the rest of China. This reflected a certain *laam chau* logic: Washington would punish China for undermining Hong Kong's autonomy by revoking its own recognition of the 'one country, two systems' policy. Advocates of the provision saw this as having a genuine deterrent effect, but critics pointed out the damage it might do to Hong Kong's economy and its citizens. It would also remove any incentive for Beijing to uphold the city's compromised, but by no means completely defunct, autonomy.

Nevertheless, with the imposition of the national-security legislation, this clause was triggered, and Trump signed an executive order stating that Washington no longer viewed Hong Kong as autonomous from the rest of China. Individual sanctions were also applied to Hong Kong and mainland officials deemed responsible for repression, including Lam. The sanctions carry a stigma in the West, but Lam received it as an honour – as did the right-wing American politicians that China 'sanctioned' in response. The move was possibly more disconcerting for Hong Kong's financial institutions, which risk being cut off from US-dollar finance if they do business with sanctioned individuals. They have complied, leaving Lam without a bank account to her name. At the same time, banks also worry that complying with the sanctions may bring them into conflict with Article 29(4) of the National Security Law, which outlaws collusion with a foreign country to impose sanctions on China. Should Beijing interpret their compliance that way, one of the main effects of Trump's move will be to increase pressure on international financial institutions to pick a side in the US–China rivalry.

Australia and Hong Kong

Australia has tended to be more circumspect towards Hong Kong than its Anglosphere allies. In the 1990s, the ALP government was divided on Governor Patten's last-minute democratic reforms and rejected calls to boycott the 1997 handover ceremony after Beijing undid some of them. Australia's response to the anti-ELAB movement reflected these traditional policy habits, which have involved criticism of Beijing at times, but also confidence-building measures to prop up the Basic Law regime.

Striking a discordant note amid the turmoil, DFAT officials spent 2019 finalising a new free-trade agreement with Hong Kong. It came into effect on 17 January, on a day that small demonstrations were calling on China to release detainees. Existing separately to the China–Australia Free-Trade Agreement, the agreement with Hong Kong represents a vote of confidence in the 'one country, two systems' principle. For Liberal MP Dave Sharma, that was part of the justification – it would 'reaffirm Hong Kong's unique status within "one country, two systems" and reaffirm its unique constitutional arrangements'.[5] But it was finalised at precisely the time that Scott Morrison was criticising China for undermining that unique status. Funnily enough, the usually hawkish Wolverines didn't raise a whimper about the agreement, and only the Greens and Labor's Peter Khalil criticised it.

Australia has always been wary of opening up its immigration system to Hong Kong, lest it provoke flight from the city, but calls grew in 2019 for Morrison to provide a 'safe haven' for refugees. In September, Greens leader Richard Di Natale called on the government to act. 'Like Bob Hawke in the wake of Tiananmen Square', he said, 'Scott Morrison now has an opportunity to demonstrate to the world some kindness and generosity.'[6] In truth, there was a degree of myth-making involved in this invocation of 1989. Contrary to popular belief, Hawke's tearful speech on the 1989 massacre in Beijing did not include an immediate offer of refugee protection for PRC nationals in Australia, only a visa extension, and it was not until 1993 that they were given residency. In the intervening period, all the usual anti-immigrant arguments were mobilised against them staying. *The Sydney Morning Herald* editorialised against any granting of permanent asylum, arguing that Australia should not 'bend to every wind of emotion that might happen to be generated for one group or another'.[7]

It's worth noting how paranoia towards PRC influence today is dredging up these old hostilities to the Tiananmen generation. Clive Hamilton is one such critic of Hawke's generosity: 'The real long-term effect of Hawke's decision was to lay the foundations for Beijing's plans to have Australia conform to its wishes', he claims.[8] While rhetorically pro–Hong Kong, therefore, China hawks have been retailing narratives that make it less likely that Australia will open its doors to refugees from the city.

While rejecting calls for a 'safe haven' for Hong Kong refugees – that is, a dedicated humanitarian intake – Morrison's eventual decision was in fact not that different from Hawke's: Hong Kongers who were already here for work or study received temporary visa extensions, but they will have to follow the normal pathway to residency. A large dose of economic self-interest informed the second element of the government's package, which was to open a special pathway for Hong Kong businesses to relocate to Australia: skills and capital remain the priority in Australia's immigration policy for Hong Kong. Morrison's decision, as activists pointed out, was more likely to advantage wealthy pro-Beijing families than to assist Hong Kong's poor – and now vulnerable – youth, who had been the mainstay of the anti-ELAB campaign. Some Hong Kongers in Australia have and will apply for protection; whether or not they receive it depends on the sluggish workings of the asylum bureaucracy. Meanwhile, there has been a surge in applications for Significant Investor Visas from Hong Kong, which require an up-front A$5 million investment. Those who try to seek refuge here without a valid visa will receive temporary protection at best. If any Hong Kongers escaping the city by speedboat were to make it to Australia's shores, they would face offshore detention and resettlement elsewhere. At worst, they might risk being returned to Hong Kong. As shocking as it sounds, Australia has in fact deported asylum seekers back to the PRC as recently as 2018.[9]

Before and after the passing of Hong Kong's national-security legislation, Australia joined the United States and other allies in issuing statements criticising China. Some of these pointedly accuse it of undermining the Sino–British Joint Declaration, which Beijing recognises as a legally binding treaty, but one that has been superseded by the Basic Law. Conservative backbenchers have been more vocal, with Tim Wilson travelling to Hong Kong for a photo-op from the front lines – a strange sight, given his record of endorsing, even encouraging, police violence against demonstrators in Australia.

Elite opinion was not all one way though. It was striking, for instance, to note the turn taken by *The Australian* in November 2019, when it ran a week-long diatribe against the anti-ELAB movement, featuring front-page headlines such as 'The Protestors, Not the Police, Are the Problem.'[10] Rhetorical support didn't necessarily translate into a warm welcome for Hong Kong activists either: Border Force interrogated student unionists travelling to Australia on a speaking tour about their possible involvement in violent demonstrations. 'I am angry,' one student said, 'because I feel like those police have a political stance towards the Hong Kong movement, and because of that, they seem to restrict my freedom to travel, my freedom of movement.'[11] Photos emerged in parts of the country of police expressing solidarity with their colleagues in the Hong Kong Police Force, hardly surprising given the Australian police's longstanding training and exchange partnerships with the city.

In the wake of the passage of Hong Kong's new legislation, Australia suspended its extradition treaty with Hong Kong. When it came to the actual letter of the law, though, Australia's own ever-expanding national-security legislation put it in a poor position to criticise. Australia's terrorism laws, like Hong Kong's, potentially criminalise much that we might think of as normal protesting activity – one of many features of the legislation that a UN special rapporteur criticised in 2012. The convergence was highlighted when David Neal, of the Law Council of Australia, testified before the

Senate on the Australian Security Intelligence Organisation Amendment
Bill, among the provisions of which was to expand the scope of ASIO's
compulsory questioning warrants to cases of foreign interference. Neal
pointed out that the bill took its definition of foreign interference from
the *ASIO Act*, where it includes any deceptive behaviour carried out in
collaboration with a foreign power that is 'detrimental to the interests of
Australia'. This, Neal argued, was even vaguer than the definition given
by the Hong Kong legislation's articles on collusion. ASIO director Mike
Burgess angrily rejected any such comparison, but the example he chose
to defend the bill only reinforced the point. Under the Hong Kong legislation, he said, 'if you damage public transport, that is a terrorism offence,
and there is a maximum sentence for that offence of life imprisonment'.[12]
Quite true, and shocking. But this is also a perfectly accurate description
of the scope and effect of Australia's counterterrorism laws.

The sad fact is that Australian security laws now serve more as a model
than as a counter-example for repressive governments in Asia. Around
the same time that Hong Kong introduced its legislation, but drawing
much less international criticism, Philippines president Rodrigo Duterte
introduced a sweeping new *Anti-Terrorism Act*. In lobbying to extend the
period of detention without charge to fourteen days, Philippines security officials referenced similar provisions in Australian laws from the
2000s, and it eventually emerged that Australia had advised the government in drafting the law. Despite Amnesty International warning that the
Philippines' 'dangerously broad counterinsurgency strategy has led to an
increase in human rights violations against human-rights defenders and
political activists across the country', Australia continues to collaborate
closely with the country on counterterrorism issues.

Of course, for many in Hong Kong this is beside the point. Their mis-
trust of China is more about certain features of the mainland's judicial
system than about the specifics of any law. But for those wishing to support them, the situation raises some of the same questions of strategy I've
highlighted elsewhere: should we frame criticisms of China in terms of
idealised, black-and-white differences between 'democracy' and 'authoritarianism', or from a standpoint that recognises the disturbing similarities
between China's anti-democratic tactics and those that Australia adopts
at home and turns a blind eye to elsewhere in Asia?

On the ground in Australia, most of the concrete support for Hong Kong came from the left at first. At two rallies in Sydney I went to one weekend in August, almost all of the non–Hong Kong participants were defenders of civil liberties in Australia as much as Hong Kong – unionists, environmentalists and socialists. When it came to connecting the issues in Hong Kong with those in Australia, though, there was a gap to be bridged. On Friday evening in Martin Place I struck up a conversation with a woman handing out flyers decrying the 'Chinalisation' of Australia, citing as evidence the buy-up of baby formula, and the presence of international students from the PRC. I put it to her that this was needlessly xenophobic and might alienate potential allies. As we went back and forth, I can't say I persuaded her, but we found common ground on a couple of points: Pauline Hanson was bad news, and only Chinese people could save China.

As the struggle in Hong Kong wore on, and Trump escalated his rhetoric against China, there was an undeniable shift to the right in the campaign. 'The only good communist is a dead communist,' one South Vietnamese activist declared at a rally in Melbourne.[13] Monash University Hong Kong specialist Kevin Carrico encouraged the movement's growing MAGA-fication by printing and distributing his own red caps emblazoned with the slogan 'Make Hong Kong Great Again'. Meanwhile, far-right provocateur Avi Yemini gained a new fan base when he produced a series of clips targeting pro-Beijing students in Melbourne for British neo-Nazi Tommy Robinson's website. As members of the American alt-right group Patriot Prayer had done, Yemini sought to capitalise on his new celebrity as an anti-totalitarian warrior by travelling to Hong Kong. Other cast-offs from the fragmenting Patriot milieu seized on the opportunity to combine advocacy for Hong Kong with attacks on political enemies – such as Victorian premier Dan Andrews – whom they represented as pawns of Beijing.

This new trend was certainly not universally welcomed. The Chinese-Australian artist Badiucao, whose drawings and multi-coloured Lennon Wall flag became symbols of the anti-ELAB campaign, was among those who were keen to draw a line between their objectives and those of the anti-Chinese right. But voices such as his often felt like the minority in a dissident milieu that was rapidly moving rightward.

The risk, of course, was that by being associated with such unsavoury allies, the Hong Kong cause would eventually become tainted in the public eye. On the eve of the United States' 2020 presidential election, staff working for media tycoon Jimmy Lai –whose *Apple Daily* was the Hong Kong's main opposition tabloid – were caught out in a deceptive scheme to push lurid stories to the Western press about the China dealings of Joe Biden's son, Hunter. It was a bad look for Lai, and a much more substantial effort to interfere in the US elections than anything the CCP was accused of doing. Hong Kong was not the bastion of Trumpism it was sometimes made out to be: polling indicated that the city preferred a Biden win by a margin of forty-two to thirty-six. But in the absence of political parties or civil society forums capable of expressing a collective view from the anti-ELAB camp, oppositionists with a large platform were free to give the world that impression.

Which Way Forward

As Beijing gradually remakes Hong Kong in its image, hope for the city tends to rest on its historical identity as a bridge between China and the world. Even socialists like Au Loong-Yu believe that the historical Sino–Western modus vivendi in Hong Kong sets limits to Beijing's ability to assimilate the city to mainland norms. Should America abandon the city, he writes in his firsthand account of the anti-ELAB campaign, *Hong Kong in Revolt*, 'Chinese companies will be immediately cash poor, and Xi Jinping's Belt and Road Initiative mega-project will be finished off. Hong Kong is Beijing's blessing, but it could also be its Achilles heel if it tries to eliminate Hong Kong's special status.'[14]

I'm not so sure of this myself. By mid-2020, business confidence was at an all-time low in Hong Kong, and the American Chamber of Commerce found that a third of its members were considering leaving the city.[15] But will the exodus eventuate, or will the city's corporate elite accommodate to the new reality? Expatriate capital is, after all, an unlikely ally in any struggle for democracy. 'Business is looking forward to an end to the disruption,' one senior Australian businessman told *The Australian Financial Review* in May 2020.[16] He was confident his colleagues felt the same way.

The emphasis on Hong Kong's special status, which is defined in essentially pro-business terms, set limits on what was otherwise a clearly progressive campaign in 2019. In a city where 20 per cent of people live below the poverty line, the absence of economic justice from anti-ELAB's vision of freedom prevented it from mobilising much of the city's working class.

Similarly, the sentiment that Hong Kong deserves certain rights and privileges because it is *different* to the rest of China, a view reinforced by localist identity politics, limited its ability to win allies on the mainland. During the debate on the extradition bill, one Hong Kong liberal even went so far as to argue that the bill might be acceptable if it were to apply to mainlanders alone! Yet despite Beijing's relentless propaganda, the views of mainlanders in Hong Kong were in fact evenly divided for and against the movement. The 7 July march to Hong Kong's high-speed rail station, where campaigners greeted mainland visitors with Mandarin slogans and simplified-character leaflets, was by all accounts a success; Au describes it as 'one of the most delightful marches I went on during the 2019 revolt'.[17]

In China itself, pro–Hong Kong views were far from uncommon in online discussion. And while any immediate revival of democracy activism in China looks unlikely, those fighting on other fronts today can see they have a common enemy in an intrusive party-state, and signal solidarity with Hong Kong by borrowing the city's slogans. Students rallying against COVID-19 restrictions on mainland campuses, for instance, raised their own 'five demands', including the democratisation of university administration.[18] Those disturbed by the thought of Hong Kong simply becoming 'another Chinese city' would do well to keep in mind that those other Chinese cities are regularly the scene of disruptive strikes and demonstrations.

How do societies make themselves more democratic? Hong Kong's theorists of *laam chau* tap into a wider line of thinking that's coming back into fashion in the West too: that hard-driving competition against China can push it towards some kind of collapse, from which a more democratic society will emerge. It's very true that the fall of the Soviet Union still haunts the CCP. But it's a dangerous delusion to pin any hope for a more democratic, less nationalistic China emerging from such a scenario.

I remember being in a postgraduate seminar in the United States
and looking at opinion polls from Russia in the 1990s, which showed a
growing hostility to democracy. For those inclined to see things in a certain way, it was possible to draw the conclusion that Russians were just
ill-disposed to democracy. But of course the respondents to the poll were
people living in a country where the transition to 'democracy' had seen
the rapid privatisation of its economy, resulting in rampant corruption
and profiteering, and a dramatic decline in living standards and life expectancy. All of this was carried out on the advice of American experts. By
deliberately associating democracy with the ravages of neoliberalism, the
West ended up discrediting the term and fostering a receptive audience
for an authoritarian, nationalist backlash led by Vladimir Putin.

The pursuit of a cold-war alliance against China can have the same effect
in the West itself: the reduction of democracy to an empty political slogan.
In the wake of the police murder of George Floyd in the United States,
the Black Lives Matter revolt gave the world the same images of teargas-
choked streets and police repression that had emerged in Hong Kong. Yet
the American politicians most given to high-minded rhetoric in support
of Hong Kong were quick to mimic Beijing in their denunciations of Black
Lives Matter activists as 'rioters'. On that year's anniversary of Tiananmen,
The New York Times published an op-ed by Senator Tom Cotton, in which
he called for the government to send in troops to put down the demonstrations. In exposing the authoritarian mindset of America's new Cold
Warriors, and sparking solidarity actions worldwide, Black Lives Matter
rendered concrete a point that the Hong Kong left had been making for
some time – that a marriage of convenience with the Western right risked
compromising the cause, and that alternative alliances with genuinely like-
minded critics of police violence were available, and needed.

In all modern cases of a society democratising, the change has come
not from international pressure but from the actions of ordinary people
from below, specifically workers. In *The Washington Post*, a recent study of
150 political movements since 1900 found that 'protest movements dominated by industrial workers outperform all other protest campaigns in
bringing about democracy'.[19] It's not that hard to grasp why working-class
involvement was a key variable in determining their outcome. By simultaneously asserting themselves at both the political and workplace levels,

workers can quickly erode the less formal mechanisms of influence and privilege that sustain authoritarian systems, and in doing so create new structures of social cohesion on the basis of horizontal solidarity. We see this now in Myanmar, with unions coming to the fore in the resistance to the recent military coup.

Activists, should they so choose, can still play a role in shifting the framing of the Hong Kong issue in this direction of grassroots solidarity. Hong Kong unions certainly need support. Leading union activists are facing jail sentences, and politically active unions themselves are facing attack. Cathay Pacific, for example, is now refusing to negotiate pay and conditions with its staff. A union-centred response also points to a way through some of the impasses that the anti-ELAB campaign ran up against: it offers the best chance of drawing in wider sections of the Hong Kong population and of crafting a message that can win wider support inside China itself.

Whether or not Hong Kong is to be considered 'part of China' in a historical or cultural sense is a debate for interested scholars and the people of Hong Kong. The fact is, though, in political terms Hong Kong is very much part of the People's Republic of China today. Various forms of international pressure may help the people of Hong Kong, but Beijing is well equipped to handle these: the challenges they present are predictable, and Beijing has had decades of practice in responding to them. It's only really a challenge from within China that can force it into genuine concessions.

In thinking about what role, if any, Australia might play in determining Hong Kong's future, much of what I say in the rest of the book should be kept in mind: a politics towards China that is guided by democratic principles would look very different to what we have today. Australia's domestic campaign against foreign interference has contributed to a global climate of paranoia that only encourages authoritarian crackdowns, which are justified in the same terms. Calls for Australia to 'decouple' from China reinforce Beijing's view that the party has little to lose by prioritising security above the rule of law in Hong Kong. Nowhere will democracy be served by a new cold war, and least of all Hong Kong. That basic fact should prompt us to seriously rethink the mode in which people outside China extend support to the people there – now and when their struggle revives.

8. SOVEREIGNTY, VALUES AND RACISM

More than once in this book, I have highlighted the astonishing regularity with which 'Australian sovereignty' is invoked in discussions of China. The ubiquity of this term raises the temperature of the political debate to a level at which alternatives to current policies are all but foreclosed – if every new law or every new measure is essential to the defence of sovereignty, what alternative is there? A second effect of this rhetoric is to obscure the essentially *conflicted* nature of sovereignty in Australia today. Indigenous sovereignty, as activists remind us, was never ceded. Whose sovereignty is at stake, then, when we rush to defend 'Australian sovereignty' in the face of China?

As an external enemy par excellence, China normalises white Australia's claim to this land and voids that of Indigenous Australians. Is there something specific to settler colonies and their historical anxieties that makes this rhetorical move more likely? Quite possibly. But the indigenous experience can never be entirely erased from consciousness. It returns as analogy, as white Australia imagines itself the victim of a foreign invasion.

Heather Rose's *Bruny* (2019), the first invasion novel of the new era, renders this analogy explicit. In the not-too-distant future, Australia has finally had to choose between China and the United States, and it has chosen China. Tasmania's Liberal Party premier has signed up to the Belt and Road Initiative and is building a bridge from Hobart to Bruny Island using Chinese steel, imported Chinese labour – and all for no obvious purpose. When the bridge is hit by a mysterious explosion and construction stalls, the premier hires his sister Astrid, who works at the United Nations, to smooth his public image. She soon becomes suspicious of her brother's friendly dealings with Chinese officials, and the influx of PRC tourists and investors to Tasmania:

> Is this how the Aborigines had felt? I wondered. All these foreigners arriving. Arriving and not leaving again. Taking up residence. Making homes in all the best places. Establishing their own rules. Making you beholden to them. Until you were worth nothing.[1]

Astrid is worldly enough, and sufficiently sceptical of the United States, to appreciate why Australia might position itself the way it has. But her suspicions grow throughout the novel. Maybe the bridge has something to do with China's designs on Antarctica? Then a shocking truth is revealed: the federal government has sold the entire state of Tasmania to China! To release population pressure and social tensions on the Chinese mainland, Beijing has decided to offer its loyal middle class (those who score well on the social credit system, that is) the opportunity to move to the more salubrious environment of Tasmania. The bridge, we discover, is to transport the existing Tasmanian population to Bruny Island, which will make room for the new arrivals. Tasmania's white Australians thus face the exact same fate as its original Indigenous population, relocated to remote island settlements.

Today's China panic engages question of Chinese-Australian history too. As the balance of the Chinese-Australian population has shifted towards immigrants from the PRC, the history of Chinese in Australia, and of anti-Chinese racism, has acquired new sensitivities. Some have voiced concerns that the CCP will exploit a narrative of Chinese 'victimhood' to advance its interests, citing the efforts of Huang Xiangmo to elicit formal apologies for past anti-Chinese racism. John Garnaut describes the question of historical apologies as a 'fault line' that 'Beijing is working'.[2] At the most extreme end of the debate, Hamilton has suggested that China intends to use (questionable) evidence of Chinese contact with northern Australia before white settlement to lay a territorial claim to the continent.[3]

Bruny gives expression to this new nervousness towards acknowledging the historical ties between China and Australia. When the Tasmanian premier gives a speech recognising the presence of Chinese in nineteenth-century Tasmania, it worries Astrid: 'It made it sound like China had staked a claim years ago and was coming back for more.'[4] Left to propagate, such anxieties can only lead in one direction: the dominant Anglo-Australian majority will increasingly police historical narratives of Chinese Australia and anti-Chinese racism.

Rose has blended many elements of today's China panic into her colonisation narrative, making it something of a fictional companion volume to Hamilton's *Silent Invasion*. Both express a sense of the inevitability of Australian dependency on China, facilitated by naive and greedy politicians. Both exhibit the same connect-the-dots view of Chinese-Australian organisations, be they religious groups or native place associations, all having vague 'links' to the CCP. What's more, Rose's plot envisages the same solution that Hamilton and his ilk propose for Australia's China worries today: faith in the intelligence agencies as democracy's last line of defence against authoritarianism. Astrid, you see, is no mere UN employee. She doubles as a CIA agent, and in the novel's conclusion she links up with a rogue member of ASIO and a squad of wetsuit-clad operatives to blow up the Bruny bridge. The vigilantism is a cathartic experience for her. As the bridge falls, Astrid's cynicism drops away, and she articulates one of the novel's key political lessons: the indispensability of America as the 'heartland of democracy'. 'Gore Vidal was right,' she muses, 'the US is a corrupted democracy, but it's still the best chance humans have of living peacefully.'[5]

There are elements of satire to *Bruny*, but its dedication to 'everyone who is still awake' and an afterword, in which Rose says she wrote the book for Tasmania and its people, give it an unmistakably earnest framing. It's certainly been read as a serious political novel, which is unsurprising, given how closely it resonates with the tone of today's media coverage of China. 'People who have read it keep sending me things from the press,' Rose told one interviewer, 'saying, "How did you know?"'[6]

Rose herself is adamant that her book is not racist, and few reviewers have dissented. Critical of corruption in Australian political life and vexed by climate change, Rose's views seem typical, in many ways, of liberal opinion in Australia. But the same of course can be said of Clive Hamilton. Although fully conscious of the distinction between the Chinese state and the Chinese people, Rose nevertheless indulges tired

racial stereotypes at times – for instance, that Chinese people lack cre-
ativity. She presents us with a fantasy of a Chinese takeover in which
almost all Chinese in Tasmania are seemingly implicated, and invites
white Australians to imagine the fate of the island's Indigenous population as their own. It's a deeply problematic narrative, with more than
a passing resemblance to the nativist and racial replacement theories of
today's far right. Yet the question of race has been almost entirely missing from *Bruny*'s critical reception. Rose's novel has received prestigious
awards and is now scheduled to be made into a television series. The situation highlights, to my mind, the great difficulty we have in thinking and
talking about racism in Australia today.

Values and Loyalty

No questions are more divisive in this whole discussion than those that
concern racism: the vehemence with which some have diagnosed an
underlying racism in Australia's response to China has been met with
equally strenuous denial by those implicated in the charge. We're not anti-
Chinese, they insist, we're anti-CCP. To introduce the 'r-word' into the
discussion is a distraction – a ploy even – that only serves the interests
of Beijing. To do so silences not just Anglo-Australian CCP critics but
also dissident Chinese voices – itself a form of racism, some go so far as
to claim. Australians simply need to set aside their 'xenophobia-phobia',
stop navel-gazing and get on with tackling the CCP.

Australia's official self-image is one of happy multiculturalism. We
were reminded of this recently, when the Senate debated a motion to
condemn right-wing extremism. The government objected to the phrase
'there has been a significant increase in far-right extremism in Australia',
and replaced it with 'Australia is one of the most successful multicultural
countries in the world'.[7] We prefer to think of racism as an archaic, irrational phenomenon, safely isolated from the mainstream. And we primarily
discuss racism, in this sense, as a feature of an individual's worldview:
someone is racist if their thoughts and actions betray a hostility to others because of their race. Official anti-racism dwells on the interpersonal
encounter – racist slurs on the street, or the bully on the bus. Racism is a
product of a poor upbringing, to be remedied by education, anti-racism

training, or exposure to the minority or migrant, through which the individual learns that they are 'people just like us'.

Defined in this way, racism is not a factor driving Australia's policy response to China today. We certainly don't find contemporary critics of the CCP demonstrating the kind of crude prejudice that we see, for example, in *The Bulletin*'s nineteenth century attacks: 'Wherever the pig-tailed pagans herd on Australasian soil, they introduce and practice vices the most detestable and damnable.'[8] A simple anti-Asian prejudice was no doubt much more prevalent among Australian elites in the nineteenth century than it is today. But at the same time, the case for Chinese exclusion was not made exclusively in those terms. Those lobbying against Asian migration constructed a socio-economic case against them: they referred to the deleterious effect of competition in the workplace, and of the possible emergence of a 'coolie' economy in northern Australia. They pointed to political baggage that was believed to render them incapable of full participation in Australian democracy. Most relevant to today's discussion, they highlighted the political risks of inviting Asians in.

Reducing racism to individual prejudice is what has enabled conservatives to maintain that policies widely recognised as racist were something different entirely. In his defence of the White Australia policy – the first substantial Act of the new Australian Commonwealth in 1901 – Keith Windschuttle argued against the consensus view of it as a racist policy and enumerated what he saw as the reasonable, rational grounds for it, among them national security. At the turn of the century, Japan occupied a place in Australian discourse not dissimilar to that which China occupies today: it was seen as an authoritarian rising power, which might exploit its expatriate citizenry as a conduit for political influence. Japan's national ideals, said the minister of defence, were 'as unlike our own as it is possible to be'. *The Age* editorialised that 'the presence of Japanese in large numbers in any part of this continent would afford an excuse for the fussy intervention of their Government'. For Windschuttle, the anti-Japanese sentiment (and policy) of this time was no racist phobia, but far-sighted geopolitical thinking, vindicated by the fact that Australia ultimately did go to war with Japan in the 1940s: 'Those Australian politicians who first identified the Japanese yellow peril as a threat to Australian security were basically right.'[9]

Racism is primarily a question of social effects, not individual intentions. The White Australia policy was racist because it erected barriers that
prevented certain people from entering and participating in Australian
society on the basis of generalised assumptions about the community
to which they belonged. These assumptions might take the form of
gross stereotypes of racial inferiority, but that is not the only way racism
functions: it also depicts particular communities as clannish, secretive,
dangerous and working to white-ant Australian society. Often, such
assumptions only become activated against a certain configuration of
international politics. From the view that China is a hostile enemy, intent
on abrogating Australia's sovereignty, it is only a short step towards heightened suspicion of anyone of Chinese background. No amount of watching
our language and carefully distinguishing criticisms of the CCP from 'the
Chinese' – however well-intentioned – will prevent this from occurring.

The notion of 'national sovereignty' embodies certain basic imperatives that provide the ultimate justification for exercising political
authority: to defend the state and its citizenry, to preserve its territory.
Little wonder, then, that it now underpins the Australian Defence Force's
extreme measures to exclude asylum seekers from its soil – Operation
Sovereign Borders. It's when sovereignty is felt to be endangered that the
most extreme acts of state power become thinkable: moving the population to a war footing, or the arbitrary expulsion or detention of those
members of the body politic identified as potentially subversive. If a society is facing a foreign invasion, this response will seem rational to many.
Likewise, if a community convinces itself that an invasion is coming,
or that a just war against the offending enemy is on the horizon, taking
such pre-emptive steps will seem like the right thing to do. For those of
the mindset that war with China is inevitable and/or desirable, treating
the Chinese-Australian community as a fifth column is simply the logical conclusion.

In Australia today, as in many parts of the world, people typically
express preferences as to the composition of the population in terms of
'values', not in terms of race. A phrase with little in the way of intellectual history, 'Australian values' came into common parlance in the 2000s,
during the global war on terror, and was institutionalised in 2007, when
the government introduced a citizenship test. For a long time, Muslims

bore the brunt of this new discourse, but the focus is now widening to include Chinese immigrants.

Calls to slash the intake of immigrants from the PRC moved from the margins to the mainstream in Peter Hartcher's 2019 essay *Red Flag*. Hartcher argued that preference should be given to immigrants 'with the most compatible values'. He took pains to insulate his proposal from any charge of racism. We could make up for the reduction of PRC immigrants, he believed, by taking in more people from Hong Kong and Taiwan – ethnically Chinese, but more likely to share Australia's values. In that sense, this wasn't so much a call for a *White* Australia policy, as a *right* Australian policy – for Hartcher, migrants from the PRC were simply the wrong kind of Australian. Note, though, the way race returned via the back door: by suggesting that the reduction of PRC immigrants be compensated for with Chinese from outside China, Hartcher was effectively reviving the idea of a racial quota – something the Department of Immigration does not practise today.

Are there such things as Australian values? Officially there are. The government's recently revised 'Australian Values Statement', which all immigrants must sign when they apply for a visa, is a collection of liberal nostrums: respect for the freedom and dignity of the individual, freedom of religion, rule of law, equality of opportunity. Not just democracy in the abstract but 'parliamentary democracy' is on the list. Mateship is not, despite Howard's efforts to inject this term into public life during his prime ministership. In its place, we find 'a "fair go" that embraces mutual respect, tolerance, compassion for those in need [and] equality of opportunity for all'. These are unobjectionable aspirations for the most part. It would certainly be controversial for anyone in public life to take a stand *against* any of them. But to call these 'values' implies something more than acceptance – that these are hallmarks of what it is to be Australian.

Since when has that been the case, though? Australia's parliament is old, but how democratic was it before the 1960s, when Indigenous Australians finally gained the vote? Today, when Indigenous Australians comprise 28 per cent of the adult prison population (but only 3 per cent of the overall population), to what extent can we say that their 'freedom and dignity' is being respected? Similarly, by various measures, including the gender pay gap, Australia is still far from realising full gender equality.

And would an outside observer, looking at Australia's refugee detention policy, see 'compassion for those in need'? Would they even see the rule of law? On more than one occasion, human-rights organisations have accused politicians of violating that 'Australian value' in the course of defending this policy. I certainly won't admit to sharing a set of common values with the people responsible for this long-running act of brutality. If someone were to extrapolate a set of 'Australian values' from the actual functioning of our system, what would they come up with?

The best we can say for this list of values is that it outlines a field of contestation, in which ongoing efforts by certain Australians to realise aspirations to justice and equality meet resistance from fellow Australians. This has always been the case. When we look at history, we find that the democratic potential of liberalism was usually realised by drawn-out, at times even bloody, struggles for recognition and the expansion of the franchise. These struggles often pitted partisans of liberty against the 'liberals' of the day.

It gets more confusing when we consider which countries Australia is said to 'share values' with. There is the club of settler colonial offshoots, such as Canada and the United States – each with their persistent racial fault lines. We share values with Israel, a state that openly discriminates against Palestinians who hold citizenship, while imposing a harsh military occupation on the rest. Duterte's strongman rule in the Philippines and Modi's in India have not deterred our diplomats from touting the values we share with these countries. When Morrison was readying for a trip that would involve promoting Australian arms exports to an Indian military that was then trampling on Kashmir's aspirations for self-determination, the political editor of *The Australian*, Greg Sheridan, reassured us that 'the Indian government is a democracy and all its major political tendencies are represented by parties in good standing'.[10] Functioning elections, then, seem to be a baseline for 'shared values' – but how functioning do they have to be? The city-state of Singapore, which permits almost no independent civil society (an activist there was recently jailed for hosting a Zoom call with Joshua Wong), is also said to be a country that Australia 'shares values' with. Even Vietnam, a single-party communist state with no democracy at all, has made the list recently. When both countries inked their Plan of Action for the Strategic Partnership in 2019, Australia described the relationship as one of 'mutual respect, mutual trust, converging interests and deepening links'.[11] In 2020, as the plan entered its third phase, Australia's foreign minister, Marise Payne, declared that it was now grounded in 'shared values'.[12]

If Australia claims to have 'shared values' with communist Vietnam, but very different values from communist China, it's hard not to conclude that talk of 'values' is simply code for political alignments. But for argument's sake, let's compare 'Chinese values' with Australian. The PRC, like Australia, has an official list of values, and like Australia it sees these as different to the values of the West: it calls them 'socialist values'. But it turns out that most of them are the same as Australia's. They include freedom, equality, democracy and the rule of law. 'Patriotism' is explicit in China's discourse, though only implicit in ours. As with the values on our list, there's nothing particularly remarkable or unique about these 'Chinese values'.

Staying at this superficial level, how then might we conjure the idea of a stark divide between Chinese and Australian values? Obviously, there's really only one way to do this: by extrapolating China's 'values' from the actual functioning of its system. Note, though, that this is precisely what we do not do for ourselves (or for our allies). When Australia fails to live up to its values, it's still our aspirations that are said to represent the deeper truth about our system. In China's case, by contrast, we identify its values in its practices, not in its professions of virtue. To embrace 'Australian values' or 'democratic values', therefore, is to adopt not so much a distinct set of values as a willingness to excuse hypocrisy.

If values talk is hard to make sense of at the level of international relations, what about at the individual level? Such language needn't always be exclusionary. When values get held up as a standard for citizenship, one response has been to insist that, yes, Chinese immigrants do share Australian values, or eventually come to embrace them after living here for a while. This is the thrust of John Fitzgerald's book *Big White Lie*, which looks at the first century of Chinese migration to Australia. The lie that John ably refutes here is that these migrants were unable to fit into Australian society and its political culture: in his view, they displayed Australian values.

As well-meaning as it is, though, this gesture to inclusivity still invests too much in the notion of Australian values. Showing how one wave of

Chinese migration measured up to this standard licenses its use against future migrants. 'Earlier generations of Chinese-heritage immigrants from Malaysia, Singapore, Hong Kong and Taiwan shared Australia's liberal democratic values,' Fitzgerald writes in a 2014 article; but he worries that recent migrants from the PRC may not.[13]

The example he provides as evidence – of a Chinese Australian who rejects 'Australia's liberal democratic values' – is telling. 'It's not right, democracy,' a member of the 1989 Tiananmen influx of immigrants complains to him. 'America talks about universal human values and criticises China, and then goes to war whenever it likes. Now look at America. China may not be democratic, but it gets results. And now that China is rich and strong, it won't be pushed around by America or anyone else. China has different values.' Fitzgerald sees in this rejection the pernicious influence of Beijing on Chinese-language media in Australia, with its propaganda message of distinctive Chinese values. But is that a satisfactory explanation?

I've had similar encounters myself. While I was gawking at the fringes of a pro-Beijing rally in Sydney, a Chinese Australian sporting a PRC flag on his cap sidled up to me. He complained that the Australian media wasn't giving people the full picture on Hong Kong – of the violence and property destruction perpetrated by the anti-ELAB side. 'You've probably got a point,' I said. 'Still,' I explained, 'I sympathise with people asking for more democracy.' That set him chortling. 'Democracy! You vote for the Liberal Party, the Labor Party, it doesn't matter – you get the same policies.' Again, it was hard to argue with that.

In both John's case and mine, what we see is not so much an abstract, philosophical rejection of liberalism, but a critique of it in practice. What these 'pro-Beijing' immigrants are doing is looking beyond the rhetoric of Western values to certain realities – America as a belligerent bully, and Australia's parliamentary democracy as a hollowed-out field offering little in the way of substantive policy choice. That is to say, they're applying to 'Australian values' the lens that we apply to China's; they are examining the actual functioning of the system and finding it wanting. But it's this critical thinking, of course, that we find unacceptable from immigrants. When we ask them to embrace our values, we're actually asking them to retain faith in our system, despite its evident flaws, and to reject the notion that there might be legitimate alternatives to it. This is why talk of values can easily give way to the more muscular language of loyalty.

The 'loyalty' of immigrants is a crude line of inquiry that many prefer to avoid. It can produce ugly scenes, such as Clive Hamilton's warning to anti-immigrant pundit Andrew Bolt that a 'significant proportion of the Chinese-Australian population ... is very patriotic, not to Australia, but to the People's Republic of China'.[14] But loyalty discourse, I believe, reveals what we really mean when we talk about 'values'. What we want to know is whether or not Chinese Australians will support Australia in a confrontation with China – not whether they support this or that specific policy. It's a more basic, tribalistic question of whose side they're on, and the ultimate test case for this, of course, is war. When Hamilton speculates at the end of *Silent Invasion* about the percentage of Chinese Australians loyal to the PRC versus Australia, it's to predict their response to any outbreak of war between the two countries. For someone like Hamilton, who believes that war is inevitable, or necessary, it's worrying to think that Chinese Australians might be more sceptical of the West's inherent virtue – and therefore its right to wage war on China – than the average Anglo-Australian. But since when does Australia expect immigrants to give the West carte blanche to wage war on their home countries? Is this an 'Australian value'? I certainly hope not.

Victims and Vectors

If the notion of Australian values is illusory, its consequences are very real. By propping up a mythic collective and obscuring lines of conflict that run through Australian society, it contains an inherent anti-immigrant bias. It also serves to divide Australia along communal lines by singling out specific groups as potentially incompatible with those values, therefore endangering social harmony. Three years ago, immigration minister Alan Tudge was still pointing to Muslims as the disruptive element: in a speech in London in 2018, he invoked the standard conservative catastrophism of a Europe occupied by unassimilable Muslims and called for a 'muscular ongoing promotion of our values' to combat the 'postmodern thinking' and 'identity politics' that has undermined the West's defences.[15]

More recently, though, Tudge has turned his focus to the Chinese diaspora, citing the threat of foreign interference to expand the citizenship
test with new questions on 'Australian values'.

It's important to note the way that the international and domestic
dimensions of the 'values' discourse interact to produce a language that
is punitive and paternalistic in equal measure. Heightened scrutiny of
Australian Muslims is often couched as a desire to shield them from
harmful outside influences: the figure of the terrorist recruiter, for example, manipulating the youth of western Sydney. The same is true of the
scrutiny of Chinese Australians. In Tudge's recent speech, he identified the
risk of foreign actors both harassing diaspora communities and exploiting
them to interfere in Australian affairs. According to Tudge, such groups
are 'both victims of interference and used as vectors to engage in foreign
influence'.[16] The neutral term 'vector' avoids branding a section of the
Chinese-Australian community as active 'agents of influence', and in that
sense it is a politically correct choice of words. But the consequence of
downplaying the question of agency, of course, is to reinforce an image
of Chinese Australians as unwitting pawns of the CCP.

During the war on terror, Muslims in the West experienced inces-
sant questioning about their attitudes towards terrorism and a string of
issues that came to be associated with radicalisation, including gender
equality and 'traditional' practices. One of the effects was to create two
equally stereotypical images: the good, loyal Muslim on the one hand and
the dangerous, subversive Muslim on the other. Those who resented the
questioning and refused to play the role of the good Muslim could easily
find themselves fingered as being among the bad, with potentially serious
implications Responding to charges of racism, the questioners insisted
they were motivated by legitimate criticisms of Islam and not the demonisation of any racial group. There is sometimes an echo of the 'Islam isn't a
race' defence in the common refrain today that 'I'm not anti-Chinese, I'm
just anti-CCP'. While strictly speaking neither Muslims nor CCP members and sympathisers are racial categories, a fixation on these identities
can easily give way to more conventional racial profiling.

Not all who advocate heightened surveillance of the Chinese-
Australian population as a security measure are oblivious to the social
consequences of doing so, but they can justify it: the CCP lays claim to all

ethnically Chinese people, so our vigilance must likewise extend across the diaspora, they argue; if Chinese Australians feel put upon or intimidated by this situation, they should take it up with Beijing. We don't *want* to arouse suspicion about Chinese people, but Xi Jinping obliges us to.

There are questions worth asking about the CCP's evolving attitude to the Chinese diaspora. Historically, the PRC was not particularly interested in the overseas Chinese. That's now changing, as its global status gives it the confidence to woo them. But we can't simply conclude that because something is part of the CCP's rhetorical self-image it is a practical reality, or that the effect of any policy mirrors its intent. Most Australians of Chinese descent were not born in China, and most go through life here without feeling any pressure to respond to overtures from Beijing. In fact, I'd argue that Australia's tendency to reduce this community to 'victims' or 'vectors' of CCP interference is doing much more to prompt Chinese Australians to reflect on their hereditary ties to China.

After 9/11, as outsiders increasingly came to view those of Muslim faith through the lens of religion, immigrants who had previously identified primarily in national terms felt themselves to be seen as Muslim. Some have described the experience of 'waking up Muslim' after 9/11. Something similar is being felt among Australian-born Chinese, who have had to grapple with their Chineseness not as a result of PRC interference but because of Australian paranoia towards it. Consider the effect, for example, of Morrison saying that Zhao Lijian's tweet criticising Australian war crimes in Afghanistan would not 'diminish our respect for and appreciation of our Chinese-Australian community'.[17] Why would anyone think it would? What do they have to do with the Twitter feed of a PRC foreign ministry employee?

In any diaspora community, there'll be some who take a keen interest in the politics of their country of origin. Just as Irish Australia had its unionists and its nationalists, and Italian Australia its monarchists and communists, some Chinese Australians have positive feelings towards the PRC and its ruling party, some are resolutely hostile to it. The distribution of views is fairly predictable: well positioned to take advantage of them, business figures tend to favour strong Australia–China relations and cultivate ties at both ends of the relationship. At the other end of the spectrum are the exiles – politically active dissidents, members of Tibet and Xinjiang advocacy groups. But there are many more who give little thought to their views on the PRC and its politics, and now face expectations that they should.

In chapter 4, I discussed the way that, in the political sphere, scrutiny of Chinese candidates' ties to the 'United Front' has sidelined all other consideration of their potential contributions. To the extent that such 'links' represent actual political views, we need to remember that they represent views about China, not Australia – that is to say, they represent a kind of diasporic nationalism. I'm not aware of any evidence, for example, showing that someone who supports the CCP's crackdown in Hong Kong is also likely, therefore, to support Australia becoming a single-party state. This kind of diasporic nationalism, as I've highlighted in this chapter, exists in a certain dialogue with the dominant discourse of 'Australian values'. It may reflect direct experiences of discrimination and racism. Seeing the truth about 'Australian values' from an immigrant standpoint can open people up to the view that it might be a better option for China to stick with 'Chinese values'.

It's still perfectly possible to criticise this kind of nationalism. The pro-Beijing gathering in Sydney's Belmore Park in August 2019 was certainly not to my taste politically. While some slogans were fairly anodyne – 'We love Hong Kong, we love China' – others were explicitly pro-police. 'Cops are my bros' was the sign one young guy held up. The gathering of 300-odd got rowdy towards the end, as it made its way through Chinatown, and a couple of hotheads took to the town hall steps to yell violent anti–Hong Kong slogans. Still, to my mind, the demonisation of these demonstrators reflected more than just a critique of nationalism. One account of the rally described its participants as fascists. Online, there were calls for deportations. Chris Zappone, Nine journalist and member of the Futures Council of ANU's National Security College, thought it was worth asking the question: 'If these people are so in favour of Beijing, what are they doing here?'[18] The fact is, diaspora communities in Australia regularly demonstrate in support of all sorts of causes, not all of which you or I might agree with. Think back to 2014, when Israeli airstrikes on the Gaza Strip killed hundreds of civilians, including many children. By any measure, this was a more disturbing act of state violence than anything taking place in Hong Kong in 2019. Yet when thousands of people rallied in Bondi to support Operation Protective Edge, no one publicly questioned their suitability for Australian citizenship. The media hardly batted an eyelid. If we can tolerate that (and we can), then we should be able to handle a small pro-Beijing rally.

To the extent that 'pro-Beijing' parts of the community have been maligned, other Chinese Australians have been held up as model citizens, allies in the struggle against the CCP. The Cold War dissident has always been a flattering figure for the West: 'He brings with him the promise of redemption and victory,' as American historian Richard Hofstadter once wrote.[19] Staunchly anti-Beijing groups provide valuable, authentically Chinese, validation for the West's newly confrontational stance towards China, and defend against any talk of racism. I certainly don't begrudge any of these people their voice in the debate – it is all the richer for it. But the construction of the dissident reinforces the message to Chinese Australians that 'you're either with us or against us'. It rests on a simplistic reduction of 'values' to a lone political criterion – where someone stands towards the CCP. It gives us a one-dimensional picture of the Chinese-Australian community that obscures much of its complexity.

One group that has inserted itself into today's debate is the Australian Values Alliance (AVA). The AVA espouses a 'love it or leave it' style of Aussie patriotism and has been praised by Hamilton as 'essential to any pushback' against the CCP.[20] The organisation came into being in 2016, around a campaign to shut down a gala event commemorating Mao Zedong, for which the Sydney and Melbourne town halls rented out their facilities. Victorious on that occasion, the AVA went on to similar campaigns to prevent the performance of Chinese operas from the Cultural Revolution era, which they say promote a 'fake image' of China. Shows such as this might not be everyone's cup of tea, but it's debatable whether a call to shut them down accords with what many see as a core Australian value: freedom of speech. The AVA has also lobbied Australian authorities to step up their surveillance and policing of Australia–PRC connections. It seems they believe freedom in Australia will be preserved by borrowing from PRC practices. Just as China restricts the activities of foreign journalists, the AVA calls for Australia to apply reciprocal restrictions on Chinese journalists. Should that come to pass – and it's not unthinkable – Chinese journalists will argue that it contravenes the principle of media freedom. In that case, who will have 'Australian values' on their side?

As the infrastructure of 'multiculturalism' decays, Australian officials often struggle to talk directly to migrant communities. The Department of Home Affairs' use of Google Translate to prepare non-English language information on COVID-19 demonstrates this. In an effort to bridge the gap, members of minority communities who talk a staunchly pro-Australian, assimilationist language can present themselves as exactly what the government needs. A recent example of this was the collaboration between NSW government agencies and Sound of Hope radio to provide services and information sessions for new migrants from China. Partnering with the Department of Human Services, the station ran the *Engage Australia* radio show and YouTube series, offering an orientation to life in Australia. It all sounds very wholesome, and it probably was, but an important fact seems to have gone unnoticed: Sound of Hope is part of the Falun Gong media empire.

A new-age amalgam of Qigong and Buddhist meditative practices, the idiosyncratic teachings of Falun Gong guru Li Hongzhi grew in popularity in China in the 1990s, until a mass gathering of devotees in Beijing in 1999 triggered a crackdown. While persecuted in China, the movement continued to grow abroad and has dedicated itself to ending the rule of the CCP. At its core, the Falun Gong remains a secretive, esoteric cult, but it now also runs a diverse range of anti-CCP media platforms. The best known of these is its flagship newspaper, *Epoch Times*, but similar organs have proliferated in the digital age, including New Tang Dynasty Television, Sound of Hope radio, and YouTube shows such as *China Uncensored*.

At a time when many traditional Chinese-language media outlets in Australia are struggling to survive, Falun Gong–affiliated publications have expanded their presence. A 2020 investigation by the ABC's *Background Briefing*, which drew on the testimony of ex-practitioners, as well as emails among Falun Gong members, confirmed that the free weekly *Vision Times* is also a Falun Gong publication. With its consistently anti-CCP stance, *Vision Times* has not only had a role in promoting alarmist reporting on China but in shaping it – it helped to introduce the dubious story of Wang Liqiang to the Australian public, for example. Paid government advertising can regularly be found in the *Vision Times*, and its general manager sits on the advisory board of DFAT's National

Foundation for Australia–China Relations, whose mission is to 'turbo-charge' ties with the People's Republic.[21]

Falun Gong members are obviously free to publish anything they like in Australia, and government agencies can collaborate with whom-ever they choose (as long as they know what they're getting themselves into). My point here is that by playing favourites in this way, we hold up an impossible standard for the 'good' Chinese Australian: they must be resolutely hostile to the CCP and supportive of every Western move against it. Those who promote these groups and individuals as yard-sticks against which to measure the rest of Chinese Australia also need to be aware of the kind of politics they're actually supporting. In July 2020, Sound of Hope's *Engage Australia* YouTube series was rebranded as *Voices*, a chat show pumping out a steady diet of Falun Gong talking points. Chinese Australians who subscribed to *Engage Australia* to learn about life in Australia – at the encouragement of the Department of Human Services – were instead fed conspiracy theories on the origins of COVID-19 and the CCP's involvement in Trump's election loss. If this is the wing of the Chinese-Australian community that best represents 'Australia values', new immigrants might well end up deciding that their values lie elsewhere.

These questions came to a head last October, when the Senate's Foreign Affairs, Defence and Trade Committee held an inquiry into issues facing diaspora communities in Australia. In its submission, the AVA focused on CCP surveillance of the diaspora, a theme that committee chairs Kimberley Kitching and Eric Abetz welcomed. The following day, three Chinese Australian testified on different issues, including barriers to the participation of Australians of Chinese background in public life and the need to rein in political suspicion of them. These were not top-ics that the 'Wolverine' Kitching and Abetz were interested in discussing. Kitching responded first, directing the conversation back to the role of the CCP. Abetz then went all-in, demanding the witnesses condemn the CCP before he would engage with their actual submissions.

In the aftermath of the grilling, most could see that Abetz had crossed a line. He responded in the predictable way, insisting that he was simply motivated by hostility towards the CCP, not Chinese people. The ques-tioning couldn't have been racially motivated, he pointed out, because he hadn't asked the same of the Chinese members of the AVA. This was obviously disingenuous: the different handling the two groups received was precisely the point. It sent the message that when they enter the public spotlight, any Chinese Australian who is not a flag-waving 'Australian values' patriot can expect to have their loyalties questioned. Amid the fallout, the AVA stood almost alone in continuing to publicly support Abetz, issuing an open letter in which they too questioned the 'allegiance' of the three witnesses he had interrogated, and praised his line of questioning as a 'perfect litmus test'.[22] Other Chinese Australians who were scheduled to testify at the hearings withdrew, declaring they had no intention of offering themselves up for a similar attack.

Abetz came in for criticism from many directions, but some of it missed the point. Some said he was wrong to do what he did because Chinese Australians who condemn the CCP risk endangering family members in China; others pointed out that his approach might compromise Australia's security by alienating the Chinese-Australian community. Well intentioned though these talking points might have been, they nevertheless had the effect of shifting an overdue and uncomfortable conversation about Australian attitudes back to the more familiar terrain of the big, bad CCP.

There was another important, unexplored question lingering in the background. The three witnesses that Abetz grilled were young, articulate English speakers, and they included criticisms of the CCP in their submissions and testimony. Would the public condemnation of Abetz have been quite so strong had his victims been more recent migrants, with poor English and 'links' to the United Front?

The biggest blind spot, though, was the reluctance to make any connection between the incident and the wider political context. Abetz's performance in the Senate hearings simply dramatised something that had been going on for some time. Chinese Australians have long been telling us they feel as if they've been depicted as a fifth column for the PRC. This is not down to the work of a boorish backbench clique in Canberra but is the result of bipartisan security policies which have the effect of casting suspicion on anyone with links to China. Abetz was only carrying a proposition that is widely endorsed, almost the orthodoxy in Australia today, to its logical conclusion: that the PRC is hell-bent on eroding Australian sovereignty and reducing it to a state of vassalage. If you buy that, then discourses and structures that stigmatise and intimidate Chinese Australians – and dissuade them from fully participating in public life – flow naturally. Such discourses and structures, of course, are the essence of racism.

Standing on the Brink

Crudely essentialist views of China and its people clearly exist in official circles. Much like 'values', ideas of culture and civilisation permeate popular punditry on international relations, but make their way into more serious pronouncements too. In 2019, the director of policy planning at the US State Department characterised the Trump administration's relationship with China as 'a fight with a really different civilisation and a different ideology'.[23] It can't be entirely coincidental that Australia's China panic coincides with a push to restore pride in 'Western civilisation' at Australia's universities, through ventures such as the Ramsay Centre. Some officials clearly believe, too, that these differences are not just cultural, but genetic. 'The East Asian mind and the Western mind are fundamentally different,' an anonymous Five Eyes security source opined to the ABC. 'Western thought is based on causality; East Asian thinking is like a spider's web.'[24]

Usually, though, it is the logic of the security scare that feeds today's China panic and ends up implicating all Chinese people. There are obvious ways in which specific anti-CCP language can give way to an all-embracing paranoia. When ASIO announced, as it did in late 2017, that it was watching ten candidates for political office with 'links' to PRC intelligence, it was hard to see how that would not arouse suspicion against *all* candidates of Chinese background. We find points of slippage too, when avowedly anti-CCP voices show us the extent to which their vigilance extends to anyone of Chinese ethnicity – for instance, when Hamilton mentions in *Silent Invasion*, apropos of nothing, that Bob Carr's wife is of Malaysian-Chinese background, or when he expresses alarm at the fact that the Australian Defence Force Academy employs ethnically Chinese janitors. When picked up on this point at a Lowy Institute forum, Hamilton was unrepentant: this was the office of a cybersecurity expert, and vigilance was required.[25]

There's a principle here that needs defending: criticising the CCP for its policies is not, in and of itself, racist. The idea that criticism of the Chinese government is in any way inherently 'anti-Chinese' has to be dismissed. I have to note the irony, though, of the Western public sphere loudly defending this principle in the case of China, while often overlooking it in the case of Israel, allowing critics of Zionism and supporters of Palestinian rights to be frequently attacked as antisemites. While he insists that criticising the CCP is not anti-Chinese, Abetz has been one of the most vocal in branding criticism of Israel as antisemitic, and in advancing a definition of antisemitism (that of the International Holocaust Remembrance Alliance) that is widely recognised as endangering free speech. Once again, foreign-policy priorities trump principle: friends of the West can silence critics with accusations of prejudice, but enemies cannot.

A misguided accusation that someone is personally motivated by racist bigotry can stifle debate, but this is far from the only way debate is discouraged. The fact that China has, on occasion, described the criticism it receives as racist has given rise to the view that criticism of racism might itself be part of a CCP conspiracy. 'What if the accusation of Australian racism is itself a weaponised narrative?' asks Chris Zappone. A 'weaponised narrative' attack, according to the US think-tank promoting the concept, 'undermines an opponent's civilisation, identity and will. By generating confusion, complexity, and political and social schisms, it confounds response on the part of the defender.'[26]

It's a straightforward logical fallacy that certain opinions should be avoided or rejected because of who else holds them, but it's a fallacy that is working its way into Australia's China debate. Anti-racist critique itself is now seen as suspicious, because China engages in it too. By this logic, self-criticism becomes an unaffordable luxury. Owning up to Australia's conflicted past, and the way it lives on in the present, could be giving aid and comfort to the enemy. Particularly in light of Australia's foreign-interference laws, which permit security agencies to investigate accusations that individuals are collaborating with a foreign principal to influence Australian politics, it's not hard to see how framing anti-racist critique as a 'weaponised narrative' serving CCP interests might have a silencing effect.

Today, if someone offers a criticism that coincides with something Beijing says, this is often seen as sufficient grounds to dismiss it as a 'CCP talking point'. An even worse sin, of course, is to express such criticisms in a Chinese forum. This was what New South Wales MP Shaoquett Moselmane did last February: he published an article on a Chinese website criticising anti-Chinese racism as the resurgence of anachronistic White Australia sentiments, and he was pilloried for it in the media.

At the time he was writing, Moselmane was pointing to something that was already obvious: the association of COVID-19 with China and Chinese people was sparking an upsurge of racism. Tabloids superimposed the PRC flag on images of the COVID-19 particles and spoke of 'Chinese virus pandamonium'. As returnees from Wuhan were diverted to Christmas Island, headlines singled out 'China kids' as domestic risk factors. Speculation that China had engineered and/or weaponised the virus was rife. Sky News seized on a 'dodgy dossier' linking COVID-19 to the Wuhan lab, possibly provided by the American embassy. Trump's open indulgence of these conspiracy theories was given support by Morrison's more cautious, but no less mischievous, proposal that China must submit to an independent inspection to determine the origins of the virus. China's entirely predictable opposition to the scheme gave Hartcher the opportunity to keep stirring the pot: 'it suggests the Beijing regime has a lot to hide', he claimed.[27] Letterboxing by Falun Gong activists, along with members of the recently established 'New Federal State of China', brought COVID-19 conspiracy theories to the kitchen tables of Australia.

As early as February 2020, Australia's Human Rights Commission was noting a serious spike in racial discrimination complaints attributable to COVID-19. A group of Asian-Australian activists launched an anti-racism survey, which recorded some 400 racist attacks in a three-month period.[28] In April, sixteen prominent Chinese Australians penned an open letter on anti-Asian racism, asking for 'fairness in our national debate, our media reporting and in our communities'.[29] This call took note of the way styles of 'Chinese influence' reportage – by now well-established – were exacerbating hostility to Chinese Australians during the crisis. The period saw a sustained campaign, for example, to blame 'United Front' organisations for depriving Australia of medical supplies by exporting them to China – or, alternatively, for doing political propaganda by importing the same goods from China.

A serious shift in public opinion towards immigrants from China was confirmed by the Scanlon Foundation's 'Mapping Social Cohesion' report for 2020, which found that almost half of Australians (47 per cent) had negative views towards this community. This was a huge increase from 2013, when only 13 per cent of Australians felt this way. A Lowy Institute poll released in March 2021 explored the consequences of this shift from the victim's perspective, finding that in the preceding twelve months, 31 per cent of Chinese Australians had suffered racial abuse, and 18 per cent – almost one in five – had been physically threatened or attacked because of their Chinese heritage.[30]

This rapid rise in racial animosity is simply inexplicable without reference to the way the Australian media has binged on the 'CCP influence' paradigm since 2017. One survey of major news outlets found stories on this topic have been rising exponentially: from forty stories in 2016, to 331 in 2017, and 747 in 2018.[31] During 2020, the suspicion that all Chinese were linked to the CCP combined in toxic ways with the stereotype of Chinese people as carriers of outlandish diseases. When Sydney man Raimond Kelly stood outside the Chinese consulate in Sydney cracking a whip, haranguing Chinese lined up there, he saw their masks as evidence that they were part of a CCP conspiracy to infect the world with COVID-19. 'You fucking knew about it, it's your plan,' he bellowed at them.[32]

Something we can also say with confidence is that any antagonism that begins with Chinese in Australia will not end there. Just as Sikhs and other non-Muslim immigrants of Middle Eastern or South Asian appearance found themselves victims of Islamophobic violence in the wake of 9/11, so too Asian Australians of a wide range of backgrounds are at risk of falling victim to the new climate of anti-Chinese racism.

The security officials, politicians and pundits responsible for this rapidly deteriorating situation have ignored the warnings for some time now, and I have little confidence they're ever going to heed them. Those committed to a path of confrontation with China increasingly invest their hope in popular sentiment to sustain the momentum: 'The crucial factor in this fight is Australian public opinion,' Hamilton writes. From this point of view, a generalised racist hostility towards Chinese immigrants may be a regrettable by-product of Canberra's 'world historical' show-down with Beijing, but certainly not something that should prompt any rethinking of it.[33]

At a time like this, the work of anti-racist activists is essential. They have highlighted the many factors that make Australia ill-equipped to contain a new wave of racial prejudice: the dominance of white perspectives in politics, and the cultural ignorance and insensitivity to issues of race that this breeds; the lack of diversity in media and the toxic, inhospitable environment this is often said to create for minority employees. They point to the need for the government to position itself as consciously anti-racist in its policies, to devise a national anti-racism strategy and to engender a culture of respect in the workplace and civil society.

These are all eminently worthwhile goals, and the activists pursuing them in an unreceptive climate deserve our full support. When Chinese Australians come out publicly and demonstrate against racism, we should stand alongside them. But there are limits to what anti-racism, in this form, can achieve. Even the most vociferous rejection of racism at the political level will count for little if it is not combined with an interrogation of the policies and postures that have generated this new wave of Australian Sinophobia. I'm convinced that, to be effective, anti-racism has to be combined with a critique of Australian foreign policies and the country's orientation to the world. Otherwise, the current trend towards an increasingly bigoted and discriminatory society will continue, to the detriment of us all.

CONCLUSION

In today's climate, when demagogic politicians are increasingly playing to the crowd on China, it's not surprising to hear people arguing that the issue is best left to specialists. The China Matters think-tank, for example, believes a select group of corporate and political figures should formulate a consistent 'China narrative' to guide Australian officialdom in a more China-centric world.[1] Since the 1960s, many books critical of Australia's approach to China have ended with a plea for the development of greater expertise on the country: more funding for more Australians to study China's language and society. The figures that get thrown around for the number of non–Chinese Australians who are functional in Mandarin are indeed paltry – 130 was one recent educated guess. A few more certainly wouldn't hurt. But the confrontation with China I've described in this book won't be remedied by better Sinology. The position that Australia now finds itself in – along with the United States and China – is not a problem of knowledge; it is a problem of politics.

Ultimately, I see the dynamics of capitalist competition as responsible for the US–China rivalry. That's not to say that every foreign-policy decision has a simple economic motive. Economic goals give rise to strategic imperatives, and it's often these imperatives that drive competition among states. Institutionalised in government bureaucracies, policy settings become habits, detached from any immediate shift in the economic winds. Abstract notions like 'credibility' enter into the calculus. But the economic dimension of today's incipient cold war is in many ways more obvious than the same dimension of the first Cold War. As a recent UN report explains, 'The dispute between the United States and China is less about tariffs and more about the technological ambitions of a middle-income developing country. Accessing foreign technology helped today's advanced economies climb the development ladder, and efforts to kick that ladder away by further reducing their policy space will face resistance from developing countries.'[2]

This economic rivalry has implications for today, as many are now watching to see how President Biden's policy on China will balance 'competition' with 'cooperation'. Whether or not the two countries are willing to sit down and discuss issues such as climate change is of considerable importance for humanity's future. At a deeper level, though, the engagement of the United States or other large states in 'competition' with China is not really a question of policy choice. It is something built into the system.

Again, there's no need for determinism. That such rivalries are systemic in nature is not to say they will inevitably result in zero-sum conflict and war. But as America's advantage in Asia is increasingly reduced to a military one, it would be foolish to assume that such outcomes are out of the question. The deep entanglement of the world's leading economies on the eve of World War I didn't prevent that disastrous conflict, and Sino–US trade is no guard against war today. To prevent a scenario like this, countervailing pressures will need to be built up. It's not easy to point to where exactly they will come from, but to get there I'm of the view that we need more Australians, not fewer, to engage with the politics surrounding China. That's what this book is for.

Malcolm Turnbull's 'The Australian People Have Stood Up' speech in late 2017 was in many ways the launch of Australia's China panic, and exemplified a basic misconception at the core of that panic: that Australia is a victim of Chinese imperialism. It is not. On its own small scale, Australia is a Pacific empire-builder itself, and it is allied to the United States, which still aims to maintain 'diplomatic, economic and military pre-eminence in the fastest-growing region of the world', as the 2018 Indo-Pacific Strategic Framework puts it. It's to this cause that Australia has been lending its weight, bringing us into conflict with Beijing, which responded first with dismay, and then with predictable fury. Not surprisingly, Australian hawks were delighted when sources let on that the Trump administration had 'incorporated lessons directly from Turnbull and his ministers into the [2018] strategy'.[3] Australia had done what it sets out to do as an ambitious sub-imperial ally of the United States: it had shown its relevance to Washington's interests.

I don't make many predictions for the future in this book, but I feel confident in saying that Australia will remain in this sub-imperial posture for as long as it seems viable. That might involve periods of relative calm at points when there is optimism that American stocks are rising. A recent lull has just been broken by the provocative cancellation of Victoria's Belt and Road memoranda. New flare-ups are probably not far away. We certainly shouldn't assume that if Washington comes to some kind of accord with Beijing it will cool the temperature here in Australia. If Australia's past responses to flagging US interest in Asia are anything to go by, it would likely react by turning up the volume on warnings against China.

We should oppose this posture and call on the government to abandon it. I say this not because the US alliance is past its use-by date, though it might be – or because it's costing the Australian economy trade dollars, though it is. I don't even rest my case on the risk of war, though we should never be blasé about that. No, we should oppose it because we need to take responsibility for our government's part in the politics that is stoking hostilities. When we peel back the rhetoric, the drivers of American and Australian foreign policy, and the instruments with which they pursue it, are no different to China's. There's no point in telling China to stop playing power politics in the region if Australia's side is doing the same thing.

Australians should tell America that we're not interested in participating in a new cold war or providing a platform for one. We should do so not with apologies and regret, but fully conscious of the way the American alliance has implicated Australian in war crimes and violations of international law, and will risk doing so again for as long as it lasts.

Our efforts should be directed towards defusing and de-escalating conflict, both in the region and worldwide. This means complying with international law, building structures that prevent big countries from bullying the small, and pushing to disarm and denuclearise the Indo-Pacific. It means fashioning an economic system that will allow developing countries to advance to living standards comparable to our own, in ways that are environmentally sustainable. We need to listen to what small countries at risk of being caught in the crossfire of a new Great Game really need, and we need to form links with civil society groups which can construct and sustain democratic institutions. We need to put forward a progressive, transformative vision of international relations.

The conclusion I'm drawing here emerges naturally from the 'China choice' I outlined in the introduction and have reflected on at other points throughout the book. Do we articulate the principles at stake in a critique of China and act consistently on that basis, or do we direct our criticisms and actions against China alone? There's nothing wrong with being apprehensive of China's rise to great-power status, or critical of the way it wields influence in the world. Great powers often behave in appalling ways. China is exhibiting the 'ambitious longings of increased power', which Commodore Perry said 'are the natural concomitants of national success'. The choice we face is whether to try to deny China this 'national success' or work to change the 'natural concomitants' of that success; whether to rally the resources of the status quo to prevent the world's most populous nation from joining the club of advanced nations or to change the way that advanced nations act in the world.

This, I'll admit, is more radical than most of the other proposals being put forward as solutions to Australia's confrontation with China, but I'm sceptical that those more conventional solutions will work. We're far too deep in the US embrace for the wonkish predictions of defence analysts to create a political consensus to withdraw from that embrace. The corporate critique, meanwhile, has been effectively maligned – and let's face it, not entirely without justification.

I don't want to be misunderstood here: I don't believe that every pro-engagement ex-politician or business figure is on the take, or anything like that. We have to remember that there are corporate interests on both sides of the debate – the tax-dodging weapons multinationals that sponsor ASPI certainly don't do so out of disinterested philanthropy. But the ringing endorsement Bob Carr received in 2013 from billionaire James Packer, calling for Carr to be put 'at the forefront of our diplomatic relations with China', didn't do a lot for the ex-foreign minister's credibility.[4] Likewise, the fact that former ambassador Geoff Raby serves on the board of a PRC mining company (and has had to register himself on the Foreign Influence Transparency Scheme as a result) limits the effectiveness of his public criticisms. The reality is that elite critics of the China panic are losing the political battle to the hawks.

But these elite critics don't go far enough anyway. The kind of position Raby outlines in *China's Grand Strategy and Australia's Future in the Global Order* suffers from the same flaws as much of mainstream liberal politics. While putting faith in a global economic system that is failing the majority and is now manifestly crumbling, it simultaneously endorses many of the premises of a more hawkish position. It buys into the discourse of Australian values. It endorses increased military spending and the principle of alliance maintenance: 'Australia needs to continue to work on its alliance relationship with the US, and to assist the US in recognising how its interests are directly aligned with Australia's own security,' Raby argues. It also advocates 'a hedging strategy for managing China', which would include cosying up to a single-party regime such as communist Vietnam. The absence of a more thoroughgoing critique gives an easy opening for more right-wing voices to step forward as the people who really know how to maintain the US alliance and 'manage' China.[5]

One of the main angles that distinguishes Raby's position, and that of many who are critical of Australia's post-2017 turn on China, is the desire to see Australia adopt a more 'independent' foreign policy. But we'd be mistaken to put Australia's conflict with China down to a lack of independence and to imagine a more 'independent' foreign policy serving us better. Australia already has an independent foreign policy: its foreign-policy establishment has *independently* decided that siding with the United States is in Australia's interests. They've done so on the basis of considerations that are not going to go away – even if ANZUS does. Australia will still want to exert economic, diplomatic and, if necessary, military influence to uphold a favourable 'regional balance' and preserve the Pacific as its 'backyard'.

Without any interrogation of these objectives, and the methods by which Australia meets them, a more 'independent' foreign policy is simply a prescription to transform Australia from a sub-imperial associate of the United States into a regional hegemon in its own right. If Hugh White's maths is correct in *How to Defend Australia*, for Australia to keep exerting influence to the degree it wants will require close to a doubling of military spending. Thanks to White's book, the nuclear question is also up for discussion again, and calls to acquire these weapons of mass destruction will probably only grow louder. If we remain within the boundaries of conventional foreign-policy thinking, an Australia without the United States is destined to become more, not less, militaristic. How is that kind of redirection of public resources going to be justified? Naturally, by keeping tensions with China on the boil.

And if not China, there are more enemies just below the horizon. One relatively unnoticed section of Hugh White's book is at the end, where he discusses scenarios yet to quite come onto the map in Australia's foreign-policy debate, including the growth of India and Indonesia, each likely to be accompanied by the same 'ambitious longings of increased power' that we now see in China. White himself believes that 'strategic independence' is only an option for Australia for a few decades. What then? Whose sidekick will Australia be in the struggle for regional primacy?

It's crucial to recognise that we're being presented here with two equally grim visions of the future. One is of an Australia standing alongside the United States in a drawn-out cold-war confrontation with an economic and military powerhouse. The other is of an Australia further sacrificing the health and education of its people so as to 'independently' seek advantage in the regional rivalries it will remain embroiled in. If, like me, you look at this menu and think 'none of the above', we need to consider the third, all too neglected option: a conscious commitment to dismantling the drivers of competition between states.

I recognise the strong sensitivities surrounding Taiwan. But we can't fall for the illusion that the way to maintain peace in the Taiwan Strait is by threatening war indefinitely. America's presence there only serves American interests, and as long as those interests keep it there, it only heightens the risk of an arms race eventually triggering conflict. Should China one day take military action to compromise Taiwan's de facto independence, we should oppose it in the same way we oppose America's wars: with demonstrations, strikes and coordinated international action, but not by calling for war on China ourselves. There are people in Taiwan who share such a vision, and aspire to 'a Taiwan independence movement that solidly rejects American military empire and instead, builds steadfast alliance with marginalised communities and struggles for justice around the world'.[6] To build the kind of forces capable of realising this vision, we need to start now. The way to win self-determination for Taiwan is not through war, which would entail an unthinkable catastrophe, but by building popular support for the principle of self-determination, in China as much as elsewhere in Asia.

Likewise, I recognise that there might be Chinese dissidents, Uyghurs and Tibetans who find what I'm proposing unattractive. But dissidents have to choose from the limited set of options that Western politics puts before them. They know us too well. They know that Western governments only really care about human rights when there's an interest involved. This needs to change, and it can only change by putting human wellbeing, not economic or security priorities, at the centre of foreign policy. This is also the only way, I believe, for criticisms of China to be truly effective. Sure, we might never persuade the CCP that we're supporting the Uyghurs in good faith, but we do need to try to persuade ordinary Chinese people of this. It's very hard to do that while we're simultaneously engaged in efforts to thwart their country's economic growth and prevent them from enjoying the kind of lives we live in the West.

A turn in the direction I'm pointing towards will do much to resolve the domestic dimensions of Australia's China panic, but let me spell out what I have in mind. First, and most importantly, we need to drop the constant accusations that China is bent on compromising Australian sovereignty and independence. As White points out, 'Countries adjust their policies under pressure from others all the time – it is what international relations is all about. Sovereignty consists in the power to choose how to respond to such pressure, not in the fact of responding at all.'[7]

I would like to say that – in all of the various issues raised by China and its presence in Australia – the 'power to choose how to respond' remains firmly in Australian hands, but of course that's not quite the case. Australian sovereignty *has* been compromised – not by China, but by its relationship with the United States. Judging from past experience, should America go to war with China, our elected representatives will likely have no ability to debate whether or not Australia joins in. Should the capabilities of Pine Gap be directed to operations against the PRC, American politicians will have the right to know about it, but Australian politicians won't. No one complaining of Beijing's infringement on Australian sovereignty should be taken seriously unless they're also complaining loudly about this situation.

Of course, incidents involving Chinese actors have highlighted issues in Australia's political system. But it's not China that is responsible for the compromised state of rule of law in this country, or the various avenues for corruption that exist. It wasn't Beijing's actions that led the CIVICUS Monitor to downgrade Australia's status in 2019 from an 'open' to a 'narrowed' democracy.[8] And it wasn't Beijing's actions that have seen Australia's position continue to slide on Transparency International's Corruption Perception Index. A single-minded fixation on China is more likely to exacerbate than mitigate the ongoing erosion of democracy and transparency we see in Australian governance. Comprehensive measures to restore the integrity of Australian institutions, by contrast, will capture any wrongdoing by Chinese actors and improve the functioning of the system.

We've been let down on this front by the Australian media, which all too often stretches the truth in its stories on China, relies too heavily on the word of anonymous intelligence sources and tends to unite disparate China-related stories into implicit or explicit grand narratives of Chinese subversion. To link, as *Four Corners* did in 2017, a story of political donors, a story of campus politics and a story of Australians finding post-political employment with Chinese corporations, presenting them as one and the *same* story – this is the plot structure that drives Sinophobia.

While critical reporting on China is necessary, we need to remember that the principle of 'speaking truth to power' first and foremost means holding to account those with power in our own country. There hasn't been nearly enough of this. Where, for example, are the investigations into Australian decision-making on China, or the role of American pressure behind the scenes? They've been entirely lacking. Nor has there been any accountability when China-related stories come unstuck. Remember Wang Liqiang, the man who *60 Minutes* said would 'expose the secret army targeting our democracy'? Well, did he? The China panic has given journalists carte blanche to lob sensational stories into the public domain without anyone ever going back and checking to see if they stood up. Australia has a free press, of course, but we also have the right to expect better from it. And to expect politicians to take a stand against irresponsible, inaccurate reporting, which is doing the public a disservice and inflaming hostilities towards Chinese Australians.

The presence of the CCP and pro-China politics in Australian public life is something that requires a political response, not a national-security one. If we welcome anti-China dissident groups to conduct their campaigning activities here, as we should, we have to extend the same rights to those who wish to promote pro-China views. Anything less puts the rights of the entire community at risk. If we're confident of the superiority of Australia's position on international issues, or the merits of its democratic system, there shouldn't be any hesitation in allowing alternative views to be aired. If politicians publicly align themselves with China's position on Taiwan, for example, let their critics debate it with them. The public can only benefit from an informed exchange of views.

Pro-CCP Chinese nationalism, like all forms of nationalism, is something I oppose. But I also recognise that if we are to combat and undermine it – in the diaspora or in China itself – there are no short-cuts we can take. Trying to bureaucratically exclude such views from the Australian public sphere – or, worse yet, excluding people who hold such views from Australia entirely – will do nothing to change anyone's mind. On the contrary, it will only confirm the scepticism of 'liberal values' that sustains this nationalism.

Australia already has laws against spying, bribery, stalking and intimidation – various infractions that Chinese 'agents' have been accused of. We should never turn a blind eye to people being bullied or threatened for their opinions. As I've argued, though, the foreign-interference laws go far too far in criminalising what I think should be considered normal political activity. I've already made the basic point here – that democracy will not be served by empowering opaque and unaccountable security agencies; that we are, in effect, simply making Australia more like China, with its own deep paranoia towards the intentions of foreign-linked actors. But let me try to make this point in a different way.

One aspect of this debate I've always found strange is the way people who worry about China subverting Australian institutions are so confident in identifying punitive new security laws as the best response. Clive Hamilton, writing in 2018, felt that it was touch-and-go whether or not Australia would survive the next decade as a sovereign, independent country. That being the case, why would anyone want to expand the already enormous powers of Australia's security agencies if there's a fair chance China might soon end up in control of them? I say this with tongue slightly in cheek – but only slightly. It's not beyond the realm of possibility that a future Australian government might decide it is in the country's interests to tighten monitoring of anti-Beijing dissident activity here. Governments now have laws at their disposal, for example, to shut down Hong Kong activists who coordinate rallies with people back home, or Uyghur advocacy groups who liaise with the World Uyghur Congress, headquartered in Europe. If we don't want Australian security agencies to act in this way, why would we so enthusiastically grant them all the powers they need to do so?

In many spheres, the cure that Australia has hit upon in responding to China is worse than the disease, and this is no more evident than when we look at universities. Here I can agree with Hamilton (and his co-author Mareike Ohlberg) when he says in *Hidden Hand* that many universities are 'led by profit-oriented people who believe their success depends on good relations with Beijing'.[9] But instead of providing universities with the public funding, at arm's length, that they need to maintain their integrity, Morrison is simply calling on them to 'rethink their business models' as they slip deeper into financial crisis.[10]

At the same time, in the name of combatting PRC intrusions, Australia has become a country that bans foreign academics on the basis of vague hints that they were trying to 'influence' someone, that treats all forms of international scholarly collaboration as potentially registrable 'foreign influence', that gives its domestic spy agency the right to vet and veto grant applications, and its foreign minister the ability to unilaterally scrap international partnerships on national-security grounds, without explanation. Anyone concerned about university autonomy and academic freedom needs to be up in arms about these trends.

In adopting this approach, the government has shown itself to be driven by foreign-policy partisanship, not principle. As long as that remains the case, we need to view with scepticism any claims that future measures – say, to abolish the Confucius Institutes – embody a concern for institutional integrity. We should keep an eye on all such collaboration – be it with China, the United States or corporate entities – to ensure they don't cross a line. But public funding, not national-security inquiries, remains key to remedying the vulnerabilities of the corporate university. We also need to remember that the alternative to trusting business-minded vice-chancellors is not to hand control to the government, but to democratise the university and enable staff and students to collectively engage with the ethical and political questions that arise from international collaborations.

We can, and should, promote this vision of the university while avoiding depicting students from the PRC as undesirable elements. Australian universities should welcome students from anywhere in the world – including China – and not as exploitable cash cows, but on the same terms as locals.

A second sphere in which discussions of funding occur is Chinese-language media. Sinophone Australians are not well served these days. On the one hand, there are a handful of struggling traditional broadsheets and newer, low-quality WeChat sites, which – whether due to editorial choice or content-sharing – mostly run a fairly anodyne line, close to that of Chinese state media. On the other hand, there is the stridently anti-CCP, pro-Trump Falun Gong media, distributed for free across the country. In between, the ABC and SBS Chinese do what they can. As in any other sector of the media, more public funding would be welcome. But not if the Chinese-Australian community and its media are reduced to a field of political warfare. All too often, when people talk about 'engaging' the Chinese-Australian community, this is what they have in mind. In one recent ASPI study, carried out with funding from the Department of Home Affairs, the authors took issue with 'misleading reporting that frames responses to interference as unjustified or unfairly targeting Chinese communities'. This, they said, was 'a substantial obstacle to successfully countering foreign interference and educating affected groups'.[11]

Hang on, though. Isn't it a legitimate view that Australia's response to foreign interference is unjustified and 'unfairly targeting Chinese communities'? After all, that's precisely what I've been arguing in this book. If Chinese-Australian media are only to be resourced on the condition that they assist the government and 'educate' their audiences on the merits of Australian policy, we're not providing Chinese Australians with what they need. We're engaging in a propaganda war and once again bringing Australian policies more into line with China's.

Such interventions will only drive a wedge deeper into the community, dividing it along lines of loyalty and disloyalty, and casting suspicion over the whole. I've highlighted in this book the lessons we can take from the last two decades of Muslim Australian experience during the war on terror. Unfortunately, this is precisely the model that some politicians have in mind for dealing with Chinese Australians.

We should 'view our Chinese communities as assets', Liberal MP Dave Sharma writes. Citing the Muslim community's cooperation with the government in its anti-extremism efforts, he argues that 'we need to have the same level of cooperation with Australia's Chinese communities'.[12] What he doesn't mention is that this same campaign has seen mosques spied upon, dubious 'de-radicalisation' programs imposed on Islamic schools, and children as young as six reported to authorities for things as innocuous as changing the way they dress.[13] The campaign has intimidated and marginalised Australian Muslims, and left them with little choice but to conform to a simplistic stereotype of the good, loyal Muslim, or else attract scrutiny. If this is a model for how we intend to 'engage' Chinese Australians, they have cause to be worried.

Our justified dismay at the political direction China is taking, and the consequences this may have for Chinese in Australia, need not – and should not – take us down this path. This is not just because such policies do damage to Australian society, but because they won't achieve any of the high-minded objectives they claim to be pursuing. The suite of contemporary responses to China add up to a sharp move to the right in Australian politics – towards a more xenophobic, racist Australia – and can only provoke a similarly nationalistic response from China.

We need something very different. Not a politics that shies away from necessary criticism of China: that has no future in Australia. But we do need to remove today's national-security lens and replace it with a more genuinely critical one. On that basis, Australia's new consciousness of China as a global actor can still point to important truths about China itself, the global system of which it is a part and the deficiencies of Australian democracy. That, in turn, points to the possibility of turning today's selective and often hypocritical critique of China into a progressive politics that lives up to the universalism we claim to embrace. Humanity simply can't afford the vision of the future that the China hawks have laid out for us. We need an alternative that combines a vision of a better China with a vision of a better Australia.

ACKNOWLEDGEMENTS

It goes without saying that I am solely responsible for the views expressed in this book, but those views are the product of conversations and debates with many people in the last three years – too many to name individually. I want to thank Columbia University's Weatherhead Centre for International Affairs for providing me with an affiliation and office space when I first commenced writing in 2019. Back home at Sydney University, James Curran and Sophie Loy-Wilson were ideal colleagues to have close to hand as the book developed. Sophie read parts of the draft, as did Clinton Fernandes and Jeff Sparrow. I couldn't ask for better friends than these to bounce ideas off. I've also benefited greatly from working with student activists at Columbia and Sydney, my colleagues in the Critical China Scholars (criticalchinascholars.org), and members of the Lausan Collective (lausan.hk). Particular thanks go to Promise Li for reading the section on Hong Kong. The work of many journalists and analysts has been important source material for the book. Australia's 'China Twitter' community, while deserving its international reputation for infighting, has at the same time been an invaluable window onto the domestic political landscape on China – I thank its participants. At Black Inc., Chris Feik has been consistently supportive and engaged. Kate Hatch's editing and Kirstie Innes-Will's work on the final proofs are also much appreciated.

NOTES

INTRODUCTION: AUSTRALIA'S CHINA PANIC

1   Cameron Stewart, 'Chinese Bullying "Won't Be Tolerated", Says DFAT Head
     Frances Adamson', *The Australian*, 11 September 2020.
2   'Lowy Institute Poll 2020', Lowy Institute (website), 24 June 2020, https://poll.
     lowyinstitute.org.
3   Sky News, '"I See the Future" as a Chinese Australia', YouTube, accessed 28 March
     2021, www.youtube.com/watch?v=6qRqy71ukJE.
4   Clive Hamilton (@CliveCHamilton), 'This Must Have Official
     Backing', Twitter, 17 June 2018, https://twitter.com/CliveCHamilton/
     status/1008244195784568832?s=20.
5   Phillip Coorey, 'Scott Morrison: "We Won't Choose" between US, China',
     The Australian Financial Review, 16 November 2018.
6   David Marr, *Power Trip: The Political Journey of Kevin Rudd*, Quarterly Essay,
     no. 38, Black Inc., Carlton, Vic., 2010.
7   Richard Baker and Philip Dorling, 'Defence "Rejected" Minister Spy Link
     Concerns', *The Sydney Morning Herald*, 7 May 2009.
8   Malcolm Turnbull, 'Power Balance in Asia: The Coalition Perspective', speech,
     Lowy Institute, 1 May 2009.
9   David Uren, *The Kingdom and the Quarry: China, Australia, Fear and Greed*,
     Black Inc., Collingwood, Vic., 2012, p. 98.
10   '(U) Secretary Clinton's March 24, 2009 Conversation with Australian Prime
     Minister Kevin Rudd', WikiLeaks (website), accessed 28 March 2021,
     https://wikileaks.org/plusd/cables/09STATE30049_a.html.
11   Mark Kenny and Philip Wen, 'Tony Abbott Lauds Wealth and Friendship in
     Speech at Business Forum in China', *The Sydney Morning Herald*, 10 April 2014;
     'Full Text of Chinese President Xi Jinping's Address to Australia's Parliament',
     The Straits Times, 19 November 2019.
12   Randa Abdel-Fattah, *Coming of Age in the War on Terror*, NewSouth Publishing,
     Sydney, 2021.
13   Kevin Rudd, 'Turnbull's Grovelling Mea Culpa on China Risks Harming
     Australia', *The Sydney Morning Herald*, 10 August 2018.
14   Sarah Ferguson and Jeanavive McGregor, 'Donald Trump's Former Strategist
     Steve Bannon Predicts Working-Class Revolt in Australia as China Rises',
     ABC News, 3 September 2018.
15   Jade Macmillan, 'Foreign Interference More of "an Existential Threat"
     to Australia than Terrorism: ASIO Chief', *ABC News*, 4 September 2019.

16   Peter Hartcher, '"Insidious": Former ASIO Boss Warns on Chinese Interference in Australia', *The Sydney Morning Herald*, 22 November 2019.

17   Nick McKenzie, Grace Tobin and Paul Sakkal, 'The Moment a Chinese Spy Decided to Defect to Australia', *The Age*, 23 November 2019.

18   Damien Cave and Jamie Tarabay, 'Suddenly, the Chinese Threat to Australia Seems Very Real', *The New York Times*, 28 November 2019.

19   Alex Joske, 'Defections Are Messy and We May Never Know the Full Story', *The Sydney Morning Herald*, 25 November 2019.

20   Commonwealth, *Parliamentary Debates*, Foreign Affairs, Defence and Trade References Committee, 3 December 2019 (Jacqui Lambie).

21   Commonwealth, *Parliamentary Debates*, Foreign Affairs, Defence and Trade References Committee, 3 December 2019 (Nick McKim).

22   Andrew Markus, Mapping Social Cohesion, Scanlon Foundation Research Institute, Melbourne, 2021, p. 11.

23   Innes Willox, 'We Must Not Trade Principles in Stand Against Beijing Bully', *The Australian*, 18 January 2021.

24   Tom Uren, 'Declassify the Garnaut ASIO report', *The Australian Financial Review*, 27 June 2018.

25   Latika Bourke, 'Hastie Urges Democracies to Engage in Political Warfare to Preserve Peace', *The Sydney Morning Herald*, 10 December 2019.

26   Paul Monk, 'Five Steps to Rebalancing Strategic Policy on China', *The Australian*, 2 January 2021.

27   Richard Denniss, 'How We Have Sold Ourselves Short', *The Australian Financial Review*, 2 September 2019.

28   Clive Hamilton, *Silent Invasion: China's Influence in Australia*, Hardie Grant Books, Melbourne, 2018, p. 278.

29   Abe David and Ted Wheelwright, *The Third Wave: Australia and Asian Capitalism*, Left Book Club Co-operative, Sydney, 1989, p. xv.

30   Paul Kelly, 'China Relations: "National Security Cowboys" Put Nation's Interests at Unnecessary Risk', *The Australian*, 9 May 2020.

31   Daniel Hurst, 'MPs' "Loose Talk" Drives Australia's Relationship with China to Very Low Point, Former Defence Chief Warns', *The Guardian*, 15 October 2020.

32   Mike Adams, Nicolas Brown and Ron Wickes, *New Frontiers: South and East Asia*, Minerals Council of Australia, Canberra, 2020, p. 59.

33   Bill Birtles, 'China Imposes Unprecedented Ban on Australian Exports', *AM*, Radio National, broadcast 6 November 2020.

34   Daniel McCulloch, Matt Coughlan and Finbar O'Mallon, 'China Iron Ore Rules Won't Harm: Minister', *The Canberra Times*, 21 May 2020; Joel Fitzgibbon, radio interview with Luke Grant on 2GB (transcript), Joel Fitzgibbon MP (website), 14 January 2021, www.joelfitzgibbon.com/news/media/transcript-radio-interview-2gb-thursday-14-january-2021.

35   Anthony Albanese, 'US–Australia Relations Under a Biden Administration', transcript of speech delivered 20 January 2021, Anthony Albanese MP (website), accessed 28 March 2021, https://anthonyalbanese.com.au/anthony-albanese-speech-us-australia-relations-under-a-biden-administration-perth-wednesday-20-january-2021.

36   Essential Media Communications, 'Most Beneficial Country to Strengthen Our Relationship With' poll results, Essential Report (website), 26 May 2020, https://essentialvision.com.au/most-beneficial-country-to-strengthen-our-relationship-with

37   Cassy O'Connor, 'Cambria Green Development', Tasmanian Greens (website),
      14 June 2018, https://tasmps.greens.org.au/parliament/cambria-green-development.

38   Mao Zedong, 'Interview with Three Correspondents from the Central News
      Agency, the Sao Tang Pao and the Hsin Min Pao', *Selected Works*, vol. 2, Foreign
      Languages Press, Beijing, 1965, p. 272.

1. CHINA AND THE WORLD

1   Alison Bashford, 'Quarantine and the Imagining of the Australian Nation',
      Health, vol. 2, no. 4, 1988, p. 398.

2   J. Xia and J. Zhou, 'Translations of Rock Engravings at North Head Quarantine
      Station', unpublished report to NSW National Parks and Wildlife Service, 1986.

3   Jeffrey Thomas Leong, *Wild Geese Sorrow*, Calypso Editions, 2018, pp. 11, 115,
      123.

4   Bill Bishop, 'Engineers of the Soul: Ideology in Xi Jinping's China by John
      Garnaut', *Sinocism*, 17 January 2019.

5   Peter Hartcher, 'Hastie's Awakening to Xi's Bid for Total Control of China – and
      Beyond', *The Sydney Morning Herald*, 10 August 2019.

6   Hoover Institution, 'Battleground of Perception: Countering Threats to Free and
      Open Societies', YouTube, 5 June 2019.

7   Domenico Losurdo, *Liberalism: A Counter-History*, Verso, London, 2011, pp. 249,
      313–14; John Stuart Mill, *Collected Works*, vol. 15, edited by Francis E. Mineka
      and Dwight N. Linley, University of Toronto Press, Toronto, 1972, p. 528.

8   Warren G. Osmond, *Frederic Eggleston: An Intellectual in Australian Politics*,
      Allen & Unwin, Sydney, 1985, pp. 226, 228.

9   Gregory Clark, *In Fear of China*, Lansdowne Press, Melbourne, 1967,
      p. 161.

10   Stephen FitzGerald, *Australia's China*, Australian National University, Canberra,
      1989, p. 8.

11   James Shinn (ed.), *Weaving the Net: Conditional Engagement with China*, Council
      on Foreign Relations, New York, 1996.

12   Raymond Vernon, *Sovereignty at Bay: The Multinational Spread of US Enterprises*,
      Basic Books, New York, 1971.

13   Clinton Fernandes, 'Apple Smarts: iPhone as Much a Creature of Public Subsidy
      as Private Brilliance', *Michael West Media*, 6 September 2019.

14   Sean O'Keefe, Frank B. Kelso, Carl E. Mundy, Jr, 'From the Sea: Preparing the
      Naval Service for the 21st Century', *Naval Institute Proceedings*, vol. 118, issue 11,
      November 1992, pp. 93–6.

15   John W. Dower, *The Violent American Century: War and Terror Since World
      War II*, Haymarket Books, Chicago, 2017, p. 82.

16   Thomas J. Christensen, *The China Challenge: Shaping the Choices of a Rising
      Power*, W.W. Norton, New York, 2016, pp. 25–6.

17   Cited in Michael J. Green, *By More Than Providence: Grand Strategy and
      American Power in the Asia-Pacific Since 1783*, Columbia University Press, New
      York, 2017, p. 48.

18   Walden Bello, *Paper Dragons: China and the Next Crash*, Zed Books, London,
      2019, p. 188.

19   Yifei Li and Judith Shapiro, *China Goes Green: Coercive Environmentalism for a
      Troubled Planet*, Polity, Cambridge, 2020, p. 201.

2. THE US-CHINA RIVALRY TODAY

1   Kurt M. Campbell and Jake Sullivan, 'Competition Without Catastrophe: How America Can Both Challenge and Coexist with China', *Foreign Affairs*, vol. 98, no. 5, September/October 2019.

2   Barack Obama, 'The National Security Strategy of the United States of America', The White House, Washingon, DC, 2015, p. 24.

3   'Summary of the 2018 National Defense Strategy of the United States of America: Sharpening the American Military's Competitive Edge', US Department of Defense, Washington, DC, 2018, p. 2.

4   Anthony Galloway, 'The Secret Plan for Countering China: Trump Should have Followed His Own Strategy', *The Sydney Morning Herald*, 13 January 2021.

5   Christensen, *The China Challenge*, p. 292.

6   Cited in James Peck, *Washington's China: The National Security World, the Cold War, and the Origins of Globalism*, University of Massachusetts Press, Amherst, 2006, p. 119.

7   Mike Pence, 'The Administration's Policy Towards China', speech, Hudson Institute, 4 October 2018.

8   John Pomfret, *The Beautiful Country and the Middle Kingdom: America and China, 1776 to the Present*, Henry Holt and Company, New York, 2016, p. 634.

9   Dower, *The Violent American Century*, p. 125.

10 Campbell and Sullivan, 'Competition Without Catastrophe'.

11 Mahmood Mamdani, *Good Muslim, Bad Muslim,* Three Leaves Press, New York, 2004, p. 239.

12 Tarun Chhabra, 'The China Challenge, Democracy, and US Grand Strategy', *Brookings*, February 2019.

13 Sean Kenji Starrs, 'American Economic Power Hasn't Declined – It Globalized! Summoning the Data and Taking Globalization Seriously', International Studies Quarterly, vol. 57, 2013, pp. 817–30.

14 Kinling Lo, 'Starbucks Can Promote US–China Trade, Chinese President Xi Jinping Says in Letter to Its Ex-Boss', *South China Morning Post*, 15 January 2021.

15 Marise Payne, 'Speech on AU/US Alliance with Secretary of State Pompeo', Minister for Foreign Affairs (website), 4 August 2019, www.foreignminister.gov.au/minister/marise-payne/transcript-eoe/speech-auus-alliance-secretary-state-pompeo.

16 Ho-Fung Hong, 'The US-China Rivalry Is About Capitalist Competition', Jacobin, 11 July 2020.

17 Hillary Clinton, 'America's Pacific Century', Foreign Policy, 11 October 2011.

18 Nyshka Chandran, '"We Can No Longer Tolerate These Chronic Trade Abuses": Trump Lashes Out at China and Others', *CNBC*, 10 November 2017.

19 Rory Medcalf, *Contest for the Indo-Pacific: Why China Won't Map the Future*, Black Inc., Carlton, Vic., 2020, p. 264.

20 Myron H. Nordquist, 'Unclos Article 121 and Itu Aba in the South China Sea Final Award: A Correct Interpretation', in S Jayakumar et al. (eds), *The South China Sea Arbitration: The Legal Dimension*, Edward Elgar, Northampton, MA, 2018, p. 202.

21 Jan van Tol et al., *Airsea Battle: A Point-of-Departure Operational Concept*, Center for Strategic and Budgetary Assessments, Washington, DC, 2010, p. x.

22 Mallory Shelbourne, 'SECDEF Nominee Austin Affirms Threat from China, Will "Update" National Defense Strategy', *USNI News*, 19 January 2021.

23 Daniel C. Sproull, 'Kinetic Energy Weapons: The Beginning of an Interagency Challenge', *InterAgency Journal*, vol. 8, no. 2, 2017, p. 62.

24 'Huawei and ZTE Pose Security Threat, Warns US Panel', *BBC News*, 8 October 2012.

25 Ewen MacAskill and Dominic Rushe, 'Snowden Document Reveals Key Role of Companies in NSA Data Collection', *The Guardian*, 2 November 2013.

26 Rob Taylor, 'At Gathering of Spy Chiefs, US, Allies Agreed to Contain Huawei', *The Wall Street Journal*, 14 December 2018.

27 'Summary of the NCSC Analysis of May 2020 US Sanction', National Cyber Security Centre (website), 14 July 2020, www.ncsc.gov.uk/pdfs/report/summary-of-ncsc-analysis-of-us-may-2020-sanction.pdf.

28 Bhavan Jaipragas, 'Pence Warns Asia-Pacific Not to Trade Sovereignty for Investment in Veiled Swipe at Beijing', *South China Morning Post*, 17 November 2018.

29 Amos Aikman, 'Secret US Poll on China Darwin Port Deal', *The Australian*, 9 March 2016.

30 James Laurenceson et al., 'Chinese Investment in Critical Infrastructure: Much Ado About Not Much?', report, Australia-China Relations Institute, Sydney, 2016.

31 Deborah Brautigam, 'A Critical Look at Chinese "Debt-Trap Diplomacy": The Rise of a Meme', Area Development and Policy, vol. 5, no. 1, 2020, pp. 1–14.

32 Vijay Prashad, 'US Is Doing Its Best to Lock Out China from Latin America and the Caribbean', *CounterPunch*, 5 November 2020.

33 Agatha Kratz, Allen Feng and Logan Wright, 'New Data on the "Debt Trap" Question', Rhodium Group (website), 29 April 2019, https://rhg.com/research/new-data-on-the-debt-trap-question.

34 Jan Wolfe, 'US Official Suggests Italy Avoid China's Belt and Road plan', *Reuters*, 10 March 2019.

35 Ovigwe Eguegu, 'Are IMF Loans Being Used to Counter China in Africa?', The Africa Report, 3 January 2020.

36 Jonathan Barrett, 'US Establishes Foothold in Solomons as Chinese Interests Expand', *Reuters*, 21 November 2019.

37 Elizabeth Redden, 'The Chinese Student Threat?', Insider Higher Ed, 15 February 2018.

38 Michael T. McCaul, China Task Force Report, China Task Force Committee, Washington, DC, 2020, p. 9.

39 Ebony Bowden, 'Trump Says Americans Will Be Forced to "Learn Chinese" if Biden Wins', *New York Post*, 11 August 2020.

40 Matthew Lee, 'Senate Confirms Linda Thomas-Greenfield as UN Ambassador', *Associated Press*, 24 February 2021.

41 Geoff Ziezulewicz, 'SECNAV Calls for Standing Up New Numbered Fleet in the Indo-Pacific', *Navy Times*, 19 November 2020.

42 Campbell and Sullivan, 'Competition Without Catastrophe'.

43 Bethany Allen-Ebrahimian, 'Former Google CEO and Others Call for US–China Tech "Bifurcation"', *Axios*, 26 January 2021.

44 Stuart Lau, 'Blinken and Sullivan to Flex US "Strength" in Summit with China's "Tiger"', Politico, 18 March 2021; Antony Blinken, 'Secretary Blinken With Yuki Morikawa of TV Asahi', *Mirage News*, 18 March 2021.

45 Bob Davis, Kate O'Keeffe and Lingling Wei, 'US's China Hawks Drive Hard-Line Policies After Trump Turns on Beijing', *The Wall Street Journal*, 16 October 2020.

3. INFLUENCING THE REGION

1   Henry Reynolds, 'It's Time to Face the Truth about ANZUS: It's Worse than No Treaty at All', *The Guardian*, 1 August 2018.
2   Hugh White, *Without America: Australia in the New Asia*, Quarterly Essay, no. 68, Black Inc., Carlton, Vic., 2017.
3   Allan Gyngell, 'History Hasn't Ended: How to Handle China', in *China Dependence: Australia's New Vulnerability*, Australian Foreign Affairs, no. 7, 2019.
4   Brendan Taylor, *The Four Flashpoints: How Asia Goes to War,* La Trobe University Press, Carlton, Vic., 2018.
5   Medcalf, *Contest for the Indo-Pacific*, p. 23.
6   Richard Marles, 'The Pacific Is Core Business', speech, Centre for Strategic and International Studies, Washington, DC, 3 May 2018.
7   Hugh White, *How to Defend Australia*, La Trobe University Press, Carlton, Vic., 2019, p. 41.
8   John Mearsheimer, 'China Debate: John Mearsheimer vs Hugh White', Centre for Independent Studies (website), 8 August 2019, www.cis.org.au/events/china-debate-john-mearsheimer-vs-hugh-white.
9   Donald Trump, 'Remarks at a Welcoming Ceremony for Prime Minister Scott Morrison of Australia', speech, White House, Washington, DC, 20 September 2019.
10   Douglas MacArthur, 'Prime Minister's War Conference Minute 23, 1 June 1942', 'Documents on Australian Foreign Policy' (website), Volume 5: July 1941–June 1942, Document no. 510, accessed 15 April 2021, https://wragge.github.io/dfat-documents-web/volumes/volume-5-1941-july-1942-june/510-prime-minister-s-war-conference-minute-23/.
11   Christopher Pyne, 'Joint Facilities: Enhancing Australia's Security and Prosperity', ministerial statement, 20 February 2019.
12   Felicity Ruby, 'Silent Partners: US Bases in Australia', in *Can We Trust America: A Superpower in Transition*, Australian Foreign Affairs, no. 8, 2020.
13   ANZUS Council, 'Press Release', 22 April 1967.
14   Peter Howson, *The Howson Diaries: The Life of Politics*, Viking Press, Ringwood, Vic., 1984, p. 223.
15   Gareth Evans, 'Australia's Regional Security', ministerial statement, 6 December 1989.
16   'Defending Australia: Defence White Paper 1994', Australian Government Publishing Service, Canberra, 1994, p. 9.
17   Albert Palazzo, 'We Went to Iraq for ANZUS', *The Interpreter*, Lowy Institute, 25 March 2013.
18   White, *How to Defend Australia*, p. 18.
19   Janaki Kremmer, 'China Casts Long Shadow of US–Australian ties', *The Christian Science Monitor*, 15 July 2005.
20   'Ambassador's Introductory Call on Opposition Leader Kim Beazley', WikiLeaks (website), 8 September 2006, https://wikileaks.org/plusd/cables/06CANBERRA1366_a.html.
21   Barack Obama, 'Remarks by President Obama to the Australian Parliament', 17 November 2020.
22   Hugh White, 'America or China? Australia Is Fooling Itself that It Doesn't Have to Choose', *The Guardian*, 27 November 2017.
23   Payne, 'Speech on AU/US Alliance with Secretary of State Pompeo'.
24   Katharine Murphy and Ben Doherty, 'Scott Morrison Echoes Trump as He Warns Nations Must Avoid "Negative Globalism"', *The Guardian*, 3 October 2019.

25 Madelaine Chiam, 'International Human Rights Treaties and Institutions in the Protection of Human Rights in Australia', in Matthew Groves, Janina Boughey and Dan Meagher (eds), *The Legal Protection of Rights in Australia*, Hart Publishing, London, 2019, p. 243.

26 Clinton Fernandes, *Island Off the Coast of Asia: Instruments of Statecraft in Australian Foreign Policy*, Monash University Publishing, Clayton, Vic., 2018.

27 Cited in Humphrey McQueen, *A New Brittania*, University of Queensland Press, St Lucia, Qld., 2004, p. 53.

28 Peter Jennings, 'China's Rapid Military Development Outpaces Even the US', *The Australian*, 5 January 2021.

29 David Wroe, 'China Eyes Vanuatu Military Base in Plan with Global Ramifications', *The Sydney Morning Herald*, 9 April 2018.

30 Graeme Smith, 'In Vanuatu, It's He Says, Xi Says', *Inside Story*, 13 April 2018.

31 Peter Jennings, 'Vanuatu: China Gains from Our Neglect of the Pacific', *The Australian*, 14 April 2018.

32 Sally Whyte, 'Australia Must Step Up If China Starts Military Build Up in Vanuatu', *The Age*, 10 April 2018.

33 Ally Foster, '60 Minutes Investigates China's Growing Influence in the South Pacific', *News.com.au*, 17 November 2019.

34 Luke Fletcher and Pichamon Yeophantong, *Enter the Dragon: Australia, China and the New Pacific Development Agenda*, Jubilee Australia, Sydney, 2019, p. 20.

35 Natalie Whiting and Stephen Dziedzic, 'Australia Ramps Up Rivalry with China for Influence in the Pacific', *ABC News*, 10 February 2019.

36 Scott Morrison, 'Australia and the Pacific: A New Chapter', speech, Townsville, Qld., 8 November 2018.

37 Oil Search, 'Submission for the Export Finance and Insurance Corporation Amendment (Support for Infrastructure Financing) Bill 2019', 28 February 2018.

38 Medcalf, *Contest for the Indo-Pacific*.

39 Greg Colton, 'Time for Australia to Forge Free Compact Agreements in the Pacific', *The Interpreter*, 24 November 2017.

40 Commonwealth, Parliamentary Debates, Foreign Affairs, Defence and Trade References Committee, 12 November 2020 (John Blaxland). See also John Blaxland, 'The Fix: A Grand Compact for the Pacific', Submission for the Inquiry into Australia's Defence Relationships with Pacific Island Nations, Australian Parliament, 2020.

41 Rebecca Strating, 'Enabling Authoritarianism in the Indo-Pacific: Australian Exemptionalism', *Australian Journal of International Affairs*, vol. 74, no. 3, 2020.

42 Paul Dibb, 'How Australia Can Deter China', *The Strategist*, 12 March 2020.

43 'Lowy Institute Poll 2020'.

44 Malcolm Turnbull, 'Prime Minister's Introduction', 2017 Foreign Policy White Paper, Department of Foreign Affairs and Trade, Canberra, 2017.

4. INTERFERING WITH DEMOCRACY

1 Commonwealth, 'ASIO Annual Report, 2019–20', Australian Security and Intelligence Organisation, Canberra, 2020, p. 2.

2 John Garnaut, 'How China Interferes in Australia', *Foreign Affairs*, 9 March 2018.

3 *Wing v The Australian Broadcasting Corporation* [2018] FCA 1340.

4 *Chau v Australian Broadcasting Corporation* (No. 3) [2021] FCA 44.

5 Tom Uren, 'Declassify the Garnaut ASIO report', *ASPI*, 27 June 2018.

6   Commonwealth, *Parliamentary Debates*, House (Malcom Turnbull), 7 December 2017.

7   Theodore Schleifer and Deirdre Walsh, 'McCain: Russian Cyberintrusions an "Act of War"', *CNN*, 31 December 2016.

8   'The October Democratic Debate Transcript', *The Washington Post*, 16 October 2019.

9   Andrew Greene, 'Former Top US Spy James Clapper Warns of China's Russian-Style Behaviour in Australia', *ABC News*, 6 June 2017.

10   Jenny Noyes, 'Hillary Clinton's Warning to Australia on Chinese Influence', *The Sydney Morning Herald*, 14 May 2018.

11   Laura Rosenberger and John Garnaut, 'The Interference Operations from Putin's Kremlin and Xi's Communist Party: Forging a Joint Response', *The Asan Forum*, 8 May 2018.

12   Garnaut, 'How China Interferes in Australia'.

13   US House of Representatives, 'Executive Session, Permanent Select Committee on Intelligence, Interview of Shawn Henry', 5 December 2017 Washington, DC.

14   Chris Kahn, 'Despite Report Findings, Almost Half of Americans Think Trump Colluded with Russia', *Reuters*, 27 March 2019.

15   Jessica Clarence, 'Who Funds Federal Parliamentarians' Overseas Travel?', *ASPI*, 26 June 2018.

16   Australia Palestine Advocacy Network, 'Federal Parliamentarians Continue to Take Lobby Trips to Israel More than Any Other country', media release, September 2020.

17   Henry Reynolds, 'The Extraordinary Ambush of China Matters', *Pearls and Irritations*, 17 July 2020.

18   Hannah Aulby, 'Undermining Our Democracy: Foreign Corporate Influence Through the Australian Mining Lobby', The Australia Institute (website), 4 September 2017, https://australiainstitute.org.au/report/undermining-our-democracy-foreign-corporate-influence-through-the-australian-mining-lobby.

19   Commonwealth, *Parliamentary Debates*, Foreign Affairs, Defence and Trade References Committee, 9 September 2019 (Nick McKim).

20   Cassy O'Connor and Rosalie Woodruff, letter to David Metcalf, 14 June 2018.

21   Mark Harrison, 'Antarctica and the China test', *The Interpreter*, 23 October 2019.

22   Primrose Riordan, 'Antarctic Chief Ices "Unfounded" China Concerns', *The Australian*, 9 April 2019.

23   Daniel Flitton, 'Victoria Takes the Initiative with China', *The Interpreter*, 25 October 2019.

24   Eliza Borrello, 'Australia's States Are Growing Closer to China as the Federal Relationship Remains Strained', *ABC News*, 10 November 2019.

25   Michael Shoebridge, 'Beijing Drives a Belt and Road between Melbourne and Canberra', *The Strategist*, 25 October 2019.

26   Ryan Manuel, 'The United Front Work Department and How It Plays a Part in the Gladys Liu Controversy', *ABC News*, 15 September 2019.

27   Angus Grigg, 'Chinese Businessman Complains MPs "Not Delivering" for Donations', *The Australian Financial Review*, 29 August 2016.

28   Paul Karp, 'Australia "Pretending" to Stand Up to China Over Disputed Islands, Labor Says', *The Guardian*, 13 July 2016.

29   Quentin McDermott, 'Sam Dastyari Defended China's Policy in South China Sea in Defiance of Labor Policy, Secret Recording Reveals', *ABC News*, 29 November 2017.

30 Henry Belot, 'Malcolm Turnbull Announces Biggest Overhaul of Espionage, Intelligence Laws in Decades', *ABC News* video, 5 December 2017.

31 Paul Maley and Nicola Berkovic, 'Security Agencies Flag Chinese Manchurian Candidates', *The Australian*, 9 December 2017.

32 Nick O'Malley and Alex Joske, 'Claims of Chinese Influence, Betrayal and Racism on the Streets of Bennelong', *The Sydney Morning Herald*, 11 December 2017.

33 Dave Sharma, 'Foreign Influence in Our Politics Must Be Checked', *The Australian*, 28 December 2017.

34 Clive Hamilton, 'Book Talk – Silent Invasion', speech, Center for Strategic and Budgetary Assessments, Washington, DC, 30 April 2018.

35 *Wing v The Australian Broadcasting Corporation* [2018] FCA 1340.

36 'Foreign Influence Transparency Scheme: Factsheet 2', Attorney-General's Department (website), February 2019, www.ag.gov.au/sites/default/files/2020-03/influence-versus-interference.pdf.

37 'An Open Letter from Concerned Scholars of China and the Chinese Diaspora', *Policy Forum*, 26 March 2018.

38 Simon Benson, 'Foreign Interference "Threat" to By-Elections, Says Christian Porter', *The Australian*, 8 June 2018.

39 Jamie Tarabay, 'Bill Shorten Wants Australia to Embrace China: But at What Cost?', *The New York Times*, 15 May 2019.

40 Steve Cannane and Echo Hui, 'Chinese Media Mocks Australia and Prime Minister in WeChat Posts', *ABC News*, 9 May 2019.

41 Jim Alouat, 'Chinese-Born Hobart City Council Candidate Defends Her Right to "Encourage" International Students to Vote for Her', *The Mercury* (Hobart), 15 September 2018.

42 Cassy O'Connor, 'Foreign Influence in Local Government Elections', Tasmanian Greens (website), 27 September 2018, https://tasmps.greens.org.au/parliament/foreign-influence-local-government-0.

43 Lucy MacDonald, 'Tasmania Independence at Risk from Chinese Investment Says Australian Academic', *ABC News*, 3 October 2018; 'Packed House Hears of Chinese "Target"', *The Mercury* (Hobart), 3 October 2018, p. 6.

44 'Matter of Respect for Australian Values,' *The Mercury* (Hobart), 13 October 2018.

45 Phil Coorey, *Insiders*, ABC, broadcast 15 September 2019.

46 Clive Hamilton, 'Why Gladys Liu Must Answer to Parliament About Alleged Links to the Chinese Government', *The Conversation*, 11 September 2019.

47 Nick McKenzie, Paul Sakkal and Grace Tobin, 'China Tried to Plant Its Candidate in Federal Parliament, Authorities Believe', *The Age*, 24 November 2019.

48 Osmond Chiu, 'What Should Australia Do About … Its Politics Being Too White?', *China Matters*, February 2020.

49 Anthony Galloway and Alex Chung, 'Beijing Influence or Racism? China Debate Hits Melbourne Council Elections', *The Age*, 12 October 2020.

50 Tom Lowrey, 'Liberal and Labor Canberra Politicians Tell of "Hurtful" Racism on the ACT Election Campaign Trail', *ABC News*, 25 September 2020.

51 George Brandis, 'Defending Liberal Democracies in an Increasingly Contested World', the 2020 Gallipoli Memorial Lecture, The Royal United Services Institute, Melbourne, 25 June 2020.

52 'China's Influence and American Interests: Promoting Constructive Vigilance', Hoover Institution (website), 29 November 2018, www.hoover.org/research/chinas-influence-american-interests-promoting-constructive-vigilance.

53   Clive Hamilton, 'World's Eyes on Australia to See If We Can Resist China', *The Australian*, 6 January 2021.

54   Ray Hadley, 'Peter Dutton Calls for Labor MP's Resignation After China Coronavirus Praise', *2GB 837AM*, 2 April 2020.

55   Peter Dutton, *Insiders*, ABC, broadcast 13 September 2020.

56   'Anti-Terror Laws', Law Council of Australia (website), accessed 28 March 2021, www.lawcouncil.asn.au/policy-agenda/criminal-law-and-national-security/anti-terror-laws.

57   Clive Hamilton and Alex Joske, 'Submission to the Parliamentary Joint Committee on Intelligence and Security Review of the National Security Legislation Amendment (Espionage and Foreign Interference) Bill 2017', 22 January 2018, p. 17.

58   John Lee, 'Australia's Gladys Liu Scandal Shows How the Chinese Communist Party Is Weaponizing Race', *CNN*, 24 September 2019.

59   Peter Hartcher, *Red Flag: Waking Up to China's Challenge*, Quarterly Essay, no. 76; Black Inc., Carlton, Vic., 2019; Tom McIlroy, 'Vetting Political Candidates Unworkable: Former ASIO Chief', *The Australian Financial Review*, 18 December 2019.

5. COLD-WAR CAMPUS

1   James Laurenceson and Michael Zhou, 'The Australia–China Science Boom', Australia–China Relations Institute (website), 22 July 2020, www.australiachinarelations.org/content/australia-china-science-boom.

2   Andrew Hastie, 'Challenge to Democracy to Counter Russia, China', *The Sydney Morning Herald*, 10 December 2019; Rowan Callick, 'Chinese Students Taught to "Snitch" on Politically Incorrect Lecturers', *The Australian*, 1 September 2017; Alex Joske, 'How the West's Research Aids China's Military', *The Strategist*, 30 October 2018.

3   Commonwealth, *Parliamentary Debates*, House of Representatives, 31 August 2020 (Bob Katter).

4   Ben Doherty, 'Foreign Interference Fears After Sydney University Cancels Western Sahara Speaker', *The Guardian*, 22 September 2019.

5   'Uni Sydney Adopts Free Speech Code', *Campus Morning Mail*, 11 December 2019.

6   'HK Police Action Demonstrates "State Level Terrorism"', *SkyNews.com.au*, 1 September 2019.

7   '2020 Year-in-Review: The Movement Will Not Be Canceled', Palestine Legal (website), accessed 28 March 2021, https://palestinelegal.org/2020-report.

8   Yojana Sharma, 'Chinese Students, Researchers with "Military Links" Barred', *University World News*, 3 June 2020.

9   Sharri Markson, 'China Exploits Australia's Lax Laws to Sign Up Researchers for Secretive Program', *The Australian*, 24 August 2020.

10   'CSIRO Response to *The Australian*', media release, CSIRO (website), 10 February 2020, www.csiro.au/en/news/news-releases/2020/csiro-response-to-the-australian.

11   Paul Daley, 'WHO Worries that Melbourne University's Links to Arms Industry Will Threaten Joint Medical Research', *The Guardian*, 22 January 2021.

12   Peter Jennings, 'Party's Over for the Bullies of Beijing', *The Australian*, 23 May 2020.

13   Marshall Sahlins, 'Confucius Institutes: Academic Malware and Cold Warfare', *Inside Higher Ed*, 26 July 2018.

14   'Australian Universities Are Accused of Trading Free Speech for Cash',
      The Economist, 21 September 2019.

15   Sam Buckingham-Jones, 'Uni Staff Blasted for Ramsay Opposition', *The Australian*,
      11 June 2018.

16   John Fitzgerald, 'ANU Says No to Ramsay, but What about Confucius Institutes',
      The Australian, 6 June 2018.

17   'Voila – UniSA and Alliance Française d'Adelaïde Partnership to Boost French
      Connection', media release, University of South Australia (website), 16 February
      2017, www.unisa.edu.au/Media-Centre/Releases/2017-Media-Releases/Voila-
      -UniSA-and-Alliance-Francaise-dAdelaide-partnership-to-boost-French-
      connection; 'French Day @ UniSA', University of South Australia (website), 15 May
      2018, www.unisa.edu.au/frenchday.

18   Peter Varghese and David A. Ritchie, 'Evaluation Report', American Australian
      Association Ltd, 2017, p. 3.

19   Primrose Riordan, 'Wrong Map Ignites University Fury', *The Australian*,
      21 August 2017; Primrose Riordan, 'Uni Lecturer Targeted Over "Separate
      Taiwan"', *The Australian*, 25 August 2017; Rachel Gray, 'China Needs
      International Pressure to End Hong Kong Wrongs', University of New South
      Wales (website), 31 July 2020, www.law.unsw.edu.au/news/china-needs-
      international-pressure-to-end-hong-kong-wrongs.

20   John Garnaut, 'Our Universities Are a Frontline in China's Ideological Wars',
      The Australian Financial Review, 30 August 2017; Merriden Varrall, 'A Chinese
      Threat to Australian Openness', *The New York Times*, 31 July 2017; Andrew
      Greene, 'DFAT Boss Warns International Students to Resist Chinese Communist
      Party's "Untoward" Influence', *ABC News*, 9 October 2017; Andrew Greene
      and Stephen Dziedzic, 'China's Soft Power: Julie Bishop Steps Up Warning to
      University Students on Communist Party Rhetoric', *ABC News*, 16 October 2017.

21   Deborah Cornwall, 'ABC Quietly Settled Chinese Student's Defamation Case',
      The Australian, 11 March 2019; Jaq James, 'ABC Defames, Gags and "Chuckles"
      at Chinese Student', Critical Social Work Publishing House (website), accessed
      28 March 2021, www.criticalsocialworkpublishinghouse.com/post/2018/04/03/
      abc-settles-with-and-gags-chinese-students-and-scholars-association-president.

22   Fran Martin, *Chinese International Students' Wellbeing in Australia: The Road to
      Recovery*, The University of Melbourne, Parkville, Vic., 2020.

23   John Garnaut, 'Our Universities Are a Frontline in China's Ideological Wars';
      Primrose Riordan, 'Monash University Suspends Lecturer Over Quiz Question',
      The Australian, 22 May 2017; Eryk Bagshaw and Fergus Hunter, 'China
      "Exporting CCP Speech Controls to Australia" as Second University Caught in
      Row', *The Sydney Morning Herald*, 5 August 2020.

24   Vicky Xiuzhong Xu, 'Chinese Nationalism Jostles with Academic Freedom in
      Australia', *The New York Times*, 15 November 2017.

25   Commonwealth, *Parliamentary Debates*, House of Representatives, 1 March 2017
      (Bob Katter); Michael Koziol, 'Fraser Anning's Final Solution Speech "Absolutely
      Magnificent", says Bob Katter', *The Sydney Morning Herald*, 15 August 2018.

26   'International Student Data 2020', Department of Education, Skills and Employment
      (website), accessed 28 March 2021, https://internationaleducation.gov.au/research/
      International-Student-Data/Pages/InternationalStudentData2020.aspx#Pivot_Table.

27   Laurie Berg and Bassina Farbenblum, 'As If We Weren't Humans: The
      Abandonment of Temporary Migrants in Australia During COVID-19', Migrant
      Worker Justice Initiative, Sydney 2020.

28 Tim Dodd, 'Five Eyes Countries Could Boost Australian Uni Research Funding', *The Australian*, 11 August 2020.
29 Euan Graham, 'Australia Has Too Few Home-Grown Experts on the Chinese Communist Party: That's a Problem', *The Conversation*, 13 August 2019.

6. HUMAN RIGHTS AND XINJIANG

1 Chris Sidoti, 'Human Rights in China', *Reform*, no. 21, 1993, p. 22.
2 Timothy Kendall, *Within China's Orbit: China Through the Eyes of the Australian Parliament*, Commonwealth Government, Canberra, 2008.
3 Michael Pillsbury, *The Hundred-Year Marathon: China's Secret Strategy to Replace America as the Global Superpower*, Henry Holt and Co., New York, 2015, p. 219.
4 Abdullah b. Muḥammad Nidayi Kashghari, *Risala-i Ḥaqqiyya*, Special Collections Library, Islamic Manuscript no. 262, University of Michigan, p. 104.
5 Alessandra Cappelletti, *Socio-Economic Development in Xinjiang Uyghur Autonomous Region: Disparities and Power Struggle in China's North-West*, Palgrave Macmillan, Singapore, 2020.
6 Abdülaziz Kolcal, 'Türkistan-i Çini Türkleri bir vazife-i mukaddase', *Ḥikmet*, no. 38, 5 January 1910, p. 8.
7 '108 Cablegram to Canberra, 30 October 1964', record of talks held at Soviet Foreign Ministry, Moscow, 28 October 1964, in Documents on Australian Foreign Policy, vol. 22, Department of Foreign Affairs and Trade, Canberra, 2002, www.dfat.gov.au/about-us/publications/historical-documents/volume-22/Pages/108-cablegram-to-canberra.
8 Robert Drewe, 'The Hidden Face of China', *The Bulletin*, 24 July 1976, pp. 36–7.
9 People's Republic of China, 'The Fight Against Terrorism and Extremism and Human Rights Protection in Xinjiang', 2019 Defence White Paper, State Council Information Office, Beijing, March 2019.
10 'Xinjiang's Prosperity Driven by China's Strength', *Global Times*, 5 July 2019.
11 Amy Qin, 'In China's Crackdown on Muslims, Children Have Not Been Spared', *The New York Times*, 28 December 2019.
12 'US Muslim Groups Accuse OIC of Abetting China's Uighur "Genocide"', *Al Jazeera*, 18 December 2020.
13 'Xinjiang: PRC Scrambles to Avoid Anti-Islam Image Abroad and Kill OIC Declaration', WikiLeaks (website), 17 July 2009, https://wikileaks.org/plusd/cables/09BEIJING2041_a.html.
14 'Public Opinion Poll No. (77)', Palestinian Center for Policy and Survey Research (website), 15 September 2020, www.pcpsr.org/en/node/817.
15 Law Council of Australia, 'Submission No. 99 to Joint Standing Committee on Foreign Affairs, Defence and Trade', Inquiry into Whether Australia Should Examine the Use of Targeted Sanctions to Address Human Rights Abuses, Parliament of Australia (website), 4 March 2020, www.aph.gov.au/Parliamentary_Business/Committees/Joint/Foreign_Affairs_Defence_and_Trade/MagnitskyAct.
16 Geoffrey Robertson and Chris Rummery, 'Why Australia Needs a Magnitsky Law', *Australia Quarterly*, vol. 89, no. 4, 2018.
17 Daniel Hurst, 'Australia Urged to Tighten Anti-Slavery Laws as UK Cracks Down on Chinese Forced Labour', *The Guardian*, 14 January 2021.
18 Aryeh Neier, *Taking Liberties: Four Decades in the Struggle for Rights*, PublicAffairs, New York, 2003, p. 285.

19 Gregory Clark, 'We Badly Need Some Context on Xinjiang', *Pearls and Irritations*, 20 November 2019.

20 Jordan Shanks, 'Banning Tik Tok', Friendlyjordies Podcast (website), 26 July 2020, https://friendlyjordies.podbean.com/e/banning-tik-tok-friendlyjordies-podcast-live.

21 Haruka Nomura, 'The Eastern Question from Shanghai: Views of the Ottoman Empire in Shenbao, 1870s–1880s', PhD dissertation, Australian National University, 2015, pp. 153–54.

22 UK Foreign, Commonwealth and Development Office, 'Countering the Root Causes of Violent Extremism Undermining Growth and Stability in China's Xinjiang Region by Sharing UK Best Practice', Development Trackers (website), accessed 19 April 2021, https://devtracker.fcdo.gov.uk/projects/GB-GOV-3-PAP-CNF-002340.

23 'France's Macron Vows to Fight "Islamist Separatism"', *BBC*, 3 October 2020; 'France Needs "Society of Vigilance" Against Islamist "Hydra" – Macron', *Reuters*, 8 October 2019.

24 Azeem Ibrahim, 'Why the Uyghur Genocide in China Matters', *TheNewArab*, 1 April 2021.

25 Stephanie Savell, 'Where We Fight: US Counterterror War Locations 2017–2018', Watson Institute for International and Public Affairs, Providence, RI, 2019.

26 Ruth Blakeley et al., *Leaving the War on Terror: A Progressive Alternative to Counter-Terrorism Policy*, Transnational Institute, Amsterdam, 2019, p. 5.

27 Michael Safi, 'Anti-Muslim Sentiment Strong and Widespread in Australian Army, Study Shows', *The Guardian*, 9 June 2016.

28 Daniel Hurst, 'UK and US Lock in Behind Australia in China Row', *The Guardian*, 2 December 2020.

7. THE BATTLE FOR HONG KONG

1 'Update on Hong Kong National Security Law: First Judgment Addressing Constitutional Matters Delivered', Hogan Lovells (website), 26 August 2020, p. 3, www.hoganlovells.com/~/media/hogan-lovells/pdf/2020-pdfs/2020_08_26_hogan-lovells-client-alert-update-on-national-security-law.pdf?la=en.

2 'About Lausan', Lausan (website), accessed 28 March 2021, https://lausan.hk/about.

3 Ashley Townshend and David Santoro, 'Operationalising Deterrence in the Indo-Pacific', United States Studies Centre, Sydney, April 2020, p. 12.

4 'Trump Says It's Up to China to Deal with Hong Kong "Riots"', *Reuters*, 2 August 2019.

5 David Crowe, 'Australia Set to Ratify Controversial Trade Deal with Hong Kong', *The Sydney Morning Herald*, 8 October 2019.

6 Rosemary Bolger, 'Call for Hong Kongers to Be Given Permanent Protection in Australia', *SBS News*, 4 September 2019.

7 Cited in Tandee Wang, 'Australia's Tiananmen Generation: Politics, the Public and Posterity', honours thesis, Australian National University, Canberra, 2020, p. 70.

8 Hamilton, *Silent Invasion*, p. 29.

9 Primrose Riordan, 'Intercepted People Smuggler Boat Carrying Chinese "Not Unusual"', *The Australian*, 16 July 2018.

10 Hedley Thomas, 'Hong Kong Mob Protesters Rule the Streets', *The Australian*, 19 November 2019.

11 Liam Cochrane and Erin Handley, 'Hong Kong Democracy Protester "Detained" Briefly by Border Force as Artists Counter Beijing', *ABC News*, 5 September 2019.

12 Commonwealth, Parliamentary Debates, Parliamentary Joint Committee on Intelligence and Security, 10 July 2020 (Mike Burgess).

13 Erin Handley and Iris Zhao, 'How Hong Kong's Protest Movement is Forging Solidarity with Australia's Uyghurs and Tibetans', *ABC News*, 7 September 2019.

14 Au Loong-Yu, *Hong Kong in Revolt: The Protest Movement and the Future of China*, Pluto Press, London, 2020, p. 149.

15 Ian Marlow, 'US Forms Worried about Hong Kong Security Law, AmCham Says', Bloomberg, 13 July 2020.

16 Michael Smith, 'Capitalist Hong Kong Survives but Freedoms Take Flight', *The Australian Financial Review*, 30 May 2020.

17 Au, *Hong Kong in Revolt*, p. 56.

18 Hong Liuxing, 'Students Protest Prison-Like Restrictions across China', Chinaworkerinfo, 22 November 2020.

19 Sirianne Dahlum, Carl Henrik Knutsen and Tore Wig, 'We Checked 100 Years of Protests in 150 Countries: Here's What We Learned about the Working Class and Democracy', *The Washington Post*, 24 October 2019.

8. SOVEREIGNTY, VALUES AND RACISM

1   Heather Rose, *Bruny*, Allen & Unwin, Crows Nest, NSW, 2019, p. 191.

2   John Garnaut (@jgarnaut), 'Beijing Is Working This Fault Line in Australia Too', Twitter, 14 November 2017, https://twitter.com/jgarnaut/status/930384838061834241?s=20.

3   Hamilton, *Silent Invasion*, pp. 22–24.

4   Rose, *Bruny*, p. 156.

5   Rose, *Bruny*, p. 393.

6   Amanda Ducker, 'Author Heather Rose Examines Political Interference in Her New Novel, *Bruny*', *The Mercury* (Hobart), 28 September 2019.

7   Angela Priestley, 'How "Far Right" References Were Deleted from Senate Motion Condemning Extremism', Women's Agenda, 4 February 2021.

8   'The Chinese in Australia: Their Vices and Their Victims', *The Bulletin*, 21 August 1886.

9   Keith Windschuttle, *The White Australia Policy*, Macleay Press, Sydney, 2004, pp. 268, 273, 276.

10 Greg Sheridan, 'Forget the Cricket, This Is Our Real Test Over India', *The Australian*, 12 December 2019.

11 Scott Morrison, 'Joint Statement between Viet Nam and Australia', Prime Minister of Australia (website), 23 August 2019, www.pm.gov.au/media/joint-statement-between-viet-nam-and-australia.

12 Marise Pane (@MarisePayne), 'Today, @FMPhamBinhMinh & I Signed the Third Plan of Action', Twitter, 5 November 2020, https://twitter.com/MarisePayne/status/1324300822432288769?s=20.

13 John Fitzgerald, 'Why Values Matter in Australia's Relations with China', *The Asan Forum*, 13 June 2014.

14 Andrew Bolt, *The Bolt Report*, Sky News, broadcast 1 March 2018.

15 Alan Tudge, 'Maintaining Social Cohesion in a Time of Large, Diverse Immigration: Lessons from Australia', speech, The Australia–UK Leadership Forum, London, 19 July 2018.

16 Stephanie Dalzell and Stephen Dziedzic, 'Minister Accuses Foreign Governments of Exploiting "Proud Australians"', *ABC News*, 28 August 2020.

17 Daniel Hurst, Katharine Murphy and Paul Karp, 'Morrison Asks for Dialogue

with China as Other Countries Pledge Support for Australia', *The Guardian*, 3 December 2020.

18 Rory Medcalf (@Rory_Medcalf), 'This Is a Powerful Analogy', Twitter, 17 August 2019, https://twitter.com/chrizap/status/1162514558369406976?s=20.

19 Richard Hofstadter, *The Paranoid Style in American Politics and Other Essays*, Alfred A. Knopf, New York, 1965, p. 35.

20 Hamilton, *Silent Invasion*, p. 279.

21 Marise Payne, 'Strengthening the Future of the Australia–China Relationship', media release, Minister for Foreign Affairs (website), 29 March 2019, www.foreignminister.gov.au/minister/marise-payne/media-release/strengthening-future-australia-china-relationship.

22 Australian Values Alliance, 'Open Letter to Prime Minister Hon. Scott Morrison', Australian Values Alliance (website), 14 November 2020, http://english.ava.org.au/2020/11/open-letter-to-prime-minister-hon-scott.html.

23 Mark Magnier, 'Slip-Up or Signal? What US Official's "Clash of Civilisations" Remarks Suggest', *South China Morning Post*, 24 May 2019.

24 Andrew Probyn and Matthew Doran, 'China's "Hybrid War": Beijing's Mass Surveillance of Australia and the World for Secrets and Scandal', *ABC News*, 14 September 2020. The article was quickly edited. For discussion of the original, see Mark Fletcher, 'East Asian Thinking, the Spiderweb, the "Five Eyes Intelligence Officer" … Did @AndrewProbyn Get Pranked?', Only the Sangfroid, 14 September 2020.

25 Geraldine Doogue, 'Forum: The Challenges of the Australia–China Relationship', *Saturday Extra*, Radio National, broadcast 1 September 2018.

26 Chris Zappone, 'Is Talk of Australia's "Anti-China" Bias a Weaponised Narrative?', *The Sydney Morning Herald*, 19 May 2018.

27 Peter Hartcher, 'China's Man in Canberra Has Unmasked the Regime's True Face', *The Sydney Morning Herald*, 28 April 2020.

28 Max Koslowski, 'Almost 400 Anti-China Attacks Since Pandemic Began', *The Sydney Morning Herald*, 7 June 2020.

29 'Open Letter on National Unity During the Coronavirus Pandemic', China Neican (website), 8 April 2020, www.neican.org/p/open-letter-on-national-unity-during.

30 Andrew Markus, 'Mapping Social Cohesion: The Scanlon Foundation Surveys 2020', Monash University, Clayton, 2021.

31 Nell O'Grady and Baopu He, 'Commodity, Victim, Aggressor: Media Representations of Chinese International Students', Honi Soit, 30 November 2019.

32 David Brophy, 'For Anti-Racism and International Solidarity: A Response to Clive Hamilton on China', *Green Left*, 9 March 2021.

33 Clive Hamilton, 'World's Eyes on Australia to See If We Can Resist China', *The Australian*, 6 January 2021.

CONCLUSION

1 Stephen FitzGerald and Linda Jakobson, 'Is There a Problem with Australia's China Narrative?', China Matters (website), June 2018, http://chinamatters.org.au/wp-content/uploads/2018/05/China-Matters-Explores-June-2018-Australias-China-narrative.pdf.

2 Secretariat of the United Nations Conference on Trade and Development, 'Trade and Development Report 2019: Financing a Global Green New Deal', United Nations Publications, New York, 2019, p. iii.

3   Laura Tingle, 'Previously Secret Details of Trump Administration's Indo-Pacific
       Strategy Revealed', *ABC News*, 12 January 2021.
4   Andrew White, 'James Packer Endorses Bob Carr for China Relations',
       The Australian, 14 March 2013.
5   Geoff Raby, *China's Grand Strategy and Australia's Future in the Global Order*,
       Melbourne University Press, Carlton, Vic., 2020, pp. 160, 177.
6   'Collective Statement on Taiwanese Independence: Building Global Solidarity
       and Rejecting US Military Empire', *Medium*, 22 February 2017.
7   Hugh White, 'Response to Correspondence', in Mark McKenna, *Moment of
       Truth: History and Australia's Future*, Quarterly Essay, no. 69, 2017, p. 136.
8   Ben Doherty, 'Australia's Civil Rights Rating Downgraded as Report Finds World
       Becoming Less Free', *The Guardian*, 8 December 2019.
9   Clive Hamilton and Mareike Ohlberg, *Hidden Hand: Exposing How the
       Communist Party Is Reshaping the World*, Hardie Grant, Melbourne, 2020, p. 269.
10   'Australian PM Calls for Rethink of University Business Model', Xinhua,
       15 February 2021.
11   Alex Joske et al., 'The Influence Environment: A Survey of Chinese-Language
       Media in Australia', Policy Brief, ASPI International Cyber Policy Centre,
       Canberra, 2020, p. 19.
12   Dave Sharma, 'What Should Australia Do About ... Its Relationship with the
       PRC', China Matters Explores, November–December 2020.
13   Abdel-Fattah, *Coming of Age in the War on Terror*, p. 98.

INDEX

Abbott, Tony 3, 5
  FITS Public Register 116–17
ABC *see* Australian Broadcasting
  Corporation (ABC)
Abetz, Eric 211–13, 214
ACPPRC *see* Australian Council
  for the Promotion of Peaceful
  Reunification of China (ACPPRC)
Afghanistan 51, 76, 90, 152, 154, 165,
  167–8, 207
  Australian war crimes 72, 167–8, 207
  Brereton Report 72, 166, 167
Africa 39, 64, 156, 162
  Forum on China–Africa Cooperation
  39
  'Prosper Africa' initiative 65
Al Jazeera 116
al-Assad, Bashar 40, 54
Alaska (US) 68
Albanese, Anthony 16
Alipay (company) 42
America *see* United States (US)
Amnesty International 188
Andrews, Daniel 103, 189
Angel Island (US) 23
Angola 65
Anning, Fraser 140
Ant Group (company) 42
Antarctica 103, 196
ANU *see* Australian National University
  (ANU)
ANZUS alliance 3, 17, 71, 75–79, 81, 82,
  92–3, 132, 141, 223
  Pyne speech 76–7, 78
APEC *see* Asia-Pacific Economic
  Cooperation (APEC)
Apple (company) 36
Apple Daily (tabloid) 181, 190
Armitage, Richard 154

Ashe, John 96
Asian financial crisis (1998) 37, 42
Asian Infrastructure Investment Bank 39
'Asian values' 147
Asia-Pacific Economic Cooperation
  (APEC) 54, 60, 63
ASIO *see* Australian Security Intelligence
  Organisation (ASIO)
ASPI *see* Australian Strategic Policy
  Institute (ASPI)
Au Loong-Yu 190, 191
  Hong Kong in Revolt (2020) 190
AUSMIN *see* Australia–United States
  Ministerial Consultations
  (AUSMIN)
Austin, Lloyd 59
Australia
  Afghanistan *see* Afghanistan
  ANZUS *see* ANZUS alliance
  ASIO *see* Australian Security
  Intelligence Organisation (ASIO)
  Assistance and Access Act 2018 61–2
  Australian Infrastructure Investment
  Fund 89
  Border Force 187
  China, relations with *see* Australia–
  China relations
  China's influence in *see* Chinese
  influence in Australia
  Chinese Cultural Society of Tasmania
  113
  Chinese investment in *see* Chinese
  investment in Australia
  Confucius Institutes *see* Confucius
  Institutes
  Defence white papers *see* white
  papers (Defence)
  Export Finance and Insurance
  Corporation 89

Five Eyes countries 62–3, 116, 142, 213
Foreign Investment Review Board 64, 102
Huawei 60–3
Intercolonial Military Committee 84
Joint Parliamentary Committee on Intelligence and Security 110
Law Council of Australia 119
Multicultural Council of Tasmania 113
multiculturalism 109, 198, 210
national security 14, 15, 16, 20, 84–5
  see also Australia–US alliance
Navy 106
News Media Bargaining Code 111
NSW Defence Innovation Network 129
Operation Sovereign Borders 200
Plan of Action for the Strategic Partnership (Australia–Vietnam) 202–3
Quadrilateral Security Dialogue 56, 74
Ramsay Centre for Western Civilisation 142, 213
refugee policy 91, 185–6, 202
Regional Assistance Mission (Solomon Islands, 2003) 87–8
Royal Australian Air Force 91, 106
Taiwan policy 55–56
Treasury 102
US, reliance on see Australia–US alliance
Zionist Federation of Australia 119
Australia, New Zealand and United States alliance see ANZUS
Australia First Party 17
Australia Institute 102
Australia–China relations 5, 10–11, 118, 148, 207
  Australia, Chinese influence in see Chinese influence in Australia
  Australia, Chinese investment in see Chinese investment in Australia
  Australia–China Business Council 16
  Australia–China Relations Institute 15, 64
  China debate today 11–18
  Chinalco iron ore bid 4
  Chinese sanctions and bans see trade relations (Australia–China)

choice, different kind of 18–22
Copenhagen Climate Summit 4
COVID-19 – international investigation 10
COVID-19 – Wuhan-lab theories 10, 215
East Turkistan Australian Association 115
engagement, end of 5–11
Fitzgibbon, suspicions about 4
Menzies government 31, 34
Rio Tinto bribery case 4
trade relations see trade relations (Australia–China)
Uyghur biopic 4
Wang Liqiang defection 8, 9, 210, 226
Whitlam, Gough 34, 79
Xinjiang Association of South Australia 115
Australian Air Force 91, 106
Australian Broadcasting Corporation (ABC) 7, 114, 210, 213, 229
  Background Briefing 210
  Chau Chak Wing defamation suit 96, 108, 110
  Four Corners 96, 97, 135–6, 145, 226
  Insiders 114
Australian Centre on China in the World 5
Australian Citizens Party 18
Australian Conservative Political Action Conference 137
Australian Council for the Promotion of Peaceful Reunification of China (ACPPRC) 105–6, 107, 109, 113
Australian Council of Trade Unions 161–62
Australian Defence Force 15, 77, 87, 200
Australian Defence Force Academy 213
Australian Federal Police 164
Australian Greens 9, 103, 137, 185
  Chinese influence 112
  policy on China 16–17
Australian Labor Party (ALP) 16, 31, 108, 116, 118, 148, 163, 185, 204
  see also Albanese, Anthony; Curtin, John; Shorten, Bill
  Dastyari, Sam 6–7, 106–8, 109
  Moselmane, Shaoquett 117, 118, 119, 215
  NSW Labor Party 7

Australian Muslims 206, 230 *see also* Muslims
Australian National University (ANU) 5, 86, 90, 136
   National Security College Futures Council 208
Australian Navy 106
Australian Security Intelligence Organisation (ASIO) 64, 133, 197, 213
   Australian Security Intelligence Organisation Act 1979 188
   Australian Security Intelligence Organisation Amendment Bill 120, 188
   Chinese influence in Australia 7–8, 13, 95, 96, 97, 107, 108, 109, 115, 117, 118
   'Power and Influence' (*Four Corners*) 96
Australian Strategic Policy Institute (ASPI) 9, 13, 14, 15, 86, 87, 104, 120, 128, 130, 222, 229
   Xinjiang Data Project 145
Australian Values Alliance (AVA) 209, 211–12
Australian Values Statement 201–2
Australia–United States Ministerial Consultations (AUSMIN) 92
Australia–US alliance 19, 71–93, 95, 116, 132, 141
   alliance diplomacy 75–9
   American Australian Association 132
   ANZUS *see* ANZUS alliance
   AUSMIN 92
   Australian American Leadership Dialogue 82, 106
   Australia's balancing act 79–83
   Australia–US Multidisciplinary University Research Initiative 129
   'Defending Australia' (1994 Defence White Paper) 80
   'Great Game' 90–1, 221
   Harvard Trade Union Program 82
   International Force East Timor 87
   military/intelligence facilities 77, 91–2
   Pacific nations 85–91
   rules and orders 83–5
   'Tuna Wars' (1980s) 86
   2017 Foreign Policy White Paper 83

US Free Compact States 90
US–Australia Free Trade Agreement (2004) 80–1

Background Briefing (ABC) 210
Badar, Uthman 124
Badiucao 189
Bannon, Steve 7, 66
Baren, China 154
Bashford, Alison 23
BDS (Boycott, Divestment, Sanctions) solidarity campaign 125
Beazley, Kim 81
Beijing 154, 167
Bello, Walden 42
Belt and Road Initiative (BRI) 1–2, 15, 18, 38, 63–6, 89, 190, 195
   'debt-trap diplomacy' 64
   MOUs (Australia) 103
Bennelong electorate 109
BHP (company) 102
Biden, Hunter 190
Biden, Joe 47, 48, 50, 52, 58, 59, 66–9, 74, 147, 190, 220, 221
   China policy 67, 68–9
   'Made in America' plan 68
Big White Lie (Fitzgerald, 2007) 203
Bishop, Julie 120
Black Lives Matter 139, 159, 170, 192
Blaxland, John 90–1
Blinken, Anthony 50, 67, 68
Bolshevik period, Russia 152
Bolt, Andrew 114, 140, 205
Borneo 78, 84
Brandis, George 116
Brazil
   BRICS 39
Brereton Report 72, 166, 167
Bretton Woods institutions 39
BRICS (Brazil, Russia, India, China and South Africa) alliance 39
Britain *see* United Kingdom (UK)
British East India Company 150
British Empire 71, 171
Brookings Institution (US) 51
Bruny (Rose, 2019) 195–8
Buddhists 150, 210
Burgess, Mike 188
Burma *see* Myanmar (Burma)
Bush administration (George W.) 36, 40, 51, 164
   War on Terror *see* War on Terror

Callick, Rowan 121–2
Cambodia 100
Cambria Green development (Tas.) 17,
    103
Campbell, Kurt 47, 50, 56, 68
Canada 167, 202
    Five Eyes countries 62–3, 116, 142,
        213
Canberra University see University of
    Canberra
Carr, Bob 222
    wife's background 213
Carrico, Kevin 130, 189
Cathay Pacific (company) 192
Cato Institute (US) 48
CCP see Chinese Communist Party
    (CCP)
Central Intelligence Agency (CIA) 79,
    183, 197
Centre Alliance (Party) 9
Centre for Continuing Education,
    University of Sydney 131
Centre for Independent Studies 75, 125
Chau Chak Wing defamation suit 96,
    108, 110
Chen Hong 118–19
Chen Quanguo 155
Cheng Jingye 149
Chiang Kai-shek 31, 104
China
    Australia, influence in see Chinese
        influence in Australia
    Australia, investment in see Chinese
        investment in Australia
    Australia, relationship with see
        Australia–China relations
    Boxer Rebellion 71
    BRICS 39
    CCP see Chinese Communist Party
        (CCP)
    'century of humiliation' 24
    China Overseas Exchange
        Association 114
    Committee for Safeguarding
        National Security 180
    Confucius Institutes 5, 66, 121, 123,
        127–34, 137, 140, 228
    Cultural Revolution 147, 209
    dissidents 4, 13–14, 17, 44, 66, 100,
        159, 169, 177, 207, 225
    economic growth 3, 11, 30, 33, 42,
        45, 49, 60, 69, 80, 225 see also GDP

    environmental issues 33, 38, 42–3
    Forum on China–Africa Cooperation
        39
    GDP 41, 42, 45, 52, 54
    human rights 4, 14, 20, 35, 39, 44, 45,
        51, 147–9, 158, 162–3
    intellectual property 33–4, 37, 60,
        69, 84, 128
    isolation to engagement 29–34
    liberalism, and 24, 26–7, 29
    Marxism, and 25, 26, 30, 31, 41, 44
    May Fourth movement 125
    Ministry of Education 130
    Ministry of Foreign Affairs (PRC)
        99, 132
    mutual dependency 34–40
    National Intelligence Law (2017)
        61
    NPCSC see National People's
        Congress of the PRC (NPCSC)
    'One China' policy 56–7
    Overseas Chinese Affairs Office 114
    Pacific, interests in 71–93
    People's Liberation Army 30, 58, 86,
        99, 128, 146, 152
    People's Public Security University,
        Beijing 164
    poverty reduction 41, 118, 146, 154
    Qing dynasty 26, 27, 28, 30, 150–2,
        163, 171
    single-party system 25, 44, 104, 202,
        208
    South China Sea 12, 16, 36, 54, 56,
        57, 58, 74, 106, 107, 114
    Soviet Union, relationship with 31
    Taiwan Strait 31, 35, 57, 58, 82, 224
    Tarim Basin 150–1
    Thousand Talents program 128
    Tiananmen see Tiananmen rebellion
        (1989)
    US, rivalry with see US–China rivalry
    whither China? 40–5
China Defence Universities Tracker
    128
China Matters 16, 100, 219
China Studies Centre, University of
    Sydney 123, 132
China Uncensored (Falun Gong) 210
Chinalco (company) 4
China's Grand Strategy and Australia's
    Future in the Global Order (Raby,
    2020) 223

Chinese Australians 2, 6, 12, 18, 20,
        99–100, 143, 189, 196, 197, 200,
        204, 205, 206–7, 208, 209, 211–13,
        215–17, 226, 229–30
    political candidates, as 8–9, 113–15
Chinese Communist Party (CCP) 7, 8,
        43, 96, 118, 127, 130, 134, 136, 140,
        141, 150, 155, 162, 163–4, 170, 171,
        190, 191, 198–9, 200, 206–7, 209,
        210, 211–14, 216, 227
    communist revolution (1949) 24,
        28, 29–30
    Cultural Revolution (1966–76) 32
    Great Leap Forward 32
    Guomindang, and 28–9, 31, 58, 104,
        172
    People's Liberation Army 30, 58, 86,
        99, 128, 146, 152
    UFWD see United Front Work
        Department (UFWD)
'Chinese Influence and American
        Interests' (Diamond, 2018) 26
Chinese influence in Australia 12, 19,
        95–120
    ASIO warnings 7–8, 13, 95, 96, 97,
        107, 108, 109
    Australian Greens 9, 103
    BRI MOUs 103
    Chau Chak Wing defamation suit
        96, 108, 110
    Chen Hong 118–19
    Dastyari/Huang Xiangmo scandal
        6–7, 106–8, 109
    Duong, Sunny 118
    foreign-interference laws 104, 108–12,
        116, 117, 119, 120, 133, 214, 227
    Lee, Jing 114–15
    Li Jianjun 118
    Liu, Gladys 114
    Manchurian candidates 112–15
    media, reports by 95–6, 115
    Migration Act 117
    Ministry of Foreign Affairs (PRC)
        99, 132
    Ministry of State Security (PRC) 99
    Moselmane, Shaoquett 117, 118,
        119, 215
    scalps, looking for 116–20
    Tang, Yongbei 113–14
    United Front Work Department 5,
        43, 104–5, 110, 113, 114, 118, 120,
        208, 212, 215–16

    Zhang, John 117, 118–19
    Zhao, Nick 8–9, 115
Chinese investment in Australia 102–3
    Cambria Green development (Tas)
        17, 193
    Port of Darwin (NT) 14, 63
Chinese Nationalist government 152,
        171–2
Chisholm electorate 114, 115
Chiu, William 106
Chow, Agnes 180–1
Christensen, Thomas 40, 48
Christmas Island 23, 215
CIA see Central Intelligence Agency (CIA)
Citizens Electoral Council 18
CIVICUS Monitor 226
Clapper, James 98
Clark, Gregory 34, 163
climate change 43, 51, 67, 90, 197, 220
        see also environment
    Paris Accord 51
Clinton, Hilary 4, 53, 98
Coalition 16, 109
Coca-Cola 52
Cold War 1, 7, 14, 20, 26, 36, 48, 49, 51,
        52, 76, 79, 80, 86, 109, 123, 153,
        159, 172, 209
    'arc of containment' policy 56
    campuses, on see universities
    South Korea 55
    Taiwan Strait 58
Cold Warriors 13, 170, 192
Colton, Greg 90
Columbia University (US) 139
Communist revolution (1949) 24, 28,
        29–30
'Confucius Classrooms' 130
Confucius Institute Headquarters
        (Hanban) 130
Confucius Institutes 5, 66, 121, 123, 137,
        140, 228
    collaborations and 127–34
Conroy, Stephen 106, 107
Conservative Political Action Conference
        137
Contest for the Indo-Pacific (Medcalf,
        2020) 90
Cooper, Andrew 116, 137
Coorey, Phil 114
Cotton, Tom 182, 192
counterterrorism 155, 156, 159, 163,
        164, 165, 166, 188 see also terrorism

COVID-19 18, 43, 45, 57, 67, 118, 121,
  135, 136, 141–2, 169, 179–80, 191,
  210, 211, 216
  'China virus' 66
  international investigation 10
  quarantine 23
  recession 92
  Wuhan-lab theories 10, 215
CrowdStrike (cybersecurity) 98
CSIRO
  Centre for Southern Hemisphere
  Oceans Research 129
Curtin, John 76, 79

Dalai Lama 123, 150
Danby, Michael 148
Dastyari, Sam 6–7, 106–8, 109
David, Abe 14
Defence Innovation Hub 129
Defence Intelligence Organisation 13
Deng Xiaoping 33
Denniss, Richard 14
Department of Defence 15, 64, 128, 129
  Information Warfare Division 129
Department of External Affairs 31, 34
Department of Foreign Affairs and Trade
  (DFAT) 1, 80, 81, 86, 91
  National Foundation for Australia–
  China Relations 210–11
Department of Home Affairs 133, 210,
  229
Department of Human Services 210,
  211
Department of Immigration 201
'Developing Northern Australia' plan 2
DFAT see Department of Foreign Affairs
  and Trade (DFAT)
Di Natale, Richard 185–6
Diamond, Larry 26
Dibb, Paul 92
dissidents 13–14, 17, 44, 66, 100, 207,
  225
  Falun Gong see Falun Gong
  Hong Kong 169, 177
  Kadeer, Rebiya 4, 159
Djibouti 54
Dower, John 36, 50
Downer, Alexander 81
Dunstan, Don 153
Duong, Sunny 118
Duterte, Rodrigo 56, 57, 188, 202
Dutton, Peter 106, 107, 117, 118, 119

East Timor see Timor-Leste
East Turkistan Islamic Movement 154,
  164
Eastern Turkistan 145, 152 see also
  Xinjiang region
Ecuador 65
EFI Bill see Espionage and Foreign
  Interference Bill 2017
Eggleston, Frederic 29
Egypt 51, 158
El Salvador 64
Ellis, Kim 103
Engage Australia radio show 210, 211
environment 17, 68, 101, 102, 189, 221
  see also climate change
  China 33, 38, 42–3
Epoch Times 210
Equatorial Guinea 65
Espionage and Foreign Interference Bill
  2017 (EFI Bill) 109, 110–11, 112
Ethiopia 65, 100
European Union 59
Evans, Gareth 79
Extradition Law Amendment Bill
  (Hong Kong)
  anti-ELAB movement 136, 138, 169,
  170, 176–81, 184, 185–7, 189–91,
  193, 204
Exxon Mobil (company) 89

Facebook 86, 98, 111 see also social
  media
  News Media Bargaining Code 111
Fairfax Media see also The Age; The
  Sydney Morning Herald
  Chau Chak Wing defamation suit
  96, 108, 110
  Wang Liqiang defection 8, 9, 210,
  226
Falun Gong 18, 145, 210–11, 215,
  229
Federal Bureau of Investigation (FBI)
  128
Federation of Trade Unions (Hong
  Kong) 178
Ferguson, Niall 26
Fernandes, Clinton 36, 84
Fitzgerald, John 131, 203–4
FitzGerald, Stephen 34
Fitzgibbon, Joel 4, 16
Five Eyes countries 62–3, 116, 142, 213
Floyd, George 192

Foreign Influence Transparency Scheme (FITS) 109, 111–12, 116–17, 222
  FITS Act 112
  FITS Bill 111
  FITS Public Register 111, 116, 133
Foreign Office (UK) 164
foreign-interference laws 108–12, 116, 117, 119, 120, 214, 227
  EFI Bill 109, 110–11, 112
  Electoral Funding and Disclosure Reform Bill 2017 109–10
  FITS see Foreign Influence Transparency Scheme (FITS)
  Foreign Relations Act 2020 (Australia) 104, 133
Forrest, Andrew ('Twiggy') 15, 101
Forum on China–Africa Cooperation 38
Four Corners (ABC) 96, 97, 135–6, 145, 226
France 63, 72, 97, 150, 164–5
  Alliance Française centres 131
  Yellow Vest uprising 183
Fraser, Malcolm 79, 105, 153
free market 14, 48
Freedom House (US) 51
Freedom of Navigation Operations 12, 16, 54, 106, 107
Friendlyjordies podcast 163

Gaddafi, Muammar 39–40
Garnaut, John 13, 95, 97, 98, 116, 135, 196
  China's 'totalitarian ideology' 25
Gaza Strip 208
G.E. Morrison Institute 16
Germany 63, 72
  Goethe-Instituts 131
global financial crisis (2007–08) 42, 53
Global Times 163
Google (company) 61
Google Translate 210
Graham, Euan 143
Greater Sunrise fields 87
Greens see Australian Greens
Gromyko, Andrei 153
Guam 54, 92
Guo Wengui 66
Guomindang 28–9, 31, 58, 104, 172
Gyngell, Allan 73

Hainan Island 5
Hambantota Port (Sri Lanka) 64

Hamilton, Clive 1–2, 14, 87, 98, 103, 109, 113, 114, 116, 120, 130–1, 186, 196, 197, 205, 209, 213, 216–17, 227
  Hidden Hand (with Ohlberg, 2020) 228
  'One Belt, One Road' 2
  Silent Invasion (2018) 7, 17, 197, 205, 213
Han dynasty, China 150
Han population, Xinjiang 155, 156
Hanban (Confucius Institute Headquarters) 130
Hanson, Pauline 1, 189 see also One Nation
Harrison, Mark 103
Hartcher, Peter 201, 215
  Red Flag (Quarterly Essay, 2019) 120, 201
Hasluck, Paul 153
Hastie, Andrew 13, 25, 100, 115, 121
Hawaii 36, 54
Hawke, Bob 79, 80, 105
  Hawke–Keating era 79
  Tiananmen crackdown 185–6
Hidden Hand (Hamilton and Ohlberg, 2020) 228
Himalayas 134
Hizb ut-Tahrir (Islamic political party) 124
H&M (company) 160
Ho-fung Hung 53
Hockey, Joe 75
Hofstadter, Richard 209
Holt, Harold 78
Hong Kong 104, 125, 126, 134, 136, 139, 149, 169–93, 201, 204, 208, 228 see also Lam, Carrie
  American Chamber of Commerce, Hong Kong 190
  annexation to anti-ELAB 171–6
  Australia and 185–90
  Basic Law 174, 180, 185, 187
  Causeway Bay Books case 177
  Chinese University of Hong Kong 179
  Confederation of Trade Unions 178
  Court of First Instance 181
  Demosisto (political party) 175
  Extradition Law Amendment Bill see Extradition Law Amendment Bill (Hong Kong)
  international front 181–5

Hong Kong *cont.*
   Lennon Wall 139, 189
   'Let's Talk About Hong Kong' forums
      138–9
   mutual destruction (*laam chau*)
      doctrine 176, 184, 191
   National Security Law 185
   pro-democracy uprising 6, 8, 18, 22
   Public Order Ordinance 180
   repression 182, 183, 184, 192
   Scholarism (student organisation) 175
   Sino–British Joint Declaration 174, 187
   Umbrella Movement 175, 177
   Yuen Long 178
Hong Kong Council of Trade Unions 180
Hong Kong Federation of Students 175
Hong Kong Human Rights and
   Democracy Act (US) 184
Hong Kong in Revolt (Au Loong-Yu,
   2020) 190
Hong Kong Police Force 169, 179, 187
Hong Kong Polytechnic University 179
Hong Kong–related student
   mobilisations 137–9
Honolulu (Hawaii) 54
Hoover Institution (US) 26, 116
Hospital Authority Employee Alliance
   (HAEA) 179
Houston, Angus 15
How to Defend Australia (White, 2019)
   223–4, 225
Howard, John 3, 80–1, 148, 201
   Afghanistan *see* Afghanistan
   Iraq War 13, 76, 79, 80
   1997 Defence White Paper 80
   Timor-Leste 87
Hoy, Peter 141
Huang Xiangmo 117, 196
   Dastyari scandal 6–7, 106–8, 109
Huawei (company) 60–3
Hudson Institute (US) 49
Hui people 157
human rights 137, 145–68 *see also*
   United Nations (UN)
   Australia 83, 202
   China 4, 14, 20, 35, 39, 44, 45, 51,
      147–9, 158, 162–3 *see also* Hong
      Kong; Uyghur people
   China's colonial frontier 150–5
   War on Terror *see* War on Terror
Human Rights Commission (Australia)
   215

Human Rights Watch 40, 159, 161–2
Hunt, Greg 15

Ibrahim, Azeem 165
IMF *see* International Monetary Fund
   (IMF)
Immigration Restriction Act 1901 23
India 51, 67, 134, 140, 150, 202, 224
   see also Modi, Narendra
   Bharatiya Janata Party 119
   BRICS 39
   Hindu Rashtriya Swayamsevak
      Sangh 119
   Hindu Swayamsevak Sangh 118
   Quadrilateral Security Dialogue 56,
      74
Indigenous Australians 195, 201
Indo-Pacific region 220–1, 223–4
Indo-Pacific Strategic Framework 220
Indonesia 2, 37, 67, 78, 79, 87, 158, 224
   'arc of containment' policy 56
Insiders (ABC) 114
intellectual property 33–4, 37, 60, 69,
   128
   TRIPS 84
International Agency for Research on
   Cancer 129
International Court of Justice 51
International Criminal Court 51
International Holocaust Remembrance
   Alliance 214
International Labour Organization
   Forced Labour Protocol, 2014 162
International Monetary Fund (IMF) 37,
   38, 39, 65, 88
Iran 51, 62
Iraq 132, 154, 155
Iraq War 36, 39, 132, 154
   Howard, John 13, 76, 79, 80
Isa, Dolkun 159
Islam 150, 151, 152, 154, 155, 156, 158,
   163–6, 206 *see also* Muslims
Islamic State (ISIS) 155
Islamophobia 156, 163, 164, 165, 166,
   216
Israel 40, 50, 65, 100, 126, 158–9, 202,
   208, 214
   Boycott, Divestment, Sanctions
      campaign 119, 125
   Ministry of Strategic Affairs and
      Public Diplomacy 119
   Operation Protective Edge 208–9

Jabhat al-Nusra 155
Japan 12, 31, 33, 35, 67, 72, 80, 137, 158,
    170, 180, 199
    Australia, investment in 14
    Liberal Democratic Party 55
    Multi-Function Polis proposal 2
    Quadrilateral Security Dialogue 56,
    74
    'Self-Defence Forces' 55
    World War II 76
Japan Foundation 131
Java 84 *see also* Indonesia
Jennings, Peter 13, 86, 87, 130
Johnson, Boris 63
Jones, Alan 140
Joske, Alex 9, 120, 122, 128
Junghar Mongols 150

Kadeer, Rebiya 4, 159
Kashmir 51, 202
Kasparov, Garry 171
Katter, Bob 123, 140
Katter's Australia Party 140
Kazakh people 156–7
Kazakhstan 156–7
Keating, Paul 15, 80
    Hawke–Keating era 79
Kelly, Raimond 216
Keneally, Kristina 109
Kenny, Chris 140
Khalil, Peter 185
Khan, Imran 38
Kiribati 86, 88, 90
Kissinger, Henry 32
Kitching, Kimberley 211
Korean War 31
Kunming, China 155

laam chau doctrine 176, 184, 191
Labor Party *see* Australian Labor Party
    (ALP)
Lai, Jimmy 181, 190
Lam, Carrie 169, 171, 177, 178–9, 180,
    184–5
Lambie, Jacqui 9
Landbridge (company) 63
LaRouche, Lyndon 18
Latin America 159
Lausan Collective 182
Law Council of Australia 161, 187
Leaving the War on Terror (Transnational
    Institute, 2017) 166

Lee, Elizabeth 115
Lee, Jing 114–15
Lee, John 120
Lee Cheuk Yan 180
Lenin 30
Lewis, Duncan 7–8
Li Hongzhi 210
Li Jianjun 118
Li Keqiang 26
Li Zhang 115
Liberal Party 16, 81, 100, 106, 109, 136,
    142, 149, 204 *see also* Abbott, Tony;
    Howard, John; Menzies, Robert;
    Morrison, Scott
    Zhao, Nick 8–9, 115
Libya 39–40
Lighthizer, Robert 60
Lin, Anastasia 125
Liu, Gladys 114
Lockheed Martin (company) 129
Lowy Institute 4, 7, 88, 90, 213, 216

Ma, Jack 42
MacArthur, Douglas 76
Macau 42, 104
Macron, Emmanuel 164–5
'Magnitsky' sanctions 161
Malaya 173
Malaysia 106, 114, 204, 213
    'arc of containment' policy 56
Mamdani, Mahmood 50
Mandarin language 121, 146, 175, 191,
    219
Manuel, Ryan 105
Manus Island (PNG) 89, 90
Mao Zedong 4, 7, 17, 24, 29, 30, 31–2,
    44, 103, 147, 172, 173, 209
Maoist period, China 147, 172–3
Markson, Sharri 128
Marles, Richard 74, 78
Marshall Islands 88
Marxism 25, 26, 30, 31, 41, 44
McCain, John 97
McCarthyism 142
McKim, Nick 9, 103
McMaster, H.R. 26
Mearsheimer, John 75
Medcalf, Rory 56, 74
    Contest for the Indo-Pacific (2020) 90
Media Entertainment and Arts Alliance
    96
Melbourne International Film Festival 4

Melbourne University *see* University
    of Melbourne
Meng Jianzhu 108
Menzies, Robert 31, 34
Microsoft 61
Middle Eastern countries 158, 216
'Milk Tea Alliance' (pan-Asian) 170
Mill, John Stuart 26, 27
    On Liberty (1859) 26
Minerals Council of Australia 15, 102
mining industry 15, 102
    coal 16, 101
    iron ore 4, 101
Modern Slavery Act 2018 (Australia)
    161–2
Modi, Narendra 119, 202
Monash University 136–7, 189
Mongolia 152
Monk, Paul 13
Morocco 124
Morrison, Scott 3, 9, 83, 89, 91, 112, 141,
    202, 207, 215, 228
    COVID-19 10, 23
    Foreign Relations Act 2020 (Australia)
    104, 133
    Hong Kong refugees
    Liu, Gladys 114
    war crimes (Afghanistan) 167, 168
Moselmane, Shaoquett 117, 118, 119, 215
MSNBC (US) 97
Mueller, Robert 98–9
Multi-Function Polis proposal 2
Murdoch, Keith 82, 132
Murdoch family 132
Murdoch press 96, 100 *see also* Sky News
Muslim Students' Association, University
    of Sydney 124
Muslims 1, 140, 145, 150–2, 154, 155,
    158–9, 163–4, 165–6, 168, 200–1,
    205–6, 230 *see also* Islam
    Uyghurs *see* Uyghur people
mutual destruction (*laam chau*) doctrine
    176, 184, 191
Myanmar (Burma) 161, 192, 193

Nakba 125
National Foundation for
    Australia–China Relations 210–11
National People's Congress of the PRC
    (NPCSC)
    Standing Committee 174, 175, 180
National Press Club addresses 149

national security (Australia) 14, 15, 16,
    20, 84
National Tertiary Education Union
    (NTEU) 138
NATO *see* North Atlantic Treaty
    Organization (NATO)
Nauru 84, 88, 90, 91
Naval Group (French defence
    contractor) 131
Navalny, Aleksei 171
Navarro, Pete 48
Neal, David 187–8
Neier, Aryeh 162
neo-Nazis 189
New Caledonia 84
New Federal State of China 66, 215
New Guinea 84 *see also* Papua New
    Guinea
New Hebrides 84
New Tang Dynasty Television (Falun
    Gong) 210
New Zealand 3, 84, 86, 88
    Five Eyes countries 62–3, 116, 142,
    213
Newlines Institute 165
Nicholls, Douglas 153
Nine Network 116
9/11 (terrorist attacks, 2001) 6, 76, 116,
    119, 120, 154, 166, 207, 216
Nixon, Richard 32, 34, 78–9, 98
Nomura, Haruka 163
North Atlantic Treaty Organization
    (NATO) 40, 67, 76
North Korea 55
North West Cape naval communications
    station 77
NSW Labor Party 7
Nuclear Non-Proliferation Treaty (UN)
    78
nuclear weapons 55, 58, 59, 77–8, 154,
    221, 223–4
    Nuclear Non-Proliferation Treaty
    (UN) 78
    Treaty on the Prohibition of Nuclear
    Weapons (UN) 78

Obama administration 47, 58, 64, 67, 81–2
    National Intelligence 98
    National Security Strategy (2015) 47
    'Pivot to Asia' 4, 53, 54, 67, 82, 91
    Trans-Pacific Partnership 53, 68
O'Connor, Cassy 103, 113

Ohlberg, Mareike 228
Oil Search (company) 89
Okinawa (Japan) 55
Old Left 17, 183
Olympic Games – Winter (Beijing, 2022) 167
On Liberty (Mill, 1859) 26
One Nation 9, 117 *see also* Hanson, Pauline
Opium Wars
    First Opium War 27, 171
    Second Opium War 27
Organisation of Islamic Cooperation 158
O'Rourke, Beto 97
Ottoman Empire 151

Packer, James 222
Pakistan 38
Palau 88, 90
Palazzo, Albert 80
Palestine 50, 125–6
Palestine Legal 126
Palestinian Authority 158–9
Palestinian people 159, 202, 214
Papua New Guinea 63, 84, 88, 91
    Australian investment 89
    Chinese investment 85–6
    Manus Island 89, 90
paranoia 2, 6, 17, 34, 186, 193, 207, 213, 227
Patagonia (company) 160
Patriot Prayer 189
Patten, Chris 174, 185
Pavlou, Drew 137, 140–1
Payne, Marise 82, 203
Pence, Mike 49, 63, 184
People's Republic of China (PRC) *see* China
'People's War on Terror' 155
Perry, Matthew C. (Commodore) 40, 220–1
Philippines 36, 56–57, 202 *see also* Duterte, Rodrigo
    Anti-Terrorism Act (Philippines) 188
    US–Philippines Mutual Defence Treaty 57
    Visiting Forces Agreement 55
Pillsbury, Michael 48, 149–50
Pine Gap, Northern Territory 225
Pine Gap satellite station 77, 225
Pomfret, John 49
Pompeo, Mike 52–3, 82, 85, 147, 181, 184

Port of Darwin (NT) 14, 63–4
Porter, Christian 110, 112, 117
'Power and Influence' (ABC) 96, 135–6
PRC (People's Republic of China) *see* China
PricewaterhouseCoopers (company) 16
progressive groups 14, 69, 124, 134, 136, 160, 191
Putin, Vladimir 97, 170, 192
Pyne, Christopher 76–7, 78

Qigong 210
Qin dynasty, China 137
Qing dynasty 26, 27, 30, 171
    end of 28
    Xinjiang, invasion of 150–2, 163
Quadrilateral Security Dialogue 56, 74
Quarantine Station (Sydney) 23
Quincy Institute (US) 48

Raby, Geoff 222–3
racism 2, 67
    anti-Chinese 17, 18, 22, 106, 137, 196, 197, 198, 210, 214, 215–17, 226
    White Australia policy 23, 199, 200, 201, 215
Raytheon (company) 129
Reagan, Ronald 66, 86, 159, 182
Red Dawn (film) 13
Red Flag (Hartcher, 2019) 120, 201
Regional Comprehensive Economic Partnership 12
Reporters without Borders' World Press Freedom Index 170
Reynolds, Henry 71–2
Richardson, Dennis 15
Rio Tinto 16, 102
    bribery case 4
Ritchie, David 132
Robb, Andrew 96
Robertson, Geoffrey 161
Robinson, Tommy 189
Rohingya people 161
Rose, Heather 195–8
Rosenberger, Laura 98
Royal United Services Institute 164
Rubio, Marco 64, 68, 182
Rudd, Kevin 7, 90, 117
    Australian Centre on China in the World 5
    Copenhagen Climate Summit 4
    2009 Defence White Paper 4

Rummery, Chris 161
Russia 29, 49, 54, 109, 153, 158, 182, 192
    see also Putin, Vladimir; Soviet Union
    Bolshevik period 152
    BRICS 39
    capitalism, and 170–1
    Moscow 170
    US election (2016), interference in
      97–8, 99
Russian Empire 90
Russian Revolution 104, 152
Ruston, Anne 88–9

Sahlins, Marshall 130
Sahrawi activists 124
Saifuddin Azizi 153–4
Sandinistas 159
Saudi Arabia 51
SBS *see* Special Broadcasting Service (SBS)
Scanlon Foundation
    'Mapping Social Cohesion' report 216
Senate (Australian) 188, 198
    Foreign Affairs, Defence and Trade
      Committee 211–13
settler colonies 1, 84, 195, 202
Shanks, Jordan 163
Sharma, Dave 109, 185, 230
Sheridan, Greg 202
'Shina pigs' appellation 137
Shoal Bay Receiving Station 77
Shoebridge, Michael 103–4
Shorten, Bill 106, 107, 112
Sidick, Erkin 125
Significant Investor Visas 186
Silent Invasion (Hamilton, 2018) 7, 17,
    197, 206, 213
Singapore 3, 56, 67, 102, 173, 202, 204
60 Minutes (current affairs program) 8,
    226
Sky News 1, 140, 215
Snowden, Edward 61
social media 112, 134, 137 *see also*
    Facebook; Twitter; YouTube
Solomon Islands 62, 90
    Regional Assistance Mission (2003)
      87–8
    Taiwan, ties cut with 65–6
Sopoaga, Enele 90
Sound of Hope radio (Falun Gong) 210,
    211
South Africa 39, 72, 102–3
    BRICS 39

South China Sea 36, 56, 57, 58, 74, 114
    Freedom of Navigation Operations
      12, 16, 54, 106, 107
South Korea 12, 33, 35, 55, 63
Soviet Union 2, 44, 76, 152, 191 *see also*
    Russia
    China, relationship with 31
    'Tuna Wars' (1980s) 86
Special Broadcasting Service (SBS) 229
Spence, Michael 5, 124
Sri Lanka 64
Stalin 17, 25, 28, 31, 152
Starbucks 52
Stern Hu 4, 7
Students' Representative Council,
    University of Sydney 136
Sudan 72
Sufi networks 151
Suga, Yoshihide 55
Suidani, Daniel 65
Sullivan, Jake 47, 50, 56, 68
Sun Yat-sen 171
Suzhou, China 123
Swinburne University 131
Sydney Ideas (public talks program)
    124–5
Sydney University *see* University of Sydney
Syria 40, 54, 155

Taboi Awi Yoto 86
Taiwan 8, 31, 36, 49, 74, 81, 99, 134, 172,
    183, 201, 204, 224–5, 227
    ACPPRC 105–6, 107, 109, 113
    'AirSea Battle' 58
    Democratic Progressive Party 58
    'One China' policy 56–7
    Pacific nations, and 65–6, 88
    Taipei Economic and Cultural Office
      100
    Taiwan Relations Act 1979 (US) 56
    US policy on 55–6, 57–8
Taiwan Strait 31, 35, 57, 58, 82, 224
Tajikistan 38–9, 54
Tang, Yongbei 113–14
Tang dynasty, China 150
Tasmania 195–8
Taylor, Brendan 74
terrorism 106, 120, 126, 154, 180, 181,
    187, 188 *see also* counterterrorism;
    9/11 (terrorist attacks, 2001); War
    on Terror
Thailand 170

Thales (company) 129
Thatcher, Margaret 173
The Age 8, 199 *see also* Fairfax Media
The Australian 64, 125, 128, 129, 187, 202
The Australian Financial Review 190
The Bulletin 153, 199
The Mercury 113
The New York Times 9, 112, 113, 135, 136–7, 192
The Sydney Morning Herald 8, 186
    see also Fairfax Media
The Times 16
The Wall Street Journal 62
The Washington Post (newspaper) 192
The Weekend Australian 109
the West 126, 147, 148, 149, 156, 158, 160, 163–6, 170, 184, 191–2, 203, 205–6, 209, 213–14
think-tanks 74, 82, 98, 116, 126, 142, 183, 214
    ASPI *see* Australian Strategic Policy Institute (ASPI)
    Australia Institute 102
    Brookings Institution (US) 51
    Cato Institute (US) 48
    Centre for Independent Studies 75, 125
    China Matters 16, 100, 219
    Council on Foreign Relations (US) 35
    G.E. Morrison Institute 16
    Hoover Institution (US) 26, 116
    Hudson Institute (US) 49
    Newlines Institute 165
    Quincy Institute (US) 48
    Royal United Services Institute 164
    Transnational Institute 166
Thomas-Greenfield, Linda 67
Thousand Talents program 128
Tiananmen rebellion (1989) 34, 125, 148, 169, 173–4, 185–6
    commemoration 180–1, 192
    exiles 66, 204
Tiananmen Square 24, 66, 155
Tibet 30, 44, 105, 125, 145, 148, 152, 155, 159, 160, 182, 207–8, 225
Tibetan people 182
TikTok 66
Timor-Leste 57, 87
Tindal military base 91–2

Tocqueville, Alexis de 26, 27
Tohti, Ilham 155, 164
trade relations (Australia–China) 18, 20, 73, 80, 100–1
    China–Australia Free Trade Agreement (2015) 5, 81, 185
    Chinese sanctions and bans 10, 15–16, 101
    Defence Trade Controls Act 2012 128, 129
Transnational Institute 166
Transparency International Corruption Perception Index 226
Treaty on the Prohibition of Nuclear Weapons (UN) 78
Trump administration 10, 48, 51, 78, 112, 128, 140, 160, 164, 182, 184–5, 189, 211, 213, 215, 220
    'America first' 11, 53–54, 60, 68
    Arms Trade Treaty 51
    China policy 7, 11, 47, 52–3, 55, 58, 60, 62, 66, 67, 68
    'China virus' 66
    Intermediate-Range Nuclear Forces Treaty 51
    Joint Comprehensive Plan of Action 51
    Mueller inquiry 98–9
    National Defense Strategy 47
    Open Skies Treaty 51
    Paris Accord 51
    'reciprocity' principle 60
    Strategic Framework for the Indo-Pacific (2018) 26, 47, 220
    Turnbull, and 75
    2016 election, Russian interference in 97–8, 99
Trumpism 190
Tsai Ing-wen 57, 58
Tudge, Alan 205–6
Turkic languages 145, 150 *see also* Uyghur people
Turkistan 150
Turnbull, Malcolm 4, 7, 13, 16, 93, 96, 220
    foreign-interference laws 104, 108–12, 116, 117, 119, 120, 133, 214, 227
    Trump, and 75
Tuvalu 88, 90
Twitter 2, 8, 60, 140, 207 *see also* social media

UFWD *see* United Front Work Department (UFWD)
Uhlmann, Chris 8
UN Convention on the Law of the Sea (UNCLOS), 57, 106
UNCLOS *see* UN Convention on the Law of the Sea (UNCLOS),
United Front Work Department (UFCD) 5, 43, 104–5, 110, 114, 118, 120, 208, 212, 215–16
  ACPPRC 105–6, 107, 109, 113
United Kingdom (UK) 164, 166, 167, 171–4
  Brexit 63, 97
  Five Eyes countries 62–3, 116, 142, 213
  Huawei 60–3
  National Cyber Security Centre 63
  Sino-British Joint Declaration 174, 187
United Nations (UN) 39, 49, 76, 83, 147, 158
  Committee on the Elimination of Racial Discrimination 157–8
  General Assembly 96
  Human Rights Commission (UNHRC) 147, 148
  Human Rights Committee 83, 158
  New International Economic Order 84
  Nuclear Non-Proliferation Treaty 78
  Treaty on the Prohibition of Nuclear Weapons 78
  Universal Declaration of Human Rights (1948) 146, 147
United States Studies Centre (University of Sydney) 132, 141, 183
United States (US) *see also* Biden administration; Bush administration (George W.); Obama administration; Trump administration
  Afghanistan *see* Afghanistan
  AirSea Battle program 58, 150
  'America Crece' initiative 65
  American Conservative Political Action Committee 116
  'arc of containment' policy 56
  Australia, alliance with *see* Australia–US alliance

Better Utilization of Investment Leading to Development Act 65
'Blue Dot Network' 65
China, rivalry with *see* US–China rivalry
China Task Force 66
CIA 79, 183, 197
'Clean Network' program 65
Congress 54, 120, 159, 160, 184
Connally Reservation (1946) 51
Conservative Political Action Committee 116
Council on Foreign Relations 35
Customs and Border Protection 160
Defense Advanced Research Projects Agency 129
Department of Commerce 62
Development Finance Corporation 65
FBI 66, 96, 99, 116, 128
Five Eyes countries 62–3, 116, 142, 213
Foreign Agents Registration Act (FARA) 111
Green New Deal 68
Marine Corps *see* US Marine Corps
National Endowment for Democracy 159, 183
National Security Council 69, 98
Navy *see* US Navy
Office of Naval Research Global 129
'Pacific Pledge' plan 65
'Pivot to Asia' 4, 53, 54, 67, 82, 91
'Prosper Africa' initiative 65
Quadrilateral Security Dialogue 56, 74
regional dominance 2, 4, 11, 16, 18, 47, 73, 74
Securities and Exchange Commission 162
State Department 128, 132, 146–7, 213
Taiwan policy 55–6, 57–8
Taiwan Relations Act 1979 56
United States Space Force 59
US–Philippines Mutual Defence Treaty 57
Uyghur Forced Labor Prevention Bill 161, 162
Uyghur Human Rights Policy Act 2020 160
Visiting Forces Agreement 55

universities 121–43
Advance (political bloc) 136
campus politics 134–41
China, discussion about 123–7
Chinese Students and Scholars
Association 134, 135–6
Confucius Institutes 5, 66, 121, 123,
127–34, 137, 140, 228
destroying/saving 141–3
Lennon Wall 139, 189
Muslim Students' Association 124
Nakba 125
Panda (political bloc) 136
Paul Ramsay Foundation 142
Universities Australia 133
University Foreign Interference
Taskforce 133
University of Adelaide 137
University of Canberra 135–6
University of Chicago 130
University of International Business and
Economics (Beijing) 131
University of Melbourne 129, 137, 139
University of New South Wales 7, 134
University of Queensland 131, 132, 137,
140–1
University of South Australia 131
University of Sydney 5, 8, 123–5, 129,
136, 137, 138–9
Centre for Continuing Education 131
chancellor 129
China Studies Centre 123, 132
Confucius Institute 123, 131–2
Muslim Students' Association 124
Students' Representative Council
136
Sydney Ideas (public talks program)
124–5
United States Studies Centre 132,
141, 183
University of Tasmania 103
University of Technology Sydney 15
Ürümchi (Xinjiang) 4, 126, 152, 153,
154, 155, 158, 164
US Indo-Pacific Command 54
US Marine Corps 36, 82, 91
US National Security Agency 61
US Navy 4, 36, 54, 55, 67, 91
Freedom of Navigation Operations
12, 16, 54, 106, 107
US State Department 13, 49, 51, 64, 81,
88, 128, 132, 146, 213

USAsia Centre 16
'US–Australia Deterrence Dialogue' 183
US–Australia Free Trade Agreement
(2004) 80–1
US–China rivalry 3, 10, 21, 47–69, 73–4
Belt and Road see Belt and Road
Initiative (BRI)
Biden reset 66–9
'Chimerica' 52
'containment' versus 'engagement'
31, 32–3, 34–7, 48–50
Huawei 60–3
military wrestle in Asia 54–9
pivot towards competition 52–4
trade war to tech war 59–63
Uyghur American Association 159
Uyghur Forced Labor Prevention Bill
(US) 161, 162
Uyghur Human Rights Policy Act 2020
(US) 160
Uyghur Human Rights Project 159
Uyghur people 7, 13–14, 18, 19, 100,
125, 139, 140, 145–7, 149, 152–68,
182, 225, 228 see also Islam;
Muslims; Xinjiang region
counterterrorism 155, 163, 164, 166
Kadeer, Rebiya 4, 159
're-education' camps 6, 145, 150–63,
166
repression of 6, 17, 18, 22, 44, 50, 51,
145, 159, 160, 163, 164, 167
World Uyghur Congress 159, 228
Uyghuristan 152, 153

Vanuatu 86–7
Varghese, Peter 132, 141
Varrall, Merriden 135
Victoria University, Melbourne
Business School 131
Vietnam 36, 54, 56, 79, 223
Communist Party 51
Plan of Action for the Strategic
Partnership (Australia–Vietnam)
202–3
Vietnam War 29, 32, 78
Vision Times (Falun Gong) 210–11
Voices (YouTube show) 211

Wang Liqiang 8, 9, 210, 226
War on Terror 76, 120
ending the global war 163–8
Warren, Elizabeth 68

Weaving the Net: Conditional Engagement with China (CFR study) 35
WeChat 66, 109, 118, 119, 229
Western media 183, 190
Western Sahara 124
Wheelwright, Ted 14
White, Hugh 15, 75, 81, 82, 225
    How to Defend Australia (2019) 223–4
    Without America (essay, 2017) 73
White Australia policy 23, 199–200, 201, 215
white papers (Defence)
    1994 80
    1997 80
    2009 4
    2016 85
Whitlam, Gough 34, 79, 105
WikiLeaks cables 158
Wilson, Tim 187
Windschuttle, Keith 199
Winter Olympics – Beijing, 2022 167
Without America (White, 2017) 73
'Wolverines' 13, 25, 185, 211
Wong, Joshua 175–6, 179, 180, 202
Woodruff, Rosalie 17
Woodside Petroleum (company) 87
World Health Organization 129
World Trade Organization (WTO) 37, 48, 59, 60, 68, 84
World Uyghur Congress 159, 228
World War I 84, 220
    Battle of Hamel 75
World War II 49, 55, 71, 72, 76, 78, 172
Wray, Christopher 66, 128
WTO *see* World Trade Organization (WTO)
Wuhan, China 215

xenophobia 1, 103, 198 *see also* yellow peril
Xi Jinping 5, 103, 114, 132, 146, 155, 160, 164, 190, 207

anti-corruption campaign 43–4
BRI *see* Belt and Road Initiative (BRI)
policy objectives 40–3
The Governance of China (speeches/ articles) 38
'Xi Jinping Thought on Socialism with Chinese Characteristics for a New Era' 41
Xinjiang Data Project 145
Xinjiang Production and Construction Corps 153, 160–1, 162
Xinjiang region 5–6, 17, 30, 125, 126, 127, 145–7, 148, 149, 150–68, 208 *see also* Ürümchi (Xinjiang); Uyghur people
    East Turkistan Australian Association 115
    Ili district 152
    Kashgar 151, 152
    Qing dynasty, invasion during 150–2, 163
    Uyghurs *see* Uyghur people
    Xinjiang Association of South Australia 115

Yang, Jennifer 114
Yaqub Beg 151
Yarkand, Xinjiang 150, 155
yellow peril 1, 199 *see also* xenophobia
Yellow Vest uprising (France) 183
Yemini, Avi 189
Yokosuka (Japan) 55
YouTube 210, 211 *see also* social media

Zappone, Chris 208, 214
Zhang, John 117, 118–19
Zhao, Nick 8–9, 115
Zhao Lijian 167, 207
Zionism, critics of 214
ZTE (company) 61, 62
Zuo Zongtang 163